BOND RISK ANALYSIS

A GUIDE TO DURATION AND CONVEXITY

LIVINGSTON G. DOUGLAS

New York Institute of Finance

Library of Congress Cataloging-in-Publication Data

Douglas, Livingston G.
  Bond risk analysis : a guide to duration and convexity /
  Livingston G. Douglas.
    p.   cm.
  ISBN 0-13-221037-1
  1. Bonds. 2. Bonds—Prices. 3. Portfolio management. I. Title
HG4651.D68   1990
332.63'23—dc20   89–39761
                                                                      CIP

This publication is designed to provide accurate and authoritative information in regard to the subject matter covered. It is sold with the understanding that the publisher is not engaged in rendering legal, accounting, or other professional service. If legal advice or other expert assistance is required, the services of a competent professional person should be sought.

From a Declaration of Principles Jointly Adopted by a Committee of the American Bar Association and a Committtee of Publishers and Associations

© 1990 by Livingston G. Douglas
Published by NYIF Corp.
A Division of Simon & Schuster, Inc.
2 Broadway, New York, NY 10004–2207

Printed in the United States of America

10   9   8   7   6   5   4   3   2

New York Institute of Finance
(NYIF Corp.)
2 Broadway
New York, NY 10004–2207

Contents

Chapter 3: The Factors That Influence Duration, *21*

Chapter 4: Duration Tables, *42*

Chapter 5: Using Duration as a Risk Measure, *59*

Preface

The purpose of this book, *Bond Risk Analysis*, is to provide a comprehensive and practical discussion of the basic concepts of duration and convexity and to apply these concepts to modern day bond portfolio management. The book addresses the critical concepts of duration and convexity in a thorough and easy-to-understand manner. It is designed for fixed-income investors—portfolio managers, traders, salesmen, pension plan sponsors and consultants, and sophisticated individual investors.

Bond Risk Analysis is structured to enhance the learning process. The book is divided into two basic sections, the first of which discusses duration and the second of which addresses convexity. Each section offers a series of chapters. The initial chapter in each section introduces the broad concept in a very simple manner. The subsequent chapters offer additional insights in a logical, building-block fashion. The final two chapters of each section apply the concept to bond portfolios and bond portfolio management strategies, respectively. These final chapters integrate the discussions of the preceding chapters into a series of in-depth illustrations of the underlying concept in real-world investment situations.

Each of the book's fourteen chapters begins with an introduction, which offers an overview of the chapter. The chapter text is coherently organized with headings and subheadings used to enhance readability. A liberal dose of exhibits (tables, graphs, and figures) support the concepts covered. Footnotes provide additional clarification of technical matters. Each chapter ends with a summary that recaps the chapter and looks ahead to subsequent chapters. Chapter appendixes analyze some of the specialized subject matter in greater detail. The book includes a glossary and index for reference purposes.

Overview of chapter topics

Part I includes Chapters 1 through 8 and covers the concept of duration. Chapter 1 introduces the concept of duration as a measure of time (e.g., 3.2 years, 10.0 years). Chapter 2 describes the calculations underlying Macaulay's duration and offers several interpretations of duration. An appendix provides the duration calculations for bonds purchased between coupon payment dates. Chapter 3 extends the previous chapter's analysis by assessing the factors that influence a bond's duration: term to maturity, coupon rate, accrued interest, market yield level, sinking fund provisions, call provisions, and passage of time. Each of these influences is supported by an extensive series of exhibits. Chapter 4 ascertains the interrelationships of these influential factors through the use of duration tables.

Chapter 5 looks at duration as a measure of a bond's inherent risk. The chapter defines and illustrates the concept of modified duration and outlines the positives and negatives of using modified duration as a measure of bond risk. Chapter 6 analyzes effective duration, a sophisticated version of duration that applies to callable bonds such as corporate bonds and mortgage-backed securities. The chapter also discusses duration to call, duration to maturity, and weighted average duration. The chapter lists the variables that influence effective duration and presents a series of applications of effective duration to corporate bonds and mortgage-backed securities (including derivative products such as CMOs, TACs, POs, and CARDS). In addition, Chapter 6 assesses the effective duration of putable bonds. Chapter appendixes elaborate on the duration of callable bonds, the Capital Management Sciences (CMS) Option Valuation Model, and on historical yield volatility.

Chapter 7 presents the calculations underlying the duration of a portfolio of bonds. An appendix shows how to derive an internal rate of return (IRR). Chapter 8 concludes the duration section with a look at applications of duration in bond portfolio management strategy. The chapter covers both passive investment strategies (cash flow matching, bond immunization, and bond indexation) and active investment strategies (total return maximization, current income maximization, yield maximization, and interest rate anticipation). An appendix analyzes the impacts and mechanics of bond swaps.

Part II encompasses Chapters 9 through 14 of the book and addresses the concept of convexity. Chapter 9 introduces convexity as the difference between a bond's actual price and the bond's price as predicted by its modified duration. Chapter 10 expands on this by detailing the mathematics of convexity and the use of convexity factors and price volatility multipliers. An appendix presents the in-depth mathematics of convexity as the second derivative of the price:yield function. Chapter 11 assesses the factors that influence a bond's convexity: duration, cash flow distribution, yield volatility, and direction of yield change. An appendix looks at the convexity of zero coupon bonds. Chapter 12 discusses the complex subject of negative convexity. The chapter defines negative convexity, illustrates the concept both numerically and graphically, outlines the factors influencing negative convexity, and applies the concept to corporate bonds and mortgage-backed securities.

Chapter 13 shows how to calculate the convexity of a bond portfolio. Chapter 14 concludes the convexity section with a series of applications of convexity in the context of bond portfolio management. The chapter analyzes both passive and active bond management strategies.

Bond Risk Analysis provides the reader with a logical, in-depth analysis of the important concepts of duration and convexity. The book's contents reflect a practical hands-on approach to these topics. The book offers a solid underpinning for both beginners and experienced professionals in the fixed-income marketplace and is designed to serve as a useful reference tool.

LIVINGSTON G. DOUGLAS

Acknowledgments

Bond Risk Analysis: A Guide to Duration and Convexity has its roots in a series of memoranda written during my tenure as a fixed-income investment specialist at the Florida State Board of Administration. I am grateful to the SBA for providing a working atmosphere in which such innovative endeavors were encouraged. Dr. Stephen Celec introduced me to the duration concept during my graduate studies in finance at the Florida State University. Steve, your deep understanding of the mathematics of bonds provided an excellent foundation upon which I could expand and develop a book such as this.

I am also indebted to Ron Ryan of Ryan Labs, Inc. for his many tutorials on the mechanics and real-world applications of bond math. David Kroon and Steve Edelman, colleagues of mine in previous money management endeavors, deserve credit for their quantitative insights in using bond math to enhance a bond portfolio's return while controlling the portfolio's risk. Duration and convexity are, of course, critical elements in this process.

The support of Capital Management Sciences, a consulting firm based in Los Angeles, California, was invaluable. Most of the effective duration calculations in this book were provided by CMS and I must thank Jim Kaplan (President), Sonia Dixon (Senior Vice President), and Daniel Anderson (Senior Consultant) for their cooperation. In addition, Greg Parseghian and Kathy Burke (The First Boston Corporation), Scott Pinkus (Goldmans, Sachs & Co.), and Mitzi Dwyer (Shearson Lehman Hutton, Inc.) contributed data for the illustrations in the book.

I appreciate the effort of the individuals who took time to review the manuscript, including Dr. Thomas Ho (President, Global Advanced Technology Corporation), Robert Kuberek (Vice President, Wilshire Associates), and Jack Malvey (Senior Vice President, Kidder Peabody & Co.). Many of your suggestions are incorporated into the chapters of the book, much to the reader's benefit.

Finally, I must thank Fred Dahl, my editor, and Bob Gulick (President, New York Institute of Finance) for their fine professional support. Both this book and my first book, *Yield Curve Analysis: The Fundamentals of Risk and Return*, are products of Fred Dahl's experienced handiwork. I trust that this book will be useful in the NYIF's fixed-income courses and seminars on bond mathematics.

PART I

Duration

CHAPTER 1

The Duration Concept

Introduction

This chapter offers a simplistic view of duration as a helpful starting point prior to delving into the mathematics and applications of duration. The use of formulas and derivations is covered in Chapter 2.

Defining duration

If one were to ask an average person what the meaning of duration is, that person would probably respond with a reference to time. For example, the duration of a journey or the duration of one's career is the typical context in which a person places duration. Indeed, *Webster's Dictionary* defines duration as:

"the time during which something exists or lasts."[1]

[1] *Webster's Ninth New Collegiate Dictionary* (Springfield, MA: Merriam-Webster Inc., 1988).

3

The word *duration* is from the Latin word *dúráre*, meaning "to last." In general usage, duration is a reference to a length or period of time.

In the context of the financial markets, *duration is a measure of the average life of an investment.* For a zero-coupon bond, the duration of the investment is the period of time remaining until the bond matures, or the term to maturity.[2] Because all of the bond's cash flow occurs on that final maturity date, the best measure of a zero-coupon bond's average life is its term to maturity.

For a coupon-bearing bond, however, the appropriate measure of the bond's duration is not so clear. Since this type of bond generates a series of semiannual cash flows, or coupons, during its lifespan in addition to a principal repayment at the final maturity date, some method of averaging must be done in order to arrive at a representative average life.

Frederick Macaulay reasoned that the best descriptive measure of a bond's average life should consider all of the bond's cash flows (coupons, principal repayment) as well as the time value of money.[3] Macaulay termed this measure *duration*. Therefore, duration in the context of financial instruments can be defined as:

"the weighted average maturity of a bond's cash flows, where the present values of the cash flows serve as the weights."

Duration in a graphical form

A timeline (see Exhibit 1-1) illustrates the duration concept for a typical bond. The duration of a bond is simply the average maturity of the bond's cash flows (keep in mind that the cash flows are adjusted for the time value of money). As a specific

[2] In this book, the reference to "bond" covers both "notes" (bonds issued with final maturities of 10 years or less) and "bonds" (bonds issued with final maturities of greater than 10 years).

[3] *See* Frederick Macaulay's *Some Theoretical Problems Suggested by the Movements of Interest Rates, Bond Yields, and Stock Prices in the United States since 1865* (New York: National Bureau of Economic Research, 1938).

example, the 10-year U.S. Treasury bond (9% due 5/15/98) has a duration of 6.80 years. In other words, the average maturity of this bond's cash flows is on 3/3/95, or 6.80 years from the date of analysis. The May 15, 1988, date is selected to allow the illustration of a duration calculation on a coupon payment date. The duration calculation for a bond evaluated on a coupon payment date (and, therefore, carrying no accrued interest) is the most basic and easiest to understand. Therefore, in the initial chapters of this book, it serves the purpose of illustrating the duration concept without needlessly complicating matters.

As the book progresses, the full impact of many factors (including accrued interest for bonds purchased between coupon payment dates) will be incorporated into the duration presentations. In actuality, May 15, 1988, was a Sunday, and May 16, 1988, prices are used to derive the market values of the bonds illustrated. Exhibit 1–2 shows the cash flow timeline for the 10-year U.S. Treasury bond.

As noted earlier in this chapter, the duration of a zero-coupon bond is dictated by its final maturity date. Exhibit 1–3 illustrates this fact for a 10-year maturity U.S. Treasury Separately Traded Registered Interest and Principal of Securities (STRIPS). The duration of this bond is 5/15/98, or 10.00 years from the date of analysis.

Exhibit 1–1. Duration is a measure of the average maturity of a bond's cash flows.

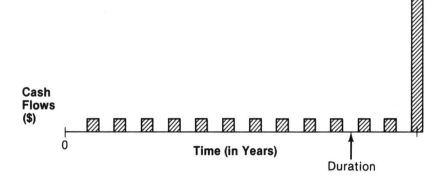

Exhibit 1-2. The duration of a 10-year U.S. Treasury bond (9% due 5/15/98). The bond is priced at par on May 15, 1988.

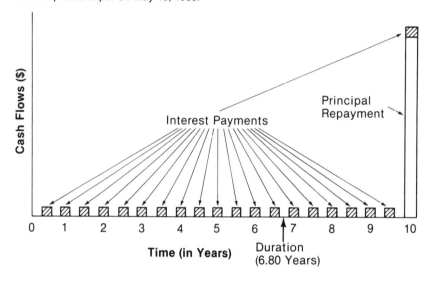

Exhibit 1-3. The duration of a 10-year U.S. Treasury STRIPS (0% due 5/15/98) as of May 15, 1988.

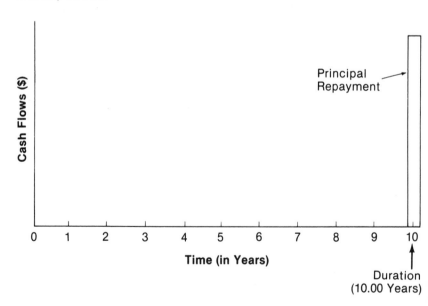

Summary

Duration is a measure of time. Specifically, duration is the weighted average maturity of a bond's cash flows, where the present values of the cash flows serve as the weights. Duration evolved out of the search for a better measure of a bond's "average" life. The duration of a zero-coupon bond is simply its remaining term to maturity. For example, a 5-year zero-coupon bond has a 5.00 duration. The duration of a coupon-bearing bond is somewhat less than its remaining term to maturity. For example, a 9% coupon, 10-year U.S. Treasury bond carries a 6.80 duration. Chapter 2 explains the calculations required to derive a duration.

The Mathematics of Duration

Introduction

This chapter illustrates the mechanics of calculating duration. In addition, it provides a series of expanded definitions of the duration concept. These tools will be helpful to the reader as the book discusses the influences on, and the applications of, duration.

Macaulay's duration

The most widespread form of duration is *Macaulay's duration.* It is calculated as the weighted average maturity of a bond's cash flows, where the present values of the cash flows serve as the weighting factors:[1]

$$\text{Duration (in years)} = \sum_{t=0.5}^{n} \left(\frac{\text{PV(CF}_t)}{\text{TPV}} \times t \right)$$

[1] For simplicity, this duration formula assumes evaluation on a coupon payment date. The chapter Appendix presents a more generalized formula for duration.

where

$PV(CF_t)$ = the present value of the cash flow received in year "t." The investment's internal rate of return (IRR) is used to calculate the present value. For a typical bond, the yield to maturity (YTM) is the bond's IRR. For a more complex investment, such as a mortgage-backed security, the discounted cash flow (DCF) yield serves as the IRR.[2]

CF_t = the nominal cash flow received in year "t"

TPV = the total present value of all of the bond's future cash flows (i.e., the bond's current market value including accrued interest)

t = the number of years (i.e., time) remaining until the receipt of cash flow CF_t

n = the number of years remaining until the final maturity of the bond (i.e., the remaining term to maturity)

The duration formula is not as ominous as it may first appear. The components of the formula can be dissected as follows:

$$\text{Duration (in years)} = \sum_{t=0.5}^{n} \left(\frac{PV(CF_t)}{TPV} \times t \right)$$

Summation   Time Period

Weighting Factor

Duration measures the weighted average maturity of a bond. Each time period (t) in which a cash flow occurs is included in the calculation. To express duration in terms of years, each time period must be expressed in years (e.g., 0.5, 1.0, 1.5).[3] The weighting

[2] For a thorough discussion of internal rates of return, including yield to maturity and DCF yield, you are encouraged to consult Chapter 3 ("Bond Yield Measures") of *Yield Curve Analysis: The Fundamentals of Risk and Return* (New York: New York Institute of Finance, 1988).

[3] Throughout this book, duration is expressed in number of years. Alternatively, one can calculate duration in terms of semiannual periods (or monthly periods) and convert it to an annual figure by an appropriate division.

factor assigns to each time period a value ranging from 0 to 1. The sum of all the weighting factors must be 1.0. Each weighting factor reflects the relative importance of the specific cash flow (CF_t) as a contributor to the bond's total present value, or price (TPV). A period in which a larger cash flow occurs typically registers a weighting factor close to 1.0. A small cash flow warrants a weighting factor closer to 0.0. In addition, a cash flow received further into the future tends to have a lower weighting factor as its influence in present value terms is diminished.[4] Finally, the summation simply adds up all the time periods, as adjusted by the weighting factors.

A sample calculation of duration

Exhibit 2–1 derives the duration of the 10-year U.S. Treasury bond (9% due 5/15/98). Column 1 lists the "*t*" values (i.e., time as expressed in years). Column 2 shows that the bond pays a $45.00 coupon semiannually (i.e., every 0.5 years) and at final maturity makes its final coupon payment ($45.00) in addition to the principal repayment ($1,000.00). Column 3 summarizes the present value (PV) factors (i.e., discounting factors) necessary to translate the future cash flows into present value equivalents. The PV factors are based on the bond's 9% YTM. Column 4 calculates the present values of the bond's future cash flows by multiplying each nominal cash flow (Column 2) by its present value factor (Column 3). The sum of the present values, by definition, equals the bond's current market value or price ($1,000.00).[5] Column 5 computes the weighting

[4] Consult Chapter 1 ("The Time Value of Money") of *Yield Curve Analysis: The Fundamentals of Risk and Return* (New York: New York Institute of Finance, 1988) for a more comprehensive discussion of present values and future values.

[5] A bond's market value is the dollar value of the bond (e.g., $975.00). The bond's par, or face, value is $1,000.00. The bond's price is the bond's market value expressed as a percentage of the bond's par value. For example, a bond valued at $800.00 is quoted at a price of 80.00. A bond valued at $1,157.50 is quoted at 115.75. A bond trading at par ($1,000.00) is quoted at a 100.00 price.

A bond's price is expressed in points (where 1 point = 1% of the bond's face value), and fractions thereof. The fraction is expressed in 32nds of a point for some bonds (U.S. Treasury bonds, federal agency bonds, and mortgage-backed securities) and in 8ths of a point (or in decimal form) for other bonds (corporate bonds and municipal bonds). Consult Chapter 2 ("The Relationship Between Bond Prices and Bond Yields") of *Yield Curve Analysis: The Fundamentals of Risk and Return* (New York: New York Institute of Finance, 1988) for additional information.

Exhibit 2-1. Calculation of the duration of the U.S. Treasury 9% due 5/15/98. On May 15, 1988, the bond was priced at par to yield 9% to maturity.

(1) t Years	(2) Cash Flow	(3) PV Factor	(4) = (2) × (3) PV (CF$_t$)	(5) = (4) / Price Weighting Factor	(6) = (1) × (5) PV-Weighted t
0.5	$ 45.00	0.9569	$ 43.06	0.0431	0.0216
1.0	45.00	0.9157	41.21	0.0412	0.0412
1.5	45.00	0.8763	39.43	0.0394	0.0591
2.0	45.00	0.8386	37.74	0.0377	0.0754
2.5	45.00	0.8025	36.11	0.0361	0.0903
3.0	45.00	0.7679	34.56	0.0346	0.1038
3.5	45.00	0.7348	33.07	0.0331	0.1159
4.0	45.00	0.7032	31.64	0.0316	0.1264
4.5	45.00	0.6729	30.28	0.0303	0.1364
5.0	45.00	0.6439	28.98	0.0290	0.1450
5.5	45.00	0.6162	27.73	0.0277	0.1524
6.0	45.00	0.5897	26.54	0.0265	0.1590
6.5	45.00	0.5643	25.39	0.0254	0.1651
7.0	45.00	0.5400	24.30	0.0243	0.1701
7.5	45.00	0.5167	23.25	0.0233	0.1748
8.0	45.00	0.4945	22.25	0.0223	0.1784
8.5	45.00	0.4732	21.29	0.0213	0.1811
9.0	45.00	0.4528	20.38	0.0204	0.1836
9.5	45.00	0.4333	19.50	0.0195	0.1853
10.0	1,045.00	0.4146	433.26	0.4333	4.3330
			$1,000.00	1.0000	6.8000
			Bond Price		Duration

factors by dividing each present value (Column 4) by the sum of all the present values ($1,000.00). The weighting factors are, in essence, the fractional contributions to the bond's total value; therefore, the sum of all the weighting factors is 1.00. Finally, Column 6 tabulates the time periods as adjusted by their respective weighting factors. The sum of all of these weighted t's is, by definition, the duration of the bond. In this case, the duration is 6.80 years.

The duration of a zero-coupon bond is its remaining term to maturity. Intuitively, this is easy to understand since all of the bond's cash flow occurs on the final maturity date. The calculation is straightforward. A 10-year STRIPS, for example, has a 10.00-year duration. Exhibit 2–2 derives the duration of this STRIPS. The principal repayment at final maturity ($1,000.00) accounts for all of the bond's present value ($414.60). The weighting factor for the tenth year ($t = 10.0$) is 1.00 (i.e., 100%), and the bond's duration is 10.00 years.

Exhibit 2-2. Calculation of the duration of the 10-year STRIPS priced on May 15, 1988, to yield 9% to maturity.

(1)	(2)	(3)	(4) = (2) × (3)	(5) = (4) / Price	(6) = (1) × (5)
t		PV		Weighting	PV-Weighted
Years	Cash Flow	Factor	PV (CF$_t$)	Factor	t
0.5	$ 0.00	0.9569	$ 0	0	0
1.0	0.00	0.9157	0	0	0
.	.	.	.	.	.
.	.	.	.	.	.
.	.	.	.	.	.
9.5	0.00	0.4333	0	0	0
10.0	1,000.00	0.4146	$ 414.60	1.0000	10.0000
			$ 414.60	1.0000	10.0000
			Bond Price		Duration

Durations for a variety of bonds

Exhibit 2–3 presents the durations of a series of U.S. Treasury bills, U.S. Treasury bonds, federal agency bonds, STRIPS, and corporate bonds (the durations of mortgage-backed securities are discussed in Chapter 6). This table supports several conclusions.

First, a U.S. Treasury bill has a duration equal to its remaining term to maturity. For example, a 3-month T-bill carries a 3-month, or 0.25-year, duration because all of the T-bill's cash flow is received at final maturity. Second, a STRIPS has a duration equal to its remaining term to maturity, for the same reason. For example, a 20-year STRIPS (0% due 5/15/08) has a duration of 20.00 years.

Exhibit 2-3. Durations of a sampling of bonds as of May 15, 1988.

Issue	Price	YTM	Duration
U.S. Treasury bill (3-month)			0.25
U.S. Treasury bill (6-month)			0.50
U.S. Treasury 6⅞% due 5/15/89	99–12	7.54	0.98
U.S. Treasury 7⅝% due 5/15/93	96–16	8.48	4.18
U.S. Treasury 9% due 5/15/98	100–00	9.00	6.80
U.S. Treasury 9⅛% due 5/15/18	100–00	9.13	10.67
STRIPS 0% due 5/15/93	65.17	8.75	5.00
STRIPS 0% due 5/15/08	15.63	9.50	20.00
Federal Farm Credit Bank (FFCB)			
14.10% due 6/1/90	110–28	8.21	1.76
Federal Home Loan Bank (FHLB)			
8¼% due 6/25/96	93–16	9.41	5.80
International Business Machines (IBM)			
9% due 5/1/98	97.50	9.50	6.71
Texas Utilities Electric (TXU)			
12% due 9/1/15	102.00	11.75	8.40
Southern Bell Telephone and Telegraph			
(SBT) 8⅝% due 9/1/26	87.00	9.95	10.20

Third, longer maturity bonds have long (i.e., high) durations. The 1-year U.S. Treasury bond (6⅞% due 5/15/89) has a 0.98 duration, the 5-year U.S. Treasury bond (7⅝% due 5/15/93) has a 4.18 duration, the 10-year U.S. Treasury bond (9% due 5/15/98) has a 6.80 duration, and the 30-year U.S. Treasury bond (9⅛% due 5/15/18) has a 10.67 duration. Duration is a measure of the average maturity of a bond's cash flows. Long maturity bonds have more cash flows that occur further into the future than do short maturity bonds. Consequently, long maturity bonds bear high durations.

Fourth, intermediate maturity bonds have middle-of-the-road durations. The IBM 10-year bond (9% due 5/1/98) has a duration of 6.71 years, and the FHLB 8-year bond (8¼% due 6/25/96) has a duration of 5.80 years. The two long-term corporate bonds (Texas Utilities Electric 12% due 9/1/15 and Southern Bell Telephone 8⅜% due 9/1/26 carry durations of 8 to 10 years. Short-term securities, such as T-bills, have durations of less than 1 year.

Duration definitions

Duration can be interpreted in several different ways.

> **Interpretation 1:** *Duration is the weighted average maturity of a bond's cash flows, where the present values of the cash flows serve as the weights.*

The duration calculation includes *all* of a bond's cash flows (coupons and principal repayment). The time value of money is incorporated into the results through weightings based on present values. Duration is an average maturity. A coupon-bearing bond may not have a specific cash flow on the duration date. For example, the 10-year U.S. Treasury bond (9% due 5/15/98) has a duration of 6.80 years. This translates into a March 3, 1995 date. The bond makes coupon payments on May 15 and November 15 of each year; no cash flow occurs on March 3, 1995.

> **Interpretation 2:** *The duration of a bond is the term to maturity of its equivalent zero-coupon bond.*

If one describes a coupon-bearing bond as a single cash flow, rather than as a series of cash flows, the term to maturity of that single cash flow serves as the duration of the bond. As with any averaging measure, of course, there is some degree of error in using a single date as a proxy for a sequence of future cash flows.

> **Interpretation 3:** *Duration is the future point in time at which, on average, an investor will have received half of the original investment, adjusted for the time value of money.*

In a sense, duration is the average point at which an investor has recouped half of the original investment in real, not nominal, terms. The bond's yield to maturity at purchase date serves as the adjustment for the time value of money.

> ***Interpretation 4:*** *Duration is the balancing point, or fulcrum, of a bond's cash flow stream, where the cash flows are expressed in terms of present value.*

The 10-year U.S. Treasury bond (9% due 5/15/98) has a cash flow structure as shown in Exhibit 2–4. Exhibit 2–5 plots the identical cash flow distribution as expressed in present value equivalents, using a discount rate of 9%. The duration of this bond is the point at which one could place a beam under the timeline (Exhibit 2–5) and obtain a perfect balance. The scale would not tip to the left or to the right. Engineers refer to this point as the fulcrum of the scale.

Exhibit 2–4. The cash flow structure of the U.S. Treasury 9% due 5/15/98.

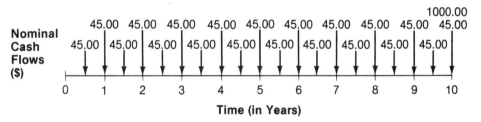

Exhibit 2–5. The cash flow structure (expressed in present value terms) of the U.S. Treasury 9% due 5/15/98. A 9% discount rate is assumed.

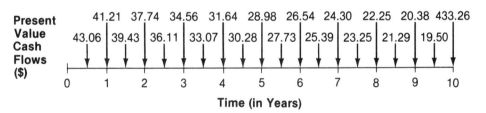

Summary

Macaulay's duration is the weighted average maturity of a bond's cash flows, where the present values of the cash flows serve as the weights. In formula terms, Macaulay's duration is a summation of the time periods (expressed in years) as weighted by the relative contribution of that period's cash flow to the bond's total market value. Each nominal cash flow is translated into a present value equivalent. The sum of all the present values equals the bond's current market value.

The duration of a pure discount bond (e.g., a zero coupon bond or a T-bill) is identical to its remaining term to maturity. The duration of a coupon-bearing bond is somewhat less than its remaining term to maturity because of the influence of coupon cash flows. Long maturity bonds have higher durations than short maturity issues.

Duration can be interpreted as: (1) the weighted average maturity of a bond's cash flows, where the present values of the cash flows serve as the weights; (2) the term to maturity of a bond's zero coupon equivalent; (3) the future point in time at which, on average, an investor will have received half of the original investment, as adjusted for the time value of money; or (4) the fulcrum of the timeline of a bond's present value cash flows.

Duration Calculations for Bonds Purchased Between Coupon Payment Dates

Semiannual-pay bonds

Chapter 2 presents the formula for Macaulay's duration in the context of a semiannual-pay bond purchased on a coupon payment date:

$$\begin{matrix} \text{Duration} \\ \text{(in years)} \end{matrix} = \sum_{t=0.5}^{n} \left(\frac{\text{PV(CF}_t)}{\text{TPV}} \times t \right)$$

This same formula can be expressed as follows:

$$\begin{matrix} \text{Duration} \\ \text{(in semiannual} \\ \text{periods)} \end{matrix} = \sum_{t=1}^{N} \left(\frac{\text{PV(CF}_t)}{\text{TPV}} \times t \right)$$

where

$\text{PV(CF}_t)$ = the present value of the cash flow received in period t. The bond's internal rate of return (per semiannual period) is used to calculate the present value.

CF_t = the nominal cash flow received in period t

TPV = the total present value of all of the bond's future cash flows (i.e., the bond's current market value including accrued interest)

t = the number of semiannual periods remaining until the receipt of cash flow CF_t

n = the number of years remaining until the final maturity of the bond

N = the number of semiannual periods remaining until the final maturity of the bond

The resulting duration is converted into an annual figure by dividing by 2.

The second equation can be rewritten in a form that separates the coupon cash flows from the principal cash flow:

$$\text{Duration (in semiannual periods)} = \sum_{t=1}^{N} \left(\frac{PV(CPN_t)}{TPV} \times t \right) + \left(\frac{PV(P)}{TPV} \times N \right)$$

where

$PV(CPN_t)$ = the present value of the coupon cash flow received in period t. The bond's internal rate of return (per semiannual period) is used to calculate the present value

CPN_t = the nominal coupon amount received in period t

$PV(P)$ = the present value of the principal payment. The bond's internal rate of return (per semiannual period) is used to calculate the present value

P = the principal amount received at final maturity (typically \$1,000.00)

For a semiannual-pay bond analyzed between coupon payment dates, duration is assessed by discounting each cash flow by a factor that reflects the initial fractional period:

$$\text{Duration (in semiannual periods)} = \sum_{t=1-f}^{N-f} \left(\frac{PV(CPN_t)}{TPV} \times t \right) + \left(\frac{PV(P)}{TPV} \times (N-f) \right)$$

where

f = the fraction of a semiannual period that has passed since the last coupon payment

t = the number of semiannual periods remaining until the receipt of cash flow CPN_t

$N - f$ = the number of semiannual periods remaining until the final maturity of the bond

Consequently, the time periods t are expressed in fractional form. For example, if a semiannual-pay bond is evaluated 2 months after its most recent coupon payment, the time periods t are 0.67, 1.67, 2.67, and so on. These figures represent the number of semiannual periods remaining until the future cash flows are received.

Annual-pay bonds

For annual-pay bonds (e.g., Eurobonds), the duration formulas are as follows:

On a Coupon Payment Date:

$$\text{Duration (in years)} = \sum_{t=1}^{N} \left(\frac{\text{PV(CPN}_t)}{\text{TPV}} \times t \right) + \left(\frac{\text{PV(P)}}{\text{TPV}} \times N \right)$$

Between Coupon Payment Dates:

$$\text{Duration (in years)} = \sum_{t=1-f}^{N-f} \left(\frac{\text{PV(CPN}_t)}{\text{TPV}} \times t \right) + \left(\frac{\text{PV(P)}}{\text{TPV}} \times N\text{-}f \right)$$

where

f = the fraction of a annual period that has passed since the last coupon payment

t = the number of annual periods remaining until the receipt of cash flow CPN_t

$N - f =$ the number of annual periods remaining until the final maturity of the bond

The present value computations are based on the bond's internal rate of return as derived on an annual basis.

CHAPTER 3

The Factors That Influence Duration

Introduction

This chapter discusses and illustrates the influences on a bond's duration. There are seven primary influences on a bond's duration: term to maturity, coupon rate, accrued interest, market yield level, sinking fund provisions, call provisions, and the passage of time. General examples as well as specific applications ascertain the relationships. Chapter 4 uses duration tables to identify the interrelationship of these effects.

Term to maturity

Duration is positively related to a bond's remaining term to maturity. Longer maturities create higher durations. Exhibit 3–1 tabulates the durations of a series of 7% coupon U.S. Treasury bonds of maturities ranging from 1 year to 50 years. A 3-year bond bears a 2.76 duration, a 10-year bond carries a 7.36 duration, and a 30-year bond sports a 12.91 duration. Exhibit 3–2 plots

Exhibit 3-1. The durations of 7% coupon U.S. Treasury bonds of various maturities. Each bond is priced at par to yield 7% to maturity.

Term to Maturity (Years)	Duration	Term to Maturity (Years)	Duration
1	0.98	9	6.83
2	1.90	10	7.36
3	2.76	15	9.52
4	3.56	20	11.05
5	4.30	25	12.14
6	5.00	30	12.91
7	5.65	40	13.84
8	6.26	50	14.31

the duration:term-to-maturity relationship. *Duration increases as maturity is extended, but it does so at a decreasing rate* (notice how the curve flattens). *For a zero coupon bond, duration increases at a constant rate as maturity lengthens.* Duration and term to maturity are identical for a zero coupon bond. Exhibit 3–3 illustrates the duration:term-to-maturity relationship for a zero coupon bond as a straight line.

Exhibit 3-2. The duration:term-to-maturity relationship for coupon-bearing bonds (data from Exhibit 3-1).

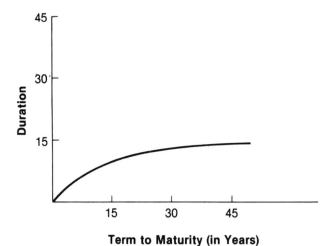

Term to Maturity (in Years)

Exhibit 3-3. The duration:term-to-maturity relationship for zero coupon bonds.

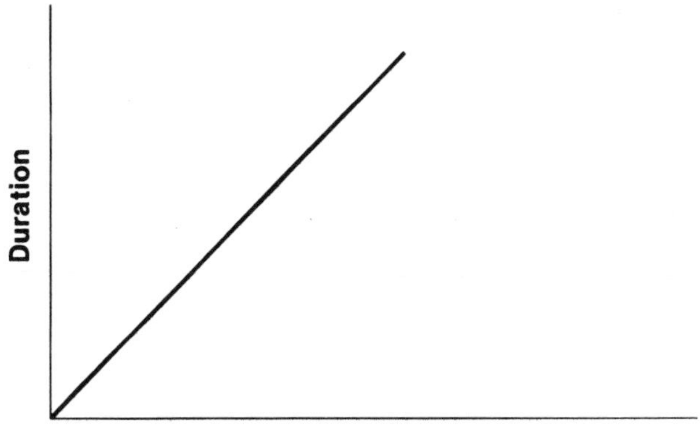

Exhibit 3–4 summarizes the durations of a series of U.S. Treasury bonds and STRIPS as of May 15, 1988. Once again, there is a positive correlation between duration and term to maturity. The 2-year U.S. Treasury (7⅞% due 5/15/90) carries a duration of only 1.89, whereas the 7-year bond (11¼% due 5/15/95) bears a modest 5.15 duration, and the 30-year issue 9⅛% due 5/15/18) has a long duration of 10.67 years.

Exhibit 3-4. The durations of a sample of U.S. Treasury bonds and STRIPS as of May 15, 1988.

Issue	*Term to Maturity (years)*	*Duration*
U.S. Treasury 6⅞% due 5/15/89	1	0.98
U.S. Treasury 7⅞% due 5/15/90	2	1.89
U.S. Treasury 8⅛% due 5/15/91	3	2.72
U.S. Treasury 7⅝% due 5/15/93	5	4.18
U.S. Treasury 11¼% due 5/15/95	7	5.15
U.S. Treasury 9% due 5/15/98	10	6.80
U.S. Treasury 11⅝% due 11/15/02	14½	7.90
U.S. Treasury 9⅛% due 5/15/18	30	10.67
STRIPS 0% due 5/15/93	5	5.00
STRIPS 0% due 5/15/98	10	10.00
STRIPS 0% due 5/15/08	20	20.00

Explanation of the duration:term-to-maturity relationship

Duration and term to maturity are positively related for two primary reasons. First, the principal repayment is a large contributor to a bond's price and is a major influence on a bond's duration. As this cash flow is postponed further into the future, it tugs the bond's duration with it.[1] Second, long maturity bonds have cash flows (coupons, principal) that occur after a short-term security matures. A 10-year bond receives 79% of its cash flow after a 5-year bond matures; a 30-year bond records 89% of its cash flow after a 5-year bond matures and captures 77% of its cash flow after a 10-year bond matures (a 7% coupon rate is assumed). These longer cash flows create a higher duration for the long maturity bond. In a timeline format, the duration fulcrum moves to the right in order to keep the cash flow stream in balance (see Exhibit 3-5). However, duration increases at a decreasing rate because long-term cash flows (of a given nominal amount) are assigned progressively lower present values.

Exhibit 3-5. Extending a bond's maturity leads to a higher duration.

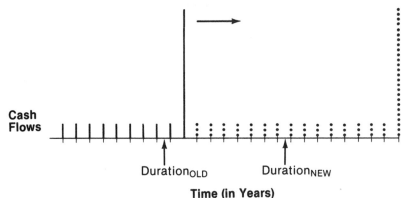

Coupon rate

Duration is inversely related to a bond's coupon rate of interest. All other factors held constant, a high coupon rate corresponds with a low duration. For example, Exhibit 3-6 calculates the

[1] In addition, the long-term coupon payments assist in this tugging process.

Exhibit 3-6. The durations of 30-year U.S. Treasury bonds bearing a variety of coupon rates. Each bond is priced to yield 7% to maturity.

Coupon Rate (%)	Duration	Coupon Rate (%)	Duration
0	30.00	11	12.08
1	20.00	12	11.95
2	17.03	13	11.85
3	15.38	14	11.75
4	14.40	15	11.67
5	13.74	16	11.60
6	13.26	17	11.53
7	12.91	18	11.47
8	12.63	19	11.42
9	12.41	20	11.37
10	12.23		

durations of a series of 30-year U.S. Treasury bonds with coupons ranging from 0% to 20%. A 4% coupon bond carries a duration of 14.40 years whereas a 14% coupon issue has a duration of only 11.75 years. Exhibit 3–7 plots the duration:coupon rate relationship. This exhibit shows that duration falls at a decreasing rate as the coupon rate increases.

Exhibit 3-7. The duration:coupon rate relationship (data from Exhibit 3-6).

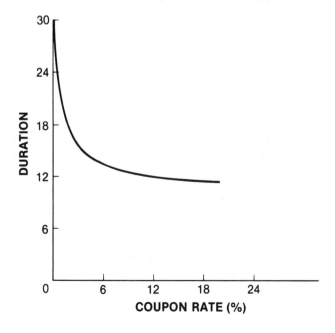

Exhibit 3–8 looks at a set of U.S. Treasury bonds and STRIPS as of May 15, 1988. Once again, lower coupon issues bear longer durations than their higher coupon counterparts of similar maturity. In the 10- to 15-year maturity sector, the U.S. Treasury 8% due 8/15/01 carries a higher duration than the U.S. Treasury 15¾% due 11/15/01 (8.01 versus 7.23). The 20- to 30-year maturity sector finds the duration of the U.S. Treasury 7¼% due 5/15/16 exceeding that of the U.S. Treasury 11¼% due 2/15/15 by approximately 1 year (10.83 versus 9.84).

Exhibit 3-8. The durations of a sample of U.S. Treasury bonds and STRIPS as of May 15, 1988.

10- to 15-Year Maturity Sector	*Coupon Rate (%)*	*Duration*
STRIPS 0% due 5/15/01	0	13.00
U.S. Treasury due 8/15/01	8	8.01
U.S. Treasury due 11/15/01	15¾	7.23
20- to 30-Year Maturity Sector	*Coupon Rate (%)*	*Duration*
STRIPS 0% due 5/15/18	0	30.00
U.S. Treasury due 5/15/16	7¼	10.83
U.S. Treasury due 2/15/15	11¼	9.84
U.S. Treasury due 11/15/11	14	9.21[a]

[a] Duration to final maturity (this bond is callable at par on 11/15/06).

Explanation of the duration:coupon-rate relationship

Duration and coupon rate are inversely related for two primary reasons: First, high coupon bonds have greater amounts of cash flow occurring before final maturity. This reduces the influence of the principal repayment at maturity. Exhibit 3–9 shows that, on a nominal basis, a 7% coupon bond has only 68% of its cash flow attributable to its coupons; a 14% coupon bond has a more sizable 81% of its cash flow traceable to its coupon cash flows. On a present value basis, the coupon contributions are 87% and 93%, respectively, for the 7% coupon bond and the 14% coupon bond.

Exhibit 3-9. The proportion of a bond's cash flow that is attributable to coupon payments and principal repayment. The breakdowns are calculated on both a nominal basis and a present value basis. A variety of coupon rates are presented for comparative purposes. Each bond is a 30-year issue priced to yield 7% to maturity.

| | Nominal Basis | | Present Value Basis | |
Issue	Coupons	Principal	Coupons	Principal
4% coupon bond	55	45	80	20
7% coupon bond	68	32	87	13
10% coupon bond	75	25	91	9
14% coupon bond	81	19	93	7

Second, the discounting process has less effect on the early cash flows (i.e., the coupon payments) than on the late cash flows (i.e., the final coupon payments and the principal repayment).[2] For example, a $50.00 coupon due in 2 years is valued at $43.57 in present value dollars; a $50.00 coupon due in 20 years is worth only $12.63 today (a 7% discount rate is assumed). Consequently, the large coupon cash flows are assigned greater weights in present value terms. Pictorially, a high coupon bond forces the duration fulcrum toward the left on the scale to maintain equilibrium (see Exhibit 3-10).

Exhibit 3-11 segregates the present values of the coupon payment stream and the principal repayment for a series of 30-year U.S. Treasury bonds of various coupon rates. This table shows that the coupon cash flows have more weight than the principal repayment at maturity, particularly for high coupon bonds. For example, a 14% coupon bond's principal repayment accounts for only 7% of the bond's market value; the remaining 93% is attributable to the coupon cash flows. However, only 79% of the price of a 4% coupon bond is attributable to its coupon cash

[2]You are encouraged to consult Chapter 1 ("The Time Value of Money") and Chapter 6 ("Bond Risk Measures: The Present") of *Yield Curve Analysis: The Fundamentals of Risk and Return* (New York: New York Institute of Finance, 1988) for more details on present value calculations and their influence on specific cash flows as yield levels change.

Exhibit 3-10. Raising a bond's coupon rate lowers the bond's duration.

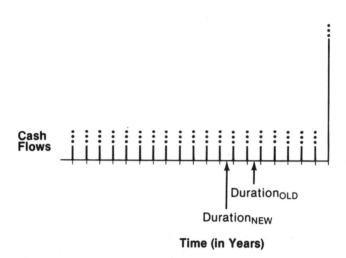

Time (in Years)

Exhibit 3-11. The present value weights of coupon payments versus principal repayment for a series of 30-year U.S. Treasury bonds of various coupon rates. Each bond is priced to yield 7% to maturity.

	Percentage of Bond Price Attributable to:		
			Bond
Coupon Rate (%)	*Coupon Payments*	*Principal*	*Duration*
0	0	100	30.00
4	79	21	14.40
7	87	13	12.91
10	91	9	12.23
14	93	7	11.75

flows. Consequently, the 14% coupon issue carries an 11.75 duration, a sharp contrast to the 14.40 duration of the 4% coupon bond.

Accrued interest

A bond's duration is inversely related to the amount of accrued interest attached to the bond. A bond purchased or sold between coupon payment dates is subject to accrued interest. The full price of a bond is the sum of the bond's quoted price (e.g., 98½, or $985.00) plus any accrued interest (e.g., 3 points, or $30.00). The duration calculation uses the full price, not the quoted price. Therefore, accrued interest has an impact on a bond's duration.

Accrued interest can be considered as an investment with a zero duration. The upcoming coupon payment essentially reimburses the owner of the bond for the accrued interest paid up front. On semiannual-pay bonds, this reimbursement occurs within 6 months. Not surprisingly, a bond with a lot of accrued interest has a lower duration than a similar bond with little or no accrued interest. The accrued interest portion of the bond's full price drags down the bond's overall duration. When the bond's coupon payment is made and the accrued interest amount disappears, the bond's duration lengthens because the bond is relieved of its zero duration component.

As an example, a 7% coupon, 30-year U.S. Treasury bond carries a 12.48 duration one day before coupon payment. After the coupon payment is made, the bond's accrued interest falls to zero, and the bond's full price falls by the amount of the coupon payment. At the same time, the bond's duration extends to 12.91 years, an upward move of 0.43 year (see Exhibit 3–12). The 30-year U.S. Treasury bond (9⅛% due 5/15/18) experiences almost a half-year duration shift on November 15, 1988, its first coupon payment date. The bond's duration jumps from 10.17 to 10.64 years when the accrued interest drops off. The buildup and payout of accrued interest can have a sizable impact on a bond's duration.[3] What a difference a (coupon payment) day can make!

Exhibit 3-12. The duration of a 7% coupon, 30-year U.S. Treasury in "full accrued" and "no accrued" states. The bond is priced at par to yield 7% to maturity.

	Duration	
Issue	*Full Accrued*	*No Accrued*
30-year U.S. Treasury bond	12.48	12.91

[3] A newly issued bond may be subject to a long or short first coupon payment. A long coupon has a greater effect on the bond's duration than a normal coupon does; a short coupon has a lesser effect on the bond's duration than a normal coupon does.

*The accrued interest effect is magnified in annual-pay bonds sucl
as Eurodollar bonds.* For example, Exhibit 3-13 compares th
durations of a U.S. corporate bond and a Eurodollar bond ir
both "full accrued" and "no accrued" states. The 10-year corporate
experiences a 0.25-year duration shift on the coupon paymen
date (7.36 versus 7.11). The 10-year Euro registers a 0.49-yea
duration advance under the same conditions (7.52 versus 7.03)
The Eurodollar bond is more susceptible to the accrued interes
effect because it pays coupons on an annual, rather than
semiannual, basis. The buildup of accrued interest is approximately
twice that of a semiannual-pay bond.[4]

Exhibit 3-13. The duration of 7% coupon, 10-year bonds in "full accrued" anc
"no accrued" states. Each bond is priced at par to yield 7% to maturity.

	Duration	
Issue	*Full Accrued*	*No Accrued*
10-year U.S. corporate bond (semiannual-pay)	7.11	7.36
10-year Eurodollar bond (annual-pay)	7.03	7.52

Explanation of duration:accrued-interest relationship

Duration and accrued interest are inversely related because accrued
interest is essentially a cash investment with a zero duration. The
greater the proportion of a bond's full price that is attributable
to accrued interest, the lower the bond's duration. In a timeline
schematic, as the coupon payment falls off the left side of the
scale, the duration fulcrum must move right in order to maintain
the balancing role that it serves (see Exhibit 3-14).

[4] Note that the duration of the Eurobond in a "no accrued" state is longer than
that of the U.S. corporate bond under similar conditions (7.52 versus 7.36). The longer
duration of the Eurobond is attributable to the fact that the Eurobond's coupon payment
is received entirely at year-end; the semiannual-pay bond receives half of its annual coupon
amount at midyear, with the remainder payable at year-end. The deferral in receipt of
coupon cash flows extends the Eurobond's duration by 0.16 year vis-à-vis its American
counterpart.

Exhibit 3-14. A coupon payment forces a natural extension of a bond's duration.

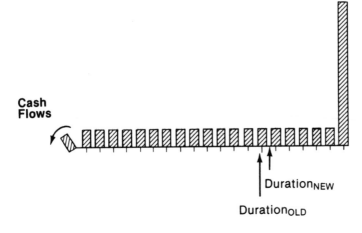

Market yield level

Duration is inversely related to the market yield level at which a bond trades. High yield environments lead to low durations; low yield environments create high durations. Exhibit 3–15 illustrates this phenomenon through the use of 30-year U.S. Treasury bonds priced at par in a variety of yield conditions ranging from 1% to 20%. For example, the duration of a current coupon 30-year bond in a 10% yield environment stands at 9.94 years. If interest rates fall to 7%, a newly issued 30-year bond bears a duration of 12.91 years. A further decline in interest rates to the 4% area gives a newly issued bond a duration of 17.73 years. Exhibit 3–16 plots the duration: market yield relationship, showing that the surge in duration accelerates as yields decline progressively further.

Exhibit 3-15. The durations of 30-year U.S. Treasury bonds priced at par in a variety of yield environments.

Yield Environment (%)	Duration	Yield Environment (%)	Duration
1	25.99	11	9.21
2	22.70	12	8.57
3	19.99	13	8.01
4	17.73	14	7.51
5	15.84	15	7.07
6	14.25	16	6.68
7	12.91	17	6.34
8	11.76	18	6.02
9	10.78	19	5.74
10	9.94	20	5.48

Exhibit 3-16. The duration:market yield relationship (data from Exhibit 3-15).

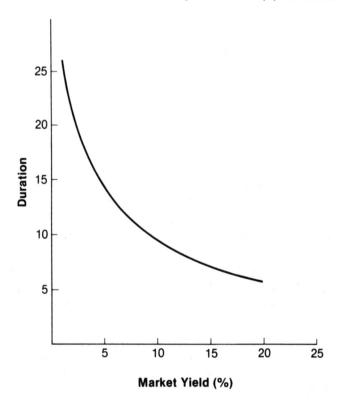

The decade of the 1980s witnessed a wide range of market yields on U.S. Treasury bonds. Exhibit 3-17 provides a capsule view of the commensurately wild fluctuations in the durations of new-issue U.S. Treasury long-term bonds during the 1980s. This table calculates the durations of a sample of issues priced at par as of the issue dates. In the 30-year bond arena, for example, the 14% due 11/15/11 was issued in November 1981 and carried a duration of only 7.51 years. The sizable collapse in yields from 1984 to 1986 led to the issuance of a 7¼% coupon bond in May 1986. This issue had a calculated duration of 12.61 years at issuance, which was much higher than the durations of its counterparts of the early 1980s.

Explanation of the duration:market yield relationship

Duration and market yield are inversely related for two primary reasons. First, duration is based on the present value weights of a bond's cash flows. Duration falls as interest rates rise because the present value discounting process assigns lower weights to the long-term cash flows and assigns higher weights to the short-term cash flows. Exhibit 3-18 illustrates the duration behavior of a 7% coupon, 30-year U.S. Treasury bond. In a 7% yield environment, the bond carries a 12.91 duration. If yields rise to 14%, the bond's duration collapses to 7.89 years.

Exhibit 3-17. Durations of a sample of U.S. Treasury bonds at issue date (each issue is priced at par).

20-Year Bonds	*Issued*	*YTM (%)*	*Duration*
U.S. Treasury 15¾% due 11/15/01	10/7/81	15.75	6.54
U.S. Treasury 11⅝% due 11/15/02	9/29/82	11.63	8.18
U.S. Treasury 9⅜% due 2/15/06	1/15/86	9.38	9.40

30-Year Bonds	*Issued*	*YTM (%)*	*Duration*
U.S. Treasury 14% due 11/15/11	11/16/81	14.00	7.51
U.S. Treasury 11¼% due 2/15/15	2/15/85	11.25	9.04
U.S. Treasury 9¼% due 2/15/16	2/15/86	9.25	10.56
U.S. Treasury 7¼% due 5/15/16	5/15/86	7.25	12.61

Exhibit 3-18. Duration of a 7% coupon, 30-year U.S. Treasury bond in a variety of yield environments.

Yield Environment (%)	Duration
7	12.91
10	10.39
14	7.89

Exhibit 3-19 shows why the 7% coupon bond's duration falls so dramatically. As interest rates rise, the present value of the principal payment falls disproportionately, driving down its relative contribution to the bond's price. Whereas at a 7% yield the principal accounts for 13% of the bond's price, a 14% yield shrinks the principal contribution to only 3%. The greater weightings assigned to the coupon cash flows (particularly the earliest coupon cash flows) pull the duration of the bond downward.

Second, the first rationale is amplified by the fact that newly issued bonds have coupon rates that reflect the surrounding yield environment. High yield environments warrant the issuance of high coupon bonds (e.g., 14% coupon issues). The coupon component of the newly issued bond is an even greater proportion of the bond's market price. Exhibit 3-20 illustrates the impact on duration by comparing the 7% coupon bond of earlier illustrations to a current coupon bond in the variety of yield environments outlined in the previous example. Vis-à-vis the 7% coupon issue, current coupon bonds experience a larger decline in duration as interest rates rise. The effect of the yield shift more readily affects the durations of current coupon issues.

Exhibit 3-19. The present value weights of coupons versus principal repayment for a 7% coupon, 30-year U.S. Treasury bond in a variety of yield environments.

Yield Environment (%)	Percentage of Bond Price Attributable to:		
	Coupon Payments	Principal Repayment	Bond Duration
7	87	13	12.91
10	93	7	10.39
14	97	3	7.89

Exhibit 3-20. Durations of a set of 30-year U.S. Treasury bonds in a variety of yield environments.

Yield Environment (%)	Duration of a:	
	7% Coupon Bond	*Current Coupon Bond*
7	12.91	12.91
10	10.39	9.94
14	7.89	7.51

Sinking fund provisions

Sinking fund provisions lower the duration of a bond by reducing the average maturity of the principal repayment.[5] The higher the percentage of the bond issue sunk before final maturity, the lower the bond's duration. For example, a 7% coupon, 20-year corporate bond (priced at par) has a duration of 11.05 years. Attaching a 90% sinker to this bond will lower its duration to 9.60 years. Exhibit 3–21 illustrates the duration calculation for such a bond. The earlier the repayment of the bond's principal, the lower the weighted average maturity of the bond's cash flows, as reflected by the bond's duration. Any additional provisions granted to the issuer (e.g., a sinking fund doubling option) will reduce the bond's duration further.

Explanation of the duration:sinking fund relationship

Two major factors explain the inverse relationship between a bond's duration and its sinking fund provisions. First, the return of principal at earlier points in time shortens the average maturity of the bond's cash flows. Second, the nominal amount of coupon cash flow decreases because the principal amount outstanding is drawn down before final maturity (coupon payments are based on the principal outstanding). Column 2 of Exhibit 3–21 illustrates

[5] The effects of sinking fund provisions apply principally to bonds with *pro-rata sinkers*. Bonds with *market sinkers* have duration impacts that are not easily generalized. Most corporate bonds grant the issuer the right to satisfy the sinking fund requirement(s) through open-market purchases of bonds.

Exhibit 3-21. Calculation of the duration of a 7% coupon, 20-year corporate bond with a sinking fund paying down 10% of the principal amount annually, beginning in Year 11. The bond is priced at par to yield 7% to maturity.

(1) t Years	(2) Cash Flow	(3) PV Factor	(4) = (2) × (3) PV (CF$_t$)	(5) = (4) / Price Weighting Factor	(6) = (1) × (5) PV-Weighted t
0.5	$ 35.00	0.9662	$ 33.82	0.0338	0.0169
1.0	35.00	0.9335	32.67	0.0327	0.0327
1.5	35.00	0.9019	31.57	0.0316	0.0474
2.0	35.00	0.8714	30.50	0.0305	0.0610
2.5	35.00	0.8420	29.47	0.0295	0.0738
3.0	35.00	0.8135	28.47	0.0285	0.0855
3.5	35.00	0.7860	27.51	0.0275	0.0963
4.0	35.00	0.7594	26.58	0.0266	0.1064
4.5	35.00	0.7337	25.68	0.0257	0.1157
5.0	35.00	0.7089	24.81	0.0248	0.1240
5.5	35.00	0.6849	23.97	0.0240	0.1320
6.0	35.00	0.6618	23.16	0.0232	0.1392
6.5	35.00	0.6394	22.38	0.0224	0.1456
7.0	35.00	0.6178	21.62	0.0216	0.1512
7.5	35.00	0.5969	20.89	0.0209	0.1568
8.0	35.00	0.5767	20.18	0.0202	0.1616
8.5	35.00	0.5572	19.50	0.0195	0.1658
9.0	35.00	0.5384	18.84	0.0188	0.1692
9.5	35.00	0.5202	18.21	0.0182	0.1729
10.0	35.00	0.5026	17.59	0.0176	0.1760
10.5	35.00	0.4856	17.00	0.0170	0.1785
11.0	135.00	0.4692	63.34	0.0633	0.6963
11.5	31.50	0.4533	14.28	0.0143	0.1645
12.0	131.50	0.4380	57.60	0.0576	0.6912
12.5	28.00	0.4231	11.85	0.0119	0.1488
13.0	128.00	0.4088	52.33	0.0523	0.6799
13.5	24.50	0.3950	9.68	0.0097	0.1310
14.0	124.50	0.3817	47.52	0.0475	0.6650
14.5	21.00	0.3687	7.74	0.0077	0.1117
15.0	121.00	0.3563	43.11	0.0431	0.6465
15.5	17.50	0.3442	6.02	0.0060	0.0930
16.0	117.50	0.3326	39.08	0.0391	0.6256
16.5	14.00	0.3213	4.50	0.0045	0.0743
17.0	114.00	0.3105	35.40	0.0354	0.6018
17.5	10.50	0.3000	3.15	0.0032	0.0560
18.0	110.50	0.2898	32.02	0.0320	0.5760
18.5	7.00	0.2800	1.96	0.0020	0.0370
19.0	107.00	0.2706	28.95	0.0290	0.5510
19.5	3.50	0.2614	0.91	0.0009	0.0176
20.0	103.50	0.2526	26.14	0.0261	0.5220
			$1,000.00	1.0000	9.6000
			Bond Price		Duration

this fact. Coupon payments commence at $35.00 semiannually ($1,000.00 principal × 7% coupon rate × 1/2 year = $35.00) and decline each year by $3.50 per semiannual payment as the principal is paid down (starting in Year 11).

The combination of these two factors forces the relative weight of the principal cash flow to increase. For a 7% coupon, 20-year corporate bond, the principal:coupon mix moves from a 25:75 ratio to a 35:65 ratio (see Exhibit 3–22).

Exhibit 3–22. The relative contributions to the price of a 7% coupon, 20-year corporate bond with (1) no sinking fund provision and (2) a 90% sinker (from Exhibit 3-21). Each bond is priced at par to yield 7% to maturity.

Issue	Percentage of Bond Price Attributable to:		Bond Duration
	Coupon Payments	Principal Repayment	
No Sinker	75	25	11.05
90% Sinker	65	35	9.60

Call provisions

Cash call and refunding call provisions lower the duration of a bond by reducing the period of time the bond may be outstanding. In the case of mortgage-backed securities, prepayment features have a similar effect. Chapter 6 discusses the impact of these provisions.

Passage of time

The passage of time eats away at a bond's duration as the bond's remaining term to maturity falls. In the case of a zero-coupon bond, the duration decline parallels the maturity reduction (see again Exhibit 3–3). In the case of coupon-bearing bonds, however, the duration drift is less uniform. Exhibit 3–23 calculates by year the duration of a 30-year, 7% coupon bond during its lifespan. As the bond moves from a 30-year issue to a 29-year issue, its duration falls by only 0.13 year. Late in its life, the issue's impending maturity forces duration declines of almost a full year per annum (see Exhibit 3–24). Exhibit 3–25 plots the duration erosion of this bond at a gradual, but accelerating, pace.

Exhibit 3-23. The duration of a 7% coupon, 30-year U.S. Treasury bond at annual points during its lifespan. Interest rates are held stable at 7%.

Remaining Term to Maturity (Years)	Duration	Remaining Term to Maturity (Years)	Duration
30	12.91	14	9.14
29	12.78	13	8.74
28	12.63	12	8.31
27	12.48	11	7.85
26	12.31	10	7.36
25	12.14	9	6.83
24	11.95	8	6.26
23	11.75	7	5.65
22	11.53	6	5.00
21	11.30	5	4.30
20	11.05	4	3.56
19	10.79	3	2.76
18	10.50	2	1.90
17	10.20	1	0.98
16	9.87	0	0.00
15	9.52		

A secondary effect of passing time is created by the buildup and dropoff of accrued interest. A coupon payment causes a temporary surge in the underlying bond's duration. On a graph,

Exhibit 3-24. The duration drift of a 7% coupon, 30-year U.S. Treasury bond in its early and late stages (data from Exhibit 3-23).

Remaining Term to Maturity (Years)	Maturity Decline	Duration Decline
30		
29	–1.00	–0.13
28	–1.00	–0.15
.		
.	.	.
.	.	.
3		
2	–1.00	–0.86
1	–1.00	–0.92
0	–1.00	–0.98

Exhibit 3-25. The behavior of duration over time (data from Exhibit 3-23).

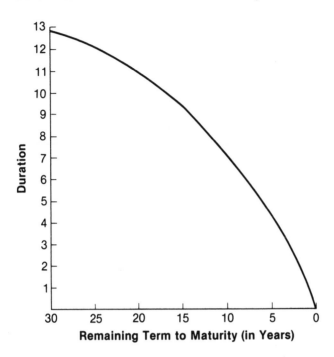

these spikes create a sawtooth pattern in the duration curve (see Exhibit 3-26). The durations of bonds with long terms to maturity are more sensitive to coupon accrual and payout than the durations of short maturity issues.

Explanation of the duration:passage-of-time relationship

As time passes, a bond's duration falls at an increasing rate. The duration decline is a natural consequence of the progressively smaller set of remaining coupon cash flows and the approaching principal repayment. The increasing dominance of the principal repayment forces an acceleration of the duration decline as the final maturity date nears. For a zero coupon bond, the duration falls at a constant rate because the principal repayment is the only future cash flow generated by the bond.

Exhibit 3-26. The behavior of duration over time (including coupon accrual and payment effects).

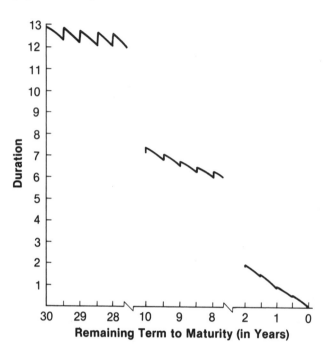

Summary

Exhibit 3-27 summarizes the factors that influence duration. Duration is positively related to a bond's remaining term to maturity. A long maturity warrants a long duration. For a coupon-bearing bond, duration increases at a decreasing rate as the bond's maturity lengthens. For a zero coupon bond, duration bears a one-to-one relationship with the term to maturity; therefore, a zero coupon bond's duration increases at a constant rate as the bond's maturity extends.

Duration is inversely related to a bond's coupon rate of interest. A higher coupon rate justifies a lower duration because the final principal repayment loses relative importance. Duration is inversely related to the amount of accrued interest on a bond. Larger amounts of accrued interest reduce a bond's duration. This

Exhibit 3-27. A summary of the influences on a bond's duration.

Factor	Duration Behavior	
	Low Duration	*High Duration*
Term to maturity	Shorter	Longer
Coupon rate	Higher	Lower
Accrued interest	Large	Small
Market yield level	Higher	Lower
Sinking fund features	Many	Few
Call provisions	Many	Few

effect is magnified in an annual-pay bond, which has a longer period of interest accumulation than a traditional semiannual-pay bond.

Duration is inversely related to the market yield level. A high market yield correlates with a low duration because the long-term cash flows lose their influence in the duration calculation. Sinking funds and call provisions lower a bond's duration by reducing the amount of time that a bond's principal remains outstanding. The passage of time erodes duration as the remaining term to maturity falls. Chapter 4 analyzes the interrelationship of these primary determinants of a bond's duration.

Duration Tables

Introduction

Chapter 3 identified the primary influences on a bond's duration. This chapter uses duration tables to ascertain the interrelationships between these variables. It also assesses the sensitivities of the primary factors. This, in turn, highlights the relative importance of the factors that determine a bond's duration.

The primary factors

There are seven primary influences on a bond's duration:
1. Term to maturity
2. Coupon rate
3. Accrued interest
4. Market yield level
5. Sinking fund provisions
6. Call provisions
7. The passage of time

Duration tables confirm the primary relationships and reveal the interaction between the major factors.

Duration tables

Exhibits 4–1, 4–2, and 4–3 are a set of duration tables that summarize more than 2,000 durations. These tables isolate the sensitivity of duration to changes in term to maturity, coupon rate, and market yield level. In addition, the tables reveal the interaction of these variables. Exhibit 4–1 presents the durations of a series of current coupon (i.e., par) bonds of a variety of maturities (1 to 50 years) across a wide span of yield levels (0% through 20%). Exhibit 4–2 organizes the durations of a sequence of bonds of various coupon rates (0% through 20%) over a broad range of maturities (1 to 50 years). A 7% yield environment is assumed.[1] Exhibit 4–3 illustrates the interactions of the coupon rate (0% through 20%) and the market yield level (0% through 20%) on the duration of a 30-year bond.

The interaction of term to maturity and market yield level

Long maturities lead to long durations. In a 10% yield environment, a 1-year bond bears a duration of 0.98 years, a 5-year bond carries a duration of 4.05 years, a 10-year bond has a duration of 6.54 years, a 20-year bond offers a 9.01-year duration, and a 50-year bond earns a 10.42 duration:

Term to Maturity (Years)	Duration (10% Yield Environment)
1	0.98
5	4.05
10	6.54
20	9.01
50	10.42

[1] A 7% interest rate environment was selected for two primary reasons. First, a long-term historical perspective of U.S. interest rates finds 7% to be a more "average" level than the 9% yields of early 1989 or the double-digit rates that existed in the early
(continued on page 49)

Exhibit 4-1. Macaulay's durations (in years) for par bonds in a variety of yield environments and for a variety of maturities.

					Maturity (Years)						
YTM (%)	1	2	3	4	5	6	7	8	9	10	11
0.0	1.00	2.00	3.00	4.00	5.00	6.00	7.00	8.00	9.00	10.00	11.00
0.5	1.00	1.99	2.98	3.97	4.94	5.92	6.89	7.85	8.81	9.77	10.72
1.0	1.00	1.99	2.96	3.93	4.89	5.84	6.78	7.71	8.63	9.54	10.44
1.5	1.00	1.98	2.95	3.90	4.84	5.76	6.67	7.57	8.45	9.32	10.18
2.0	1.00	1.97	2.93	3.86	4.78	5.68	6.57	7.43	8.28	9.11	9.93
2.5	0.99	1.96	2.91	3.83	4.73	5.61	6.47	7.30	8.12	8.91	9.69
3.0	0.99	1.96	2.89	3.80	4.68	5.54	6.37	7.17	7.95	8.71	9.45
3.5	0.99	1.95	2.87	3.77	4.63	5.46	6.27	7.05	7.80	8.52	9.22
4.0	0.99	1.94	2.86	3.74	4.58	5.39	6.17	6.93	7.65	8.34	9.01
4.5	0.99	1.94	2.84	3.71	4.53	5.33	6.08	6.81	7.50	8.16	8.80
5.0	0.99	1.93	2.82	3.68	4.49	5.26	5.99	6.69	7.36	7.99	8.59
5.5	0.99	1.92	2.81	3.65	4.44	5.19	5.90	6.58	7.22	7.82	8.40
6.0	0.99	1.91	2.79	3.62	4.39	5.13	5.82	6.47	7.08	7.66	8.21
6.5	0.98	1.91	2.77	3.59	4.35	5.06	5.73	6.36	6.95	7.51	8.03
7.0	0.98	1.90	2.76	3.56	4.30	5.00	5.65	6.26	6.83	7.36	7.85
7.5	0.98	1.89	2.74	3.53	4.26	4.94	5.57	6.16	6.70	7.21	7.68
8.0	0.98	1.89	2.73	3.50	4.22	4.88	5.49	6.06	6.58	7.07	7.52
8.5	0.98	1.88	2.71	3.47	4.18	4.82	5.42	5.96	6.47	6.93	7.36
9.0	0.98	1.87	2.70	3.45	4.13	4.76	5.34	5.87	6.35	6.80	7.20
9.5	0.98	1.87	2.68	3.42	4.09	4.71	5.27	5.78	6.24	6.67	7.05
10.0	0.98	1.86	2.67	3.39	4.05	4.65	5.20	5.69	6.14	6.54	6.91
10.5	0.98	1.86	2.65	3.37	4.02	4.60	5.13	5.60	6.03	6.42	6.77
11.0	0.97	1.85	2.64	3.34	3.98	4.55	5.06	5.52	5.93	6.30	6.64
11.5	0.97	1.84	2.62	3.32	3.94	4.49	4.99	5.44	5.83	6.19	6.51
12.0	0.97	1.84	2.61	3.29	3.90	4.44	4.93	5.36	5.74	6.08	6.38
12.5	0.97	1.83	2.59	3.27	3.86	4.39	4.86	5.28	5.65	5.97	6.26
13.0	0.97	1.82	2.58	3.24	3.83	4.35	4.80	5.20	5.56	5.87	6.14
13.5	0.97	1.82	2.56	3.22	3.79	4.30	4.74	5.13	5.47	5.77	6.03
14.0	0.97	1.81	2.55	3.20	3.76	4.25	4.68	5.05	5.38	5.67	5.92
14.5	0.97	1.81	2.54	3.17	3.72	4.20	4.62	4.98	5.30	5.57	5.81
15.0	0.97	1.80	2.52	3.15	3.69	4.16	4.56	4.91	5.22	5.48	5.71
15.5	0.96	1.79	2.51	3.13	3.66	4.11	4.51	4.85	5.14	5.39	5.61
16.0	0.96	1.79	2.50	3.10	3.62	4.07	4.45	4.78	5.06	5.30	5.51
16.5	0.96	1.78	2.48	3.08	3.59	4.03	4.40	4.72	4.99	5.22	5.41
17.0	0.96	1.78	2.47	3.06	3.56	3.98	4.35	4.65	4.91	5.13	5.32
17.5	0.96	1.77	2.46	3.04	3.53	3.94	4.29	4.59	4.84	5.05	5.23
18.0	0.96	1.77	2.45	3.02	3.50	3.90	4.24	4.53	4.77	4.98	5.15
18.5	0.96	1.76	2.43	3.00	3.47	3.86	4.19	4.47	4.70	4.90	5.06
19.0	0.96	1.75	2.42	2.98	3.44	3.82	4.15	4.41	4.64	4.83	4.98
19.5	0.96	1.75	2.41	2.95	3.41	3.79	4.10	4.36	4.57	4.75	4.90
20.0	0.96	1.74	2.40	2.93	3.38	3.75	4.05	4.30	4.51	4.68	4.82

Exhibit 4-1. (cont.)

					Maturity (Years)							
YTM (%) 12	13	14	15	16	17	18	19	20	30	40	50
0.0	12.00	13.00	14.00	15.00	16.00	17.00	18.00	19.00	20.00	30.00	40.00	50.00
0.5	11.66	12.60	13.54	14.47	15.40	16.32	17.24	18.15	19.06	27.90	36.30	44.30
1.0	11.34	12.22	13.10	13.97	14.83	15.68	16.52	17.35	18.18	25.99	33.07	39.47
1.5	11.03	11.86	12.68	13.49	14.28	15.07	15.84	16.60	17.35	24.27	30.22	35.35
2.0	10.73	11.51	12.28	13.03	13.77	14.50	15.20	15.90	16.58	22.70	27.72	31.83
2.5	10.44	11.18	11.90	12.60	13.29	13.95	14.60	15.24	15.86	21.28	25.51	28.81
3.0	10.17	10.86	11.53	12.19	12.82	13.44	14.04	14.62	15.18	19.99	23.55	26.20
3.5	9.90	10.55	11.19	11.80	12.39	12.95	13.50	14.04	14.55	18.81	21.82	23.94
4.0	9.65	10.26	10.85	11.42	11.97	12.49	13.00	13.49	13.95	17.73	20.27	21.98
4.5	9.40	9.98	10.54	11.07	11.57	12.06	12.52	12.97	13.39	16.74	18.89	20.27
5.0	9.17	9.71	10.23	10.73	11.20	11.65	12.07	12.48	12.87	15.84	17.66	18.77
5.5	8.94	9.45	9.94	10.40	10.84	11.25	11.65	12.02	12.37	15.01	16.55	17.44
6.0	8.72	9.21	9.66	10.09	10.50	10.88	11.24	11.58	11.90	14.25	15.55	16.27
6.5	8.51	8.97	9.40	9.80	10.18	10.53	10.86	11.17	11.47	13.55	14.66	15.24
7.0	8.31	8.74	9.14	9.52	9.87	10.20	10.50	10.79	11.05	12.91	13.84	14.31
7.5	8.12	8.52	8.90	9.25	9.57	9.88	10.16	10.42	10.66	12.31	13.11	13.49
8.0	7.93	8.31	8.67	8.99	9.29	9.57	9.83	10.07	10.29	11.76	12.44	12.74
8.5	7.75	8.11	8.44	8.75	9.03	9.29	9.52	9.74	9.94	11.26	11.83	12.07
9.0	7.57	7.91	8.23	8.51	8.77	9.01	9.23	9.43	9.62	10.78	11.27	11.47
9.5	7.41	7.73	8.02	8.29	8.53	8.75	8.95	9.14	9.30	10.35	10.76	10.92
10.0	7.24	7.55	7.82	8.07	8.30	8.50	8.69	8.86	9.01	9.94	10.29	10.42
10.5	7.09	7.37	7.63	7.86	8.07	8.26	8.44	8.59	8.73	9.56	9.86	9.96
11.0	6.94	7.21	7.45	7.67	7.86	8.04	8.20	8.34	8.46	9.21	9.46	9.55
11.5	6.79	7.05	7.27	7.48	7.66	7.82	7.97	8.10	8.21	8.87	9.09	9.16
12.0	6.65	6.89	7.11	7.30	7.47	7.62	7.75	7.87	7.98	8.57	8.75	8.81
12.5	6.52	6.74	6.94	7.12	7.28	7.42	7.54	7.65	7.75	8.28	8.43	8.48
13.0	6.39	6.60	6.79	6.95	7.10	7.23	7.34	7.44	7.53	8.01	8.14	8.18
13.5	6.26	6.46	6.64	6.79	6.93	7.05	7.15	7.25	7.33	7.75	7.87	7.90
14.0	6.14	6.33	6.49	6.64	6.77	6.88	6.97	7.06	7.13	7.51	7.61	7.63
14.5	6.02	6.20	6.35	6.49	6.61	6.71	6.80	6.88	6.95	7.29	7.37	7.39
15.0	5.90	6.07	6.22	6.35	6.46	6.55	6.64	6.71	6.77	7.07	7.15	7.16
15.5	5.79	5.95	6.09	6.21	6.31	6.40	6.48	6.54	6.60	6.87	6.93	6.95
16.0	5.69	5.84	5.97	6.08	6.18	6.26	6.33	6.39	6.44	6.68	6.74	6.75
16.5	5.58	5.73	5.85	5.95	6.04	6.12	6.18	6.24	6.29	6.50	6.55	6.56
17.0	5.48	5.62	5.73	5.83	5.91	5.98	6.04	6.10	6.14	6.34	6.37	6.38
17.5	5.38	5.51	5.62	5.71	5.79	5.86	5.91	5.96	6.00	6.17	6.21	6.21
18.0	5.29	5.41	5.51	5.60	5.67	5.73	5.78	5.83	5.86	6.02	6.05	6.05
18.5	5.20	5.31	5.41	5.49	5.56	5.61	5.66	5.70	5.73	5.88	5.90	5.91
19.0	5.11	5.22	5.31	5.39	5.45	5.50	5.54	5.58	5.61	5.74	5.76	5.76
19.5	5.03	5.13	5.21	5.28	5.34	5.39	5.43	5.46	5.49	5.61	5.63	5.63
20.0	4.94	5.04	5.12	5.19	5.24	5.29	5.32	5.35	5.38	5.48	5.50	5.50

Exhibit 4-2. Macaulay's durations (in years) for bonds of various maturities and various coupon rates. The YTM of each bond is 7%.

Coupon Rate (%)	|	|	|	|	*Maturity (Years)*						
	1	2	3	4	5	6	7	8	9	10	11
0	1.00	2.00	3.00	4.00	5.00	6.00	7.00	8.00	9.00	10.00	11.00
1	1.00	1.98	2.96	3.92	4.87	5.80	6.71	7.61	8.49	9.34	10.17
2	1.00	1.97	2.92	3.85	4.75	5.62	6.47	7.29	8.07	8.83	9.55
3	0.99	1.95	2.88	3.78	4.64	5.47	6.26	7.02	7.73	8.42	9.06
4	0.99	1.94	2.85	3.72	4.55	5.33	6.08	6.78	7.45	8.08	8.67
5	0.99	1.93	2.82	3.66	4.46	5.21	5.92	6.59	7.21	7.80	8.35
6	0.99	1.91	2.79	3.61	4.38	5.10	5.78	6.41	7.01	7.56	8.08
7	0.98	1.90	2.76	3.56	4.30	5.00	5.65	6.26	6.83	7.36	7.85
8	0.98	1.89	2.73	3.51	4.24	4.91	5.54	6.12	6.67	7.18	7.65
9	0.98	1.88	2.70	3.47	4.17	4.83	5.44	6.00	6.53	7.02	7.48
10	0.98	1.87	2.68	3.43	4.12	4.75	5.35	5.89	6.41	6.89	7.33
11	0.97	1.86	2.66	3.39	4.06	4.68	5.26	5.80	6.30	6.76	7.20
12	0.97	1.84	2.63	3.35	4.01	4.62	5.18	5.71	6.20	6.65	7.08
13	0.97	1.83	2.61	3.32	3.97	4.56	5.11	5.63	6.11	6.56	6.98
14	0.97	1.82	2.59	3.29	3.92	4.51	5.05	5.55	6.03	6.47	6.88
15	0.97	1.82	2.57	3.26	3.88	4.46	4.99	5.49	5.95	6.39	6.80
16	0.96	1.81	2.55	3.23	3.84	4.41	4.93	5.49	5.95	6.31	6.72
17	0.96	1.80	2.54	3.20	3.81	4.36	4.88	5.37	5.82	6.25	6.65
18	0.96	1.79	2.52	3.17	3.77	4.32	4.83	5.31	5.76	6.18	6.58
19	0.96	1.78	2.50	3.15	3.74	4.28	4.79	5.26	5.71	6.13	6.52
20	0.96	1.77	2.49	3.13	3.71	4.25	4.75	5.22	5.66	6.07	6.47

Coupon Rate (%)	|	|	|	*Maturity (Years)*								
	12	13	14	15	16	17	18	19	20	30	40	50
0	12.00	13.00	14.00	15.00	16.00	17.00	18.00	19.00	20.00	30.00	40.00	50.00
1	11.98	11.77	12.52	13.25	13.95	14.62	15.26	15.87	16.44	20.30	21.08	20.07
2	10.24	10.89	11.51	12.10	12.65	13.17	13.65	14.10	14.52	17.03	17.44	16.96
3	9.67	10.24	10.78	11.28	11.75	12.19	12.59	12.96	13.31	15.38	15.89	15.78
4	9.22	9.74	10.22	10.67	11.09	11.48	11.84	12.17	12.48	14.40	15.04	15.15
5	8.86	9.34	9.79	10.20	10.59	10.95	11.28	11.59	11.87	13.74	14.49	14.76
6	8.56	9.01	9.43	9.83	10.19	10.53	10.85	11.14	11.41	13.26	14.12	14.50
7	8.31	8.74	9.14	9.52	9.87	10.20	10.50	10.79	11.05	12.91	13.84	14.31
8	8.20	8.51	8.90	9.26	9.60	9.92	10.22	10.50	10.76	12.63	13.63	14.17
9	7.91	8.32	8.69	9.05	9.38	9.69	9.98	10.26	10.52	12.41	13.47	14.06
10	7.75	8.15	8.52	8.86	9.19	9.50	9.79	10.06	10.32	12.23	13.33	13.97
11	7.61	8.00	8.36	8.70	9.03	9.33	9.62	9.89	10.15	12.08	13.22	13.89
12	7.49	7.87	8.22	8.56	8.88	9.18	9.47	9.74	10.00	11.95	13.13	13.83
13	7.38	7.75	8.10	8.44	8.76	9.06	9.34	9.61	9.87	11.85	13.05	13.78
14	7.28	7.65	8.00	8.33	8.65	8.95	9.23	9.50	9.76	11.75	12.98	13.73
15	7.19	77.55	7.90	8.23	8.55	8.85	9.13	9.40	9.66	11.67	12.92	13.69
16	7.10	7.47	7.82	8.14	8.46	8.76	9.04	9.31	9.57	11.60	12.87	13.63
17	6.96	7.32	7.67	7.99	8.30	8.60	8.89	9.16	9.42	11.47	12.78	13.60
18	6.90	7.26	7.60	7.93	8.24	8.54	8.82	9.09	9.35	11.42	12.74	13.57
19	6.84	7.20	7.54	7.87	8.18	8.48	8.76	9.03	9.29	11.37	12.71	13.55

Exhibit 4-3. Macaulay's durations (in years) for a 30-year maturity bond in a variety of yield environments and for a variety of assumed coupon rates.

					Coupon Rate (%)					
YTM (%)	0	1	2	3	4	5	6	7	8	9
0.0	30.00	26.60	24.47	23.00	21.96	21.15	20.52	20.00	19.59	19.24
0.5	30.00	26.31	24.06	22.55	21.47	20.66	20.02	19.51	19.09	18.75
1.0	30.00	25.99	23.63	22.08	20.97	20.15	19.51	19.01	18.59	18.75
1.5	30.00	25.66	23.18	21.58	20.46	19.63	19.00	18.49	18.08	17.24
2.0	30.00	25.29	22.70	21.06	19.93	19.10	18.47	17.97	17.57	17.24
2.5	30.00	24.91	22.21	20.53	19.39	18.57	17.94	17.45	17.06	16.73
3.0	30.00	24.49	21.69	19.99	18.84	18.03	17.41	16.93	16.54	16.23
3.5	30.00	24.05	21.15	19.43	18.29	17.48	16.87	16.41	16.03	15.73
4.0	30.00	23.59	20.60	18.86	17.73	16.93	16.34	15.88	15.52	15.23
4.5	30.00	23.10	20.02	18.28	17.17	16.39	15.81	15.37	15.02	14.73
5.0	30.00	22.58	19.44	17.70	16.60	15.84	15.28	14.86	14.52	14.25
5.5	30.00	22.04	18.85	17.12	16.04	15.30	14.76	14.36	14.03	13.77
6.0	30.00	21.48	18.24	16.54	15.49	14.77	14.25	13.86	13.56	13.31
6.5	30.00	20.90	17.64	15.96	14.94	14.25	13.75	13.38	13.09	12.86
7.0	30.00	20.30	17.03	15.38	14.40	13.74	13.26	12.91	12.63	12.41
7.5	30.00	19.68	16.42	14.82	13.87	13.24	12.79	12.45	12.19	11.98
8.0	30.00	19.05	15.81	14.26	13.35	12.75	12.32	12.01	11.76	11.57
8.5	30.00	18.41	15.21	13.71	12.84	12.28	11.88	11.58	11.35	11.17
9.0	30.00	17.76	14.62	13.18	12.36	11.82	11.45	11.17	10.95	10.78
9.5	30.00	17.11	14.04	12.67	11.88	11.38	11.03	10.77	10.57	10.41
10.0	30.00	16.46	13.48	12.17	11.43	10.96	10.63	10.39	10.20	10.06
10.5	30.00	15.81	12.93	11.68	10.99	10.55	10.25	10.02	9.85	9.72
11.0	30.00	15.17	12.39	11.22	10.57	10.16	9.88	9.67	9.51	9.39
11.5	30.00	14.54	11.88	10.78	10.17	9.79	0.53	9.34	9.19	9.08
12.0	30.00	13.93	11.39	10.35	9.79	9.44	9.20	9.02	8.89	8.78
12.5	30.00	13.32	10.91	9.95	9.43	9.10	8.88	8.72	8.59	8.50
13.0	30.00	12.74	10.46	9.56	9.08	8.78	8.58	8.43	8.32	8.23
13.5	30.00	12.18	10.03	9.20	8.75	8.48	8.29	8.15	8.05	7.97
14.0	30.00	11.63	9.62	8.85	8.44	8.19	8.02	7.89	7.80	7.73
14.5	30.00	11.11	9.23	8.52	8.15	7..92	7.76	7.65	7.56	7.49
15.0	30.00	10.61	8.87	8.21	7.87	7.66	7.51	7.41	7.33	7.27
15.5	30.00	10.14	8.52	7.92	7.60	7.41	7.28	7.19	7.12	7.06
16.0	30.00	9.69	8.19	7.64	7.35	7.18	7.06	6.98	6.91	6.86
16.5	30.00	9.27	7.88	7.38	7.12	6.96	6.85	6.78	6.72	6.67
17.0	30.00	8.87	7.59	7.13	6.90	6.75	6.66	6.59	6.53	6.49
17.5	30.00	8.49	7.32	6.90	6.69	6.56	6.47	6.41	6.36	6.32
18.0	30.00	8.13	7.06	6.68	6.49	6.37	6.29	6.23	6.19	6.16
18.5	30.00	7.80	6.82	6.48	6.30	6.19	6.12	6.07	6.03	6.00
19.0	30.00	7.49	6.60	6.28	6.13	6.03	5.96	5.92	5.88	5.85
19.5	30.00	7.20	6.39	6.10	5.96	5.87	5.81	5.77	5.74	5.71
20.0	30.00	6.92	6.19	5.93	5.80	5.72	5.67	5.63	5.60	5.58

Exhibit 4-3. (cont.)

					Coupon Rate (%)						
YTM (%) 10	11	12	13	14	15	16	17	18	19	20
0.0	18.94	18.68	18.46	18.26	18.09	17.93	17.79	17.67	17.56	17.45	17.36
0.5	18.45	18.20	17.98	17.78	17.61	17.46	17.33	17.20	17.09	16.99	16.90
1.0	17.96	17.71	17.49	17.30	17.14	16.99	16.86	16.74	16.63	16.54	16.45
1.5	17.46	17.22	17.01	16.82	16.66	16.52	16.39	16.27	16.17	16.08	15.99
2.0	16.96	16.72	16.52	16.34	16.18	16.05	15.92	15.81	15.71	15.62	15.54
2.5	16.46	16.23	16.03	15.86	15.71	15.58	15.46	15.35	15.25	15.17	15.09
3.0	15.96	15.74	15.55	15.38	15.24	15.11	15.00	14.89	14.80	14.72	14.64
3.5	15.47	15.26	15.07	14.91	14.77	14.65	14.54	14.44	14.36	14.28	14.20
4.0	14.98	14.78	14.60	14.45	14.31	14.20	14.09	14.00	13.92	13.84	13.77
4.5	14.50	14.30	14.13	13.99	13.86	13.75	13.65	13.56	13.48	13.41	13.35
5.0	14.03	13.84	13.68	13.54	13.42	13.31	13.22	13.14	13.06	12.99	12.93
5.5	13.56	13.38	13.23	13.10	12.98	12.88	12.80	12.72	12.65	12.58	12.53
6.0	13.11	12.94	12.79	12.67	12.56	12.47	12.38	12.31	12.24	12.18	12.13
6.5	12.66	12.50	12.37	12.25	12.15	12.06	11.98	11.91	11.85	11.80	11.75
7.0	12.23	1208	11.95	11.85	11.75	11.67	11.60	11.53	11.47	11.42	11.37
7.5	11.82	11.67	11.55	11.45	11.36	11.29	11.22	11.16	11.10	11.06	11.01
8.0	11.41	11.28	11.17	11.07	10.99	10.92	10.85	10.80	10.75	10.70	10.66
8.5	11.02	10.90	10.79	10.71	10.63	10.56	10.50	10.45	10.40	10.36	10.32
9.0	10.65	10.53	10.44	10.35	10.28	10.22	10.17	10.12	10.07	10.03	10.00
9.5	10.28	10.18	10.09	10.01	9.95	9.89	9.84	9.80	9.76	9.72	9.69
10.0	9.94	9.84	9.76	9.69	9.63	9.57	9.53	9.49	9.45	9.42	9.39
10.5	9.61	9.52	9.44	9.37	9.32	9.27	9.23	9.19	9.16	9.13	9.10
11.0	9.29	9.21	9.14	9.08	9.02	8.98	8.94	8.91	8.87	8.85	8.82
11.5	8.99	8.91	8.84	8.79	8.74	8.70	8.67	8.63	8.61	8.58	8.56
12.0	8.70	8.62	8.57	8.52	8.47	8.44	8.40	8.37	8.35	8.32	8.30
12.5	8.42	8.35	8.30	8.25	8.22	8.18	8.15	8.12	8.10	8.08	8.06
13.0	8.16	8.10	8.05	8.01	7.97	7.94	7.91	7.89	7.87	7.85	7.83
13.5	7.90	7.85	7.81	7.77	7.74	7.71	7.68	7.66	7.64	7.62	7.61
14.0	7.67	7.62	7.58	7.54	7.51	7.49	7.46	7.44	7.42	7.41	7.39
14.5	7.44	7.39	7.36	7.33	7.30	7.27	7.25	7.24	7.22	7.21	7.19
15.0	7.22	7.18	7.15	7.12	7.10	7.07	7.05	7.04	7.02	7.01	7.00
15.5	7.02	6.98	6.95	6.92	6.90	6.88	6.87	6.85	6.84	6.82	6.81
16.0	6.82	6.79	6.76	6.74	6.72	6.70	6.68	6.67	6.66	6.65	6.64
16.5	6.64	6.61	6.58	6.56	6.54	6.52	6.51	6.50	6.49	6.48	6.47
17.0	6.46	6.43	6.41	6.39	6.37	6.36	6.35	6.34	6.33	6.32	6.31
17.5	6.29	6.27	6.25	6.23	6.21	6.20	6.19	6.18	6.17	6.16	6.15
18.0	6.13	6.11	6.09	6.07	6.06	6.05	6.04	6.03	6.02	6.01	6.01
18.5	5.98	5.96	5.94	5.93	5.91	5.90	5.90	5.89	5.88	5.87	5.87
19.0	5.83	5.81	5.80	5.79	5.78	5.77	5.76	5.75	5.74	5.74	5.73
19.5	5.69	5.68	5.66	5.65	5.64	5.64	5.63	5.62	5.62	5.61	5.61
20.0	5.56	5.55	5.54	5.53	5.52	5.51	5.50	5.50	5.49	5.49	5.48

This effect is magnified in low yield environments. An extension in maturity has a greater influence on a bond's duration the lower the general level of yields:

Term to Maturity (Years)	Duration	
	5% Yield Environment	*15% Yield Environment*
1	0.99	0.97
5	4.49	3.69
10	7.99	5.48
20	12.87	6.77
50	18.77	7.16

For example, moving from a 10-year bond to a 20-year bond entails a 24% increase in duration if yields are currently in the 15% area (6.77 versus 5.48). The same extension in maturity creates a 61% surge in duration if market yields are approximately 5% (12.87 versus 7.99). The impact of a maturity extension is substantially influenced by the general level of yields. Low yield environments create more dramatic shifts in duration. Exhibit 4–4 illustrates this interrelationship.

Duration is inversely related to the market yield level. This effect is magnified in long maturity issues. Changes in market yield are most influential on the duration of bonds of long maturity.

Market Yield (%)	Duration	
	3-Year Bond	*30-Year Bond*
0	3.00	30.00
5	2.82	15.84
10	2.67	9.94
15	2.52	7.07
20	2.40	5.48

to mid-1980s. Second, several foreign bond markets (e.g., Japan and Germany) currently offer interest rates in the 4% to 6% range. A yield assumption that is reasonably close to an average yield of several of the major international bond markets, including the United States, makes the examples more useful.

Exhibit 4-4. The positive relationship between duration and term to maturity is enhanced in low yield environments (data from Exhibit 4-1).

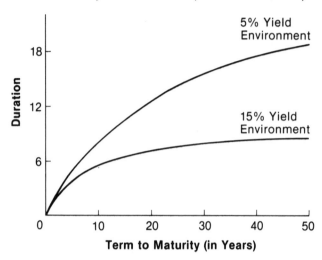

For example, if yields decline from the 15% level to the 5% level, a 3-year bond experiences a 12% increase in duration (2.82 versus 2.52). Under the same conditions, a 30-year bond registers a dramatic 124% surge in duration (15.84 versus 7.07). In sum, the natural correlation of long maturities and high durations is accentuated in low yield environments. This interrelationship is illustrated in Exhibit 4-5.

Exhibit 4-5. The inverse relationship between duration and market yield level is magnified in long maturity issues (data from Exhibit 4-1).

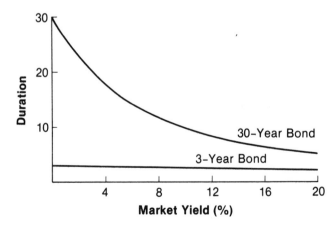

The interaction of coupon rate and term to maturity

Duration is inversely related to a bond's coupon rate of interest.
For a 10-year bond, a 5% coupon justifies a 7.80 duration, a
10% coupon warrants a 6.89 duration, and a 15% coupon deserves
a 6.39 duration:

Coupon Rate (%)	Duration
0	10.00
5	7.80
10	6.89
15	6.39
20	6.07

This effect is magnified in long maturity issues. The longer
the term to maturity of an issue, the more substantial is the impact
on a bond's duration from altering the coupon rate:

Coupon Rate (%)	Duration	
	5-Year Bond	30-Year Bond
0	5.00	30.00
5	4.46	13.74
10	4.12	12.23
15	3.88	11.67
20	3.71	11.37

A 5-year bond experiences a 26% drop in duration as its coupon
rate is raised from 0% to 20% (3.71 versus 5.00). A 30-year bond's
duration falls by 62% under the same conditions (11.37 versus
30.00). Exhibit 4-6 plots this interrelationship.

Exhibit 4-6. The inverse relationship between duration and coupon rate is magnified in long maturity issues (data from Exhibit 4-2).

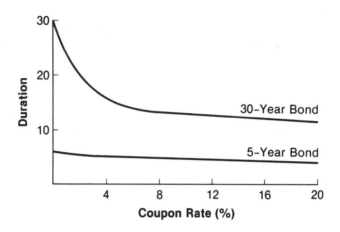

Duration is positively related to a bond's term to maturity. This effect is magnified in low coupon issues:

	Duration	
Term to Maturity (Years)	5% Coupon Bond	15% Coupon Bond
1	0.99	0.97
5	4.46	3.88
10	7.80	6.39
20	11.87	9.66
50	14.76	13.69

A 5% coupon bond experiences a 75% surge in duration as its maturity is extended from 5 years to 10 years (7.80 versus 4.46). A 15% coupon bond registers only a 65% shift in duration under the same conditions (6.39 versus 3.88). Exhibit 4-7 plots this interrelationship.

The interaction of market yield level and coupon rate

Low yields lead to high durations. A 30-year, 10% coupon bond carries a 7.22 duration in a 15% yield environment, a 9.94 duration in a 10% yield environment, and a 14.03 duration in a 5% yield environment:

Market Yield (%)	Duration
0	18.94
5	14.03
10	9.94
15	7.22
20	5.56

Exhibit 4-7. The positive relationship between duration and term to maturity is magnified in low coupon issues (data from Exhibit 4-2).

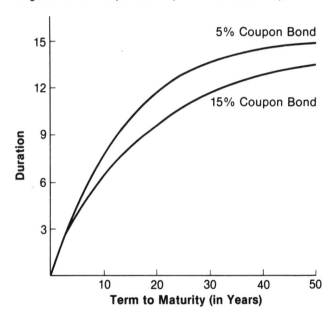

This effect is magnified in low coupon issues. Changes in market yield have a more material effect on the durations of low coupon bonds than on the durations of high coupon bonds:

	Duration	
Market Yield (%)	*5% Coupon Bond*	*15% Coupon Bond*
0	21.15	17.93
5	15.84	13.31
10	10.96	9.57
15	7.66	7.07
20	5.72	5.51

Exhibit 4-8. The inverse relationship between duration and market yield level is magnified in low coupon issues (data from Exhibit 4-3).

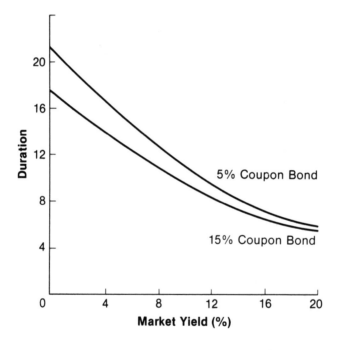

A yield decline from the 10% level to the 5% level creates a 45% surge in duration for a 5% coupon bond (15.84 versus 10.96). An identical yield decline leads to only a 39% increase in duration for the higher coupon 15% issue (13.31 versus 9.57). Exhibit 4-8 plots this interrelationship.

The interaction of accrued interest and term to maturity

Accrued interest acts as a drag on a bond's duration. This effect is particularly noticeable in long maturity bonds. Using 7% coupon bonds priced at par, the effects are as follows:

	Duration		
Issue	Full Accrued	No Accrued	Duration Change
3-year bond	2.67	2.76	+0.09
10-year bond	7.11	7.36	+0.25
30-year bond	12.48	12.91	+0.43

The coupon payment (and dropoff of accrued interest) forces a greater extension of duration in long maturity bonds than in short maturity bonds. The buildup of accrued interest creates a more severe drag on a long maturity bond's duration than on a short maturity bond's duration. In this case, a 3-year bond registers only a 0.09 duration increase, a 10-year bond experiences a 0.25 duration advance, and a 30-year bond records a 0.43 duration surge when the accrued interest drag is alleviated on the coupon payment date.

The accrued interest effect is more dramatic in high coupon bonds. Given a 7% yield level, a series of 30-year bonds illustrate this phenomenon:

	Duration			
Issue	Full Accrued	No Accrued	Duration Change	Duration Change (%)
5% coupon bond	13.30	13.74	+0.44	+3.31
10% coupon bond	11.81	12.23	+0.42	+3.56
15% coupon bond	11.25	11.67	+0.42	+3.73

The coupon payment forces a 3.73% increase in duration for a 15% coupon bond and creates only a 3.31% advance in duration for a 5% coupon issue.

Early redemption provisions

Sinking fund provisions shorten the average time until principal repayment and lower a bond's duration as was illustrated in Chapter 3. Chapter 6 discusses call provisions.

Exhibit 4-9. The factor sensitivity of various maturity noncallable bullet bonds.

	Short-Term Bonds	Intermediate-Term Bonds	Long-Term Bonds
Most sensitive factor(s)	Term to maturity	Term to maturity, market yield	Market yield
Moderately sensitive factor(s)		Accrued interest	Accrued interest, coupon rate
Least sensitive factor(s)	Coupon rate, accrued interest, market yield	Coupon rate	Term to maturity

Factor sensitivity for short-term, intermediate-term, and long-term bonds

The relative importance of the factors influencing a bond's duration are a function of the bond's term to maturity. Exhibit 4–9 summarizes the sensitivity of a variety of bonds to changes in the seven underlying factors given at the beginning of this chapter. Exhibit 4–10 provides supporting data for the assertions. (Noncallable bullet bonds are the focus of the analysis; the influences of sinking funds and call features are not easily generalized and are assessed in Chapter 6.)

Short-term bonds are dominated by the maturity factor and by the passage of time. Coupon, accrued interest, and market yield effects pale in relative importance. For intermediate-term bonds, the maturity factor still emerges as most influential; however, changes in market yield become increasingly important as the term lengthens. Coupon and accrued interest are less significant for this category. Long-term bonds are most affected by a shift in market yield, and accrued interest emerges as a

Exhibit 4–10. The duration impacts (in years) on a short-term (3-year) bond, an intermediate-term (10-year) bond, and a long-term (30-year) bond. Each issue is initially priced at par to yield 7% to maturity. The impacts are based on a 1-year change in remaining term to maturity, a 100BP change in coupon rate, a coupon payment, and a 100BP change in market yield.

| | Duration Change for a: | | |
| | 3-Year | 10-Year | 30-Year |
Factor	Bond	Bond	Bond
Term to maturity	0.86	0.53	0.13
Coupon rate	0.03	0.19	0.32
Accrued interest	0.09	0.25	0.43
Market yield	0.01	0.11	0.93

sensitive factor. In contrast, coupon and maturity effects lag in relative importance.

Summary

Several factors determine a bond's duration: term to maturity, coupon rate, accrued interest, market yield level, sinking fund provisions, call provisions, and the passage of time. Duration tables assist in identifying the interrelationships among these variables.

The positive relationship between duration and term to maturity is enhanced in low coupon bonds and in low market yields. The inverse relationship between duration and coupon rate is amplified in low coupon bonds. The inverse relationship between duration and market yield is magnified in low coupon bonds and in long maturity bonds. The effect of accrued interest is more dramatic in high coupon bonds and in long maturity issues. Early redemption provisions (e.g., sinking funds, and refunding calls) and the passage of time lower a bond's duration.

Duration sensitivities are as follows. The duration of a short-term bond is most sensitive to the remaining term to maturity and is least sensitive to the coupon rate, accrued interest, and market yield. The duration of an intermediate-term bond is most sensitive to the remaining term to maturity and the market yield

level. Its duration is least sensitive to the coupon rate of interest.
The duration of a long-term bond is most affected by the market
yield level and is least affected by the remaining term to maturity.
Its duration is moderately influenced by the coupon rate and
accrued interest.

CHAPTER 5

Using Duration
As a Risk Measure

Introduction

Chapters 1 through 4 introduced the concept of duration, analyzed the mathematics of duration, identified the influences on duration, and assessed the interrelationship of the factors affecting duration. In these chapters, duration was described as the weighted average maturity of a bond's cash flows, where the present values of the cash flows serve as the weights.

Duration can be used as a measure of a bond's riskiness. A longer duration implies a higher degree of price sensitivity and, therefore, greater market risk. The use of duration as a risk measure is widespread. This chapter describes and illustrates modified duration, which is a revised version of Macaulay's duration. The chapter points out the usefulness of modified duration, the assumptions underlying modified duration, and the advantages and limitations of using modified duration as a measure of bond risk.

Duration as an indicator of bond risk

The appropriate measure of a bond's inherent risk has evolved over time. The most primitive yardstick is the term to maturity. The weighted average maturity (of the bond's principal repayments) moves one step further by considering the timing of a bond's principal cash flows. The weighted average cash flow (or weighted average term to maturity) incorporates all of a bond's cash flows (coupons and principal repayments) into its derivation, rendering it superior to a weighted average maturity. Duration elevates the degree of sophistication by weighting all of a bond's cash flows according to their values adjusted for the time value of money. Duration is currently the most popular measure of bond risk.

The modified duration concept

Macaulay's duration requires a modification in order to be more accurate as a measure of bond risk. This revised version of duration, called *modified duration*, is calculated as follows:[1]

$$\frac{\text{modified}}{\text{duration}} = \frac{\text{duration}}{1 + \dfrac{\text{IRR}}{m}}$$

where
duration = the Macaulay's duration of the bond
IRR = the internal rate of return for the bond (expressed in decimal form)
m = the number of times per year that interest is compounded. For an annual-pay bond, $m = 1$; for a semiannual-pay bond, $m = 2$; for a quarterly-pay bond, $m = 4$; for a monthly-pay bond, $m = 12$.

[1] This division adjusts the Macaulay's duration for the noncontinuous compounding of interest. The divisor becomes larger the less frequent is the periodic compounding of interest. For example, with a 10% yield, the divisor is 1.10 for an annual-pay bond, 1.05 for a semiannual-pay bond, 1.025 for a quarterly-pay bond, and 1.0083 for a monthly-pay bond. Indeed, a pure discount bond's duration requires no adjustment if the bond's yield is stated on a continuously compounded basis.

For a typical semiannual-pay bond:

$$\frac{\text{modified}}{\text{duration}} = \frac{\text{duration}}{1 + \dfrac{\text{YTM}}{2}}$$

where
YTM = the yield to maturity of the bond (expressed in decimal form)

For example, a 3-year, 10% coupon bond priced at par to yield 10% to maturity bears a 2.67 duration and a 2.54 modified duration:

$$\frac{\text{modified}}{\text{duration}} = \frac{2.67}{\left(1 + \dfrac{0.10}{2}\right)}$$

$$= \frac{2.67}{1.05}$$

$$= 2.54$$

A 30-year, 10% coupon bond priced at par to yield 10% to maturity carries a 9.94 duration and a 9.47 modified duration:

$$\frac{\text{modified}}{\text{duration}} = \frac{9.94}{\left(1 + \dfrac{0.10}{2}\right)}$$

$$= \frac{9.94}{1.05}$$

$$= 9.47$$

The amount of adjustment necessary to arrive at a modified duration is directly related to (1) the underlying duration and

(2) the market yield level. High duration bonds and high yield environments require larger than normal modifications.

Exhibit 5-1 calculates modified durations for a series of U.S. Treasury bonds and corporate bonds. The U.S. Treasury bonds issued in the high yield environment of late 1981 (15¾% due 11/15/01, 14% due 11/15/11) experience approximately half-year duration adjustments to arrive at a modified status. A low duration bond such as the 2-year U.S. Treasury (7⅞% due 5/15/90) needs only a 0.07-year reduction to reach a 1.82 modified duration. A high duration bond such as the 20-year STRIPS (0% due 5/15/08) requires almost a full year's adjustment to create the modified duration (19.10) represented by that security (see Exhibit 5-1).

Exhibit 5-1. Modified durations for a sample of U.S. Treasury bonds and corporate bonds.

Date	Issue	YTM(%)	Duration	Modified Duration
10/7/81	U.S. Treasury 15¾% due 11/15/01	15.75	6.54	6.06
11/16/81	U.S. Treasury 14% due 11/15/11	14.00	7.51	7.02
5/15/86	U.S. Treasury 7¼% due 5/15/16	7.25	12.61	12.17
5/15/88	U.S. Treasury 9⅛% due 5/15/18	9.13	10.67	10.20
5/15/88	STRIPS 0% due 5/15/08	9.45	20.00	19.10
5/15/88	U.S. Treasury 7⅞% due 5/15/90	7.94	1.89	1.82
5/15/88	U.S. Treasury 7⅝% due 5/15/93	8.48	4.18	4.01
5/15/88	U.S. Treasury 9% due 5/15/98	9.00	6.80	6.51
5/15/88	Texas Utilities Electric (TXU) 12% due 9/1/15	11.75	8.40	7.93
5/15/88	Southern Bell Telephone and Telegraph 8⅜% due 9/1/26	9.95	10.20	9.72

Using modified duration as a measure of bond risk

Modified duration can be used as a measure of the sensitivity of a bond's price to changes in market yield.[2] The mathematical

---

[2] The bond's price is a full price and includes accrued interest; yield refers to the bond's yield to maturity.

relationship is rather straightforward:

$$\begin{array}{c} \text{percentage change} \\ \text{in bond price} \end{array} = - \left(\begin{array}{c} \text{modified} \\ \text{duration} \end{array} \right) \times \frac{\text{BP change in yield}}{100}$$

For example, a bond with a modified duration of 5 years registers approximately a 5% rise in price if yields fall 100 basis points (BP):

$$\begin{array}{c} \text{percentage change} \\ \text{in bond price} \end{array} = -(5.00) \times \left(\frac{-100}{100} \right)$$

$$= -5.00 \times (-1)$$

$$= 5.00$$

If yields fall 200BP, the bond's price rises by approximately 10% (i.e., $-5.00 \times (-200/100) = 10.00$).

Three observations are worth noting. First, bond prices are inversely related to bond yields. As interest rates rise, bond prices fall. As a result, the modified duration figure (on the right side of the equation) must be preceded by a minus sign to establish this inverse relationship. Second, modified duration acts as a multiplier. The larger the modified duration, the greater the price impact for a given change in interest rates. Third, for a bond of a given duration, large shifts in yield lead to great percentage changes in price. Insofar as price sensitivity is viewed as an indication of the riskiness of a bond investment, modified duration acts as a measure of that inherent risk.

Illustrations of modified duration

In Exhibit 5–1 the 2-year U.S. Treasury bond (7⅞% due 5/15/90), with a modified duration of 1.82, experiences approximately a

1.82% change in price for every 100 BP change in yield. For example, a 150BP rise in yield creates a 2.73% price loss:

$$\text{percentage change in bond price} = -1.82 \times \left(\frac{150}{100}\right)$$

$$= -1.82 \times 1.50$$

$$= -2.73$$

A similar rise in yield forces a 9.77% price decline in the 10-year U.S. Treasury bond (9% due 5/15/98), which has a modified duration of 6.51 years:

$$\text{percentage change in bond price} = -6.51 \times \left(\frac{150}{100}\right)$$

$$= -6.51 \times 1.50$$

$$= -9.77$$

The identical 150BP surge in interest rates is responsible for a sizable 28.65% loss on a 20-year zero coupon bond (STRIPS 0% due 5/15/08):

$$\text{percentage change in bond price} = -19.10 \times \left(\frac{150}{100}\right)$$

$$= -19.10 \times 1.50$$

$$= -28.65$$

The long duration of a 20-year STRIPS (19.10 modified duration) is the culprit behind the large percentage change in price.

Modified duration and the price:yield curve

The inverse relationship between a bond's price and its yield is plotted as a smooth curve that is convex to the origin of the graph (see Exhibit 5-2). Exhibit 5-3 calculates the prices of the 10-year U.S. Treasury bond (9% due 5/15/98) over a wide range of market yields (4% to 14%). These price:yield pairings are plotted in Exhibit 5-4.

In Exhibit 5-4, a line is drawn tangent to the price:yield curve at the price:yield coordinates depicting today's price (100.00) and today's yield (9%). *The slope of this tangent line represents the modified duration of the underlying bond.*[3] A tangent line is used to measure the slope of a curve at a point along that curve. Modified duration, therefore is a good indicator of the rate of change in the price of a bond given a small change in yield. As the yield shifts, the appropriate line of tangency (and that line's slope) changes. This fact confirms that a bond's modified duration changes as its yield fluctuates. As noted in Chapters 3 and 4, duration and market yield are inversely related.

Exhibits 5-2 through 5-4 support several conclusions. First, the modified duration line (i.e., the tangent line) expresses a bond's price:yield relationship as a straight line. As such, the modified duration is merely an estimate of the true underlying relationship, which is always a curve. The larger the change in yield, the greater the degree of error in using the straight line as the estimate of the bond's price behavior.

Second, each price:yield combination on the curve has its own tangent line. Every single basis point change in yield generates a different tangent line and, consequently, a different slope (i.e.,

---

[3] For purposes of illustrating the modified duration concept, this statement is acceptable. In reality, however, the slope of the tangent line is [– (modified duration) × the bond's current market price]. Convention has it that a downward sloping line carries a positive modified duration and an upward sloping line deserves a negative modified duration. A typical bond has a positive modified duration. A negative modified duration suggests a direct, rather than inverse, relationship between a bond's price and the market yield level.

If one plots a bond's percentage change in price (rather than the absolute dollar price) on the y-axis and plots the basis point change in "market" yield (i.e., the yield to maturity of a comparable noncallable U.S. Treasury bond) on the x-axis, then the modified duration of the bond does represent the slope of the tangent line, as preceded by a minus sign.

Exhibit 5-2. The price:yield curve for a typical noncallable bond.

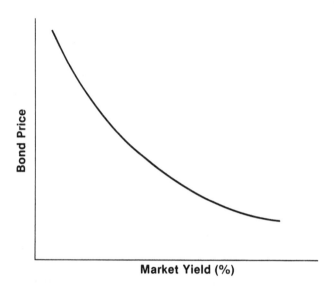

modified duration). Third, as time passes, the price:yield curve changes its shape and position. A bond's inherent price sensitivity evolves over time. Duration is hardly a static concept!

Exhibit 5-3. Prices for the U.S. Treasury 9% due 5/15/98 over a wide range of yield levels.

Yield (%)	Bond Price
4	140.88
5	131.18
6	122.32
7	114.21
8	106.80
9	100.00
10	93.77
11	88.05
12	82.80
13	77.96
14	73.51

Exhibit 5-4. The price:yield curve for a typical noncallable bond.

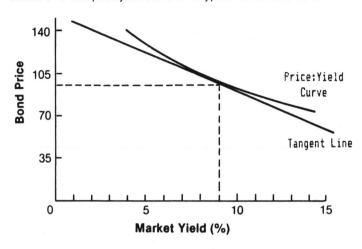

The advantages and limitations of modified duration

Exhibit 5-5 calculates both the actual prices and the duration-predicted prices for the 10-year U.S. Treasury bond used in previous illustrations. The prediction errors attributable to modified duration magnify as the bond's yield moves further away from the current level. For example, a 10BP change in yield finds virtually no prediction error; a 100BP yield shift sees approximately a 0.30 point difference between actual prices and predicted prices; a 400BP yield shift creates a sizable 4 to 5 point discrepancy between actual prices and predicted prices. Graphically, the prediction error is the gray area between the duration tangent line and the price:yield curve (see Exhibit 5-6). The bond's price is always at least as high as that predicted by the bond's modified duration. The price action is always better than the modified duration suggests. The favorable price surprises are termed *positive convexity* or, simply, *convexity*. The term convexity arises from the curvature of the price:yield curve away from the origin of the graph.

The primary advantage of modified duration is its usefulness as a proxy for a bond's price sensitivity given small to modest fluctuations in market yield. Its superiority over traditional risk measures such as term to maturity and weighted average maturity stems from its consideration of all of a bond's cash flows and the time value of money.

The limitations of modified duration arise from the assumptions upon which the concept is based:

1. *Instantaneous yield change.* Although it is possible to experience sizable intraday yield shifts in turbulent financial markets, yield shifts typically occur over time.

2. *Small change in yield (e.g., 10BP or less).* In the volatile environment of the 1980s, marginal changes in yield were unusual. Large changes (100 to 300BP) in yield became common.

3. *Parallel shift in yield.* It would be a rarity to find all bond yields moving in tandem. In reality, short-term bond yields fluctuate more than long-term bond yields, U.S. Treasury bond yields fluctuate more than corporate bond yields, on-the-run bond yields fluctuate more than off-the-run bond yields, and so on. Nonparallel yield shifts often occur.

Despite its inherent limitations, modified duration is a useful measure of bond risk. Chapters 9 through 14 elaborate on the convexity effects introduced in this chapter.

Exhibit 5-5. Actual prices and duration-predicted prices over a wide range of yields for the U.S. Treasury 9% due 5/15/98. On May 15, 1988, the bond is priced at par to yield 9% and the bond has a 6.51 year modified duration.

YTM (%)	(1) Yield Change (BP)	(2) Actual Bond Price	(3) Duration- Predicted Bond Price [a]	(4) = (2) – (3) Unexplained Price Change
0.00	−900	190.00	158.59	+31.41
1.00	−800	175.95	152.08	+23.87
2.00	−700	163.16	145.57	+17.59
3.00	−600	151.51	139.06	+12.45
4.00	−500	140.88	132.55	+ 8.33
5.00	−400	131.18	126.04	+ 5.14
6.00	−300	122.32	119.53	+ 2.79
7.00	−200	114.21	113.02	+ 1.19
8.00	−100	106.80	106.51	+ 0.29
8.90	− 10	100.65	100.65	0
8.99	− 1	100.07	100.07	0
9.00	0	100.00	100.00	0

Exhibit 5-5. (cont.)

YTM (%)	(1) Yield Change (BP)	(2) Actual Bond Price	(3) Duration- Predicted Bond Price [a]	(4) = (2) - (3) Unexplained Price Change
9.00	0	100.00	100.00	0
9.01	+ 1	99.93	99.93	0
9.10	+ 10	99.35	99.35	0
10.00	+100	93.77	93.49	+ 0.28
11.00	+200	88.05	86.98	+ 1.07
12.00	+300	82.80	80.47	+ 2.33
13.00	+400	77.96	73.96	+ 4.00
14.00	+500	73.51	67.45	+ 6.06
15.00	+600	69.42	60.94	+ 8.48
16.00	+700	65.64	54.43	+11.21
17.00	+800	62.15	47.92	+14.23
18.00	+900	58.92	41.41	+17.51

[a] Calculated as follows:

$$\text{current market price (100.00)} + \left(100 \times \frac{\text{BP change in yield}}{100} \times (-6.51)\right)$$

Exhibit 5-6. A typical price:yield curve, duration tangent line, and positive convexity region for a noncallable bond.

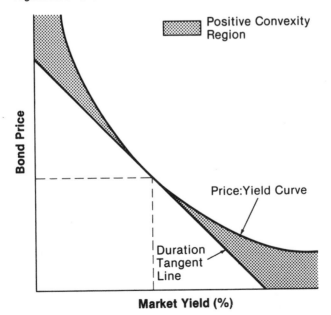

Positive Convexity Region

Bond Price

Price:Yield Curve

Duration Tangent Line

Market Yield (%)

Summary

Modified duration, a revised version of Macaulay's duration, is commonly used as a measure of bond risk. Modified duration estimates the sensitivity of a bond's price to a 100BP change in market yield. A bond with a 7.00 modified duration experiences approximately a 7% change in price for every 100BP change in market yield. A bond with a high duration has more market risk than a bond with a low duration

Graphically, modified duration is the slope of the line tangent to the price:yield curve at the current combination of price and yield. The curvilinear price:yield relationship confirms that modified duration serves only as an estimate of the true underlying relationship between price and yield. The prediction error is termed convexity, the subject of the second half of the book.

Although requiring a complex calculation, modified duration is easy to interpret. Its incorporation of the time value of money and its consideration of all of a bond's future cash flows render it superior to traditional risk measures such as term to maturity, weighted average maturity, and weighted average cash flow. The accuracy of modified duration is constrained by the assumption of a small, instantaneous parallel change in yield.

CHAPTER 6

Effective Duration

Introduction

The preceding chapters applied duration to noncallable securities. The duration characteristics of noncallable bonds are reasonably straightforward and are appropriate for the introductory sections of the book. However, many fixed-income securities incorporate features that make duration analysis a difficult task.

This chapter provides a simplified analysis of the durations of callable bonds and putable bonds. Call provisions are common to corporate bonds and mortgage-backed securities, and there are some U.S. Treasury bonds and federal agency bonds with call options attached. Put features are primarily associated with corporate bonds.

This chapter introduces and illustrates the concept of effective, or option-adjusted, duration. Both the advantages and limitations of effective duration are discussed. Appendix A provides additional insight into the derivation of the effective duration of a callable (or putable) bond. Appendix B describes the Capital Management Sciences (CMS) option valuation model for fixed-income securities. Appendix C looks at volatility, which has an important influence on effective duration.

Definitions of effective duration

There are many ways of explaining the concept of effective duration. Before delving into specific calculations and illustrations, you should consider the following definitions of effective duration:

> *Interpretation 1:* For an option-free bond (i.e., a bond lacking any option provisions), effective duration is the bond's modified duration to maturity.

> *Interpretation 2:* Effective duration is a measure of the average maturity of a bond's cash flows (duration as a measure of time). For a callable bond, the average maturity of the bond's cash flows is shortened by the possibility of early redemption of the issue.

> *Interpretation 3:* Effective duration is a sophisticated weighted average of the modified durations that a callable (or putable) bond can have.

> *Interpretation 4:* Effective duration is a simple weighted average of the modified duration of the option-free bond component and the modified duration of the option component (refer to Appendix A).

> *Interpretation 5:* Effective duration is a measure of the price sensitivity of a bond. For a callable bond, effective duration lies between the modified duration to call and the modified duration to maturity. Effective duration approaches the modified duration to call as yields fall, and effective duration approaches the modified duration to maturity as yields rise. For a putable bond, effective duration lies between the modified duration to put date and the modified duration to maturity. Effective duration approaches the modified duration to put date as yields rise, and effective duration approaches the modified duration to maturity as yields fall.

> *Interpretation 6:* Effective duration is the slope of the tangent line to the callable (or putable) bond's price:yield curve at the point representing the current market price and current market yield.

A combination of these interpretations provides a basic grasp of the effective duration concept. This chapter discusses effective duration as applied to (1) corporate bonds and (2) mortgage-backed securities. The chapter concludes with a summary of the advantages and limitations of effective duration.

Effective duration of corporate bonds

Callable bonds

The price sensitivity of a callable bond. A call option gives the holder the right to buy a bond back at a prespecified price over a predetermined period. A new-issue 10% coupon, 30-year utility bond gives the issuer the following option:

1. An immediate cash call at 110 (with cash call prices declining annually thereafter to a minimum call price of 100).
2. A refunding call in 5 years at 107 (with refunding call prices declining thereafter to a minimum call price of 100).

Call options limit the price appreciation of the bond in a bull market. In a bear market, downside price losses are restrained as the probability of early redemption falls.

Exhibit 6–1 compares the expected price behavior of a 30-year noncallable bond and a 30-year callable issue. If interest rates decline 200BP, the callable bond experiences a 10.08% gain in value as compared to the 22.62% gain registered by the noncallable issue. The issuer's right to call away the bond at a prespecified price limits

Exhibit 6–1. The price behaviors of a 30-year callable bond and a 30-year noncallable bond. Each bond bears a 10% coupon and is priced at par. U.S. Treasury bond yields are assumed at 9%.

Issue	*Percentage Change in Bond Price for a Market Yield Change (in BP) of:*					
	−300	*−200*	*−100*	*+100*	*+200*	*+300*
Noncallable bond	+37.42	+22.62	+10.32	−8.72	−16.16	−22.55
Callable bond[a]	+10.41	+10.08	+ 6.40	−7.02	−13.88	−20.15

[a] Callable bond price data courtesy of Capital Management Sciences.

the price advance of the callable issue. If interest rates rise 200BP, the callable bond suffers only a 13.88% price decline in comparison to the 16.16% price loss of the noncallable issue. Callable bonds are less volatile than noncallable bonds of similar maturity.

Assessing the duration of a callable bond. There are three ways to calculate the duration of a callable bond:

1. Calculate the bond's *duration to call* and the bond's *duration to maturity.*[1] Use the duration to call as the representative duration if the bond's market price exceeds the crossover price; use duration to maturity as the representative duration if the bond's market price is less than or equal to the *crossover price.*[2]
2. Calculate a *weighted average duration* based on a subjective assessment of the probability of call.
3. Calculate an *effective,* or *option-adjusted duration* by using an option valuation model.

The Southern Bell Telephone 10¾% due 12/18/25 (callable at 108.40 on 12/18/90) illustrates each of these three approaches (see Exhibit 6-2).

Exhibit 6-2. The yield and duration statistics for the Southern Bell Telephone 10¾% due 12/20/25. The bond is priced at 105.63 on December 30, 1988. The issue is refundable at 108.40 on 12/18/90.

Holding Period	Yield (%)	Modified Duration
To refunding call (12/18/90)	11.40	1.73
To final maturity (12/18/25)	10.16	9.51

[1] Typically, a bond has a series of call dates and a series of call prices. The DTC is evaluated using the first call date (and the first call price). The DTM assumes that the bond remains outstanding until the final maturity date.

[2] The crossover price is the price at which the YTC and YTM are equal. This yield level is appropriately termed the *crossover yield.* A more naive approach relies on the call price as the demarcation point. At market prices above the first call price, the bond is evaluated on a "first call date" basis, and the YTC and DTC statistics are used. At market prices at or below the first call price, the bond is evaluated on a "maturity date" basis, and the YTM and DTM figures are used. The most naive approach relies on the par value (100) as the differentiating point.

SELECTING EITHER THE DURATION TO CALL OR THE DURATION TO MATURITY. The simplest way to assess a callable bond's duration is by selecting either the bond's duration to call (DTC) or the bond's duration to maturity (DTM) as the representative duration. These durations are calculated as follows:

$$\text{DTC} = \sum_{t = 0.5}^{c} \left(\frac{\text{PV(CF}_t)}{\text{TPV}} \times t \right)$$

$$\text{DTM} = \sum_{t = 0.5}^{n} \left(\frac{\text{PV(CF}_t)}{\text{TPV}} \times t \right)$$

where
c = the number of years remaining until the call date
n = the number of years remaining until the final maturity date

The modified versions are computed as follows:

$$\text{modified DTC} = \frac{\text{DTC}}{\left(1 + \dfrac{\text{YTC}}{2} \right)}$$

$$\text{modified DTM} = \frac{\text{DTM}}{\left(1 + \dfrac{\text{YTM}}{2} \right)}$$

where
YTC = the yield to call (expressed in decimal form)
YTM = the yield to maturity (expressed in decimal form)

The DTC differs from the DTM in two important respects. First, the cash flows of the DTC truncate on the call date; therefore, the DTC is shorter than the DTM. Second, the call price typically exceeds par value.

Exhibit 6–2 calculates the yields and modified durations of the Southern Bell Telephone (SBT) 10¾% due 12/18/25 as of December 30, 1988. Based on a market price of 105.63, the bond has two unique durations:

1. Modified DTC: 1.73
2 Modified DTM: 9.51

The call provision can shorten the modified duration by 7.78 years (9.51 – 1.73 = 7.78). The duration of choice is a function of the bond's market price. If the market price exceeds the crossover price, the modified DTC serves as the bond's duration. If the bond's market price is at or below the crossover price, the modified DTM acts as the bond's duration. For the SBT 10¾% bond, the modified DTM (9.51) is selected because the bond is trading below the crossover price (105.63 < 108.45).

CALCULATING A WEIGHTED AVERAGE DURATION. This approach to assessing a callable bond's duration uses the concepts of DTC and DTM by assigning a probability to the call rather than a simple "yes" (use the DTC) or "no" (use the DTM). A weighted average duration is calculated using the probability of call:

$$\begin{matrix} \text{weighted average} \\ \text{duration} \\ \text{(AVGDUR)} \end{matrix} = \Big[\text{DTC} \times P_c \Big] + \Big[\text{DTM} \times (1 - P_c) \Big]$$

where

P_c = the probability of call (expressed in decimal form)

$1 - P_c$ = the probability of no call (expressed in decimal form)

A modified version is derived by using the modified DTC and the modified DTM in the calculation. The probability of call is a subjective estimate and ranges from 0.00 (0% chance) to 1.00 (100% chance).

Exhibit 6–3 summarizes the modified durations of the Southern Bell Telephone 10¾% due 12/18/25 at a series of yield levels. Exhibit 6–4 calculates the weighted average modified durations of this bond in various yield environments by applying a probability of call to the modified durations of Exhibit 6–3.

Exhibit 6-3. The modified durations of the Southern Bell Telephone 10¾% due 12/18/25 in a variety of yield environments (data as of December 30, 1988).

U.S. Treasury Yield (%)	Bond Price	Modified Duration	
		To Call Date (12/18/90)	To Maturity Date (12/18/25)
6	118.02	1.79	10.45
7	114.98	1.78	10.23
8	111.01	1.76	9.93
9	105.63	1.73	9.51
10	99.28	1.70	9.02
11	92.64	1.66	8.48
12	86.18	1.62	7.93

In an 8% U.S. Treasury yield environment, for example, the bond has a 4.21 weighted average modified duration:

$$\text{modified (AVGDUR)} = \left[\frac{\text{modified}}{\text{DTC}} \times P_c \right] + \left[\frac{\text{modified}}{\text{DTM}} \times (1 - P_c) \right]$$

$$= (1.76 \times 0.70) + (9.93 \times 0.30)$$

$$= 1.23 + 2.98$$

$$= 4.21$$

Exhibit 6-4. The weighted average durations of the Southern Bell Telephone 10¾% due 12/18/25 in a variety of yield environments (data from Exhibit 6-3).

U.S. Treasury Yield (%)	Bond Price	Probability of Call (P_c)	Weighted Average Duration[a]
6	118.02	1.00	1.79
7	114.98	0.90	2.63
8	111.01	0.70	4.21
9	105.63	0.50	5.62
10	99.28	0.30	6.82
11	92.64	0.10	7.80
12	86.18	0.00	7.93

[a] Calculated as DTC (probability of call) + DTM (1 - probability of call).

In this case, a 70% probability of call warrants a higher weighting to the modified DTC.

These tables support several conclusions. First, the weighted average duration is bounded by the DTC and the DTM. Second, the "true" duration of a callable bond cannot be known with certainty because the bond's future cash flow stream may or may not be shortened by a call provision.

Third, the best estimate of the bond's duration is influenced by the surrounding yield environment. The probability of call increases as interest rates decline. In a 12% U.S. Treasury yield environment, the investor regards an early redemption as impossible (0% probability of call). When the 10¾% bond trades at 105.63 (with U.S. Treasury bonds yielding 9%), the investor assigns a 50:50 chance to the call. If U.S. Treasury bond rates fall to 6%, the investor considers the early redemption as a certainty (100% probability of call).

If the current market yield level is low, the probability of a refunding call is high because interest rates would have to rise substantially in order to make the early redemption unattractive to the issuer of the bond. If the current market yield level is high, the probability of a refunding call is low because interest rates would have to decline substantially in order to make a refinancing profitable to the issuer. The expected future volatility of interest rates (to be discussed) is an important factor to consider when assessing the probability of call.

Finally, the probability of call is a subjective estimate. Individual investors have different predilections regarding the likelihood of early redemption. For an investor who believes that the future trend in interest rates is downward, the probability of call is higher. Conversely, a bearish investor views the call provision as a lesser concern.

THE CONCEPT OF EFFECTIVE DURATION. Effective duration is a sophisticated version of the weighted average modified duration. It attempts to quantify the price sensitivity of a bond that is subject to the influences of attached options. A callable bond's price sensitivity is assessed by separating the callable bond into its raw components: a noncallable bond and a call option (or a set of call options). The price sensitivity of the noncallable bond component is easy to observe (see the examples in prior chapters that used noncallable U.S. Treasury bonds). A bond option valuation model analyzes the price sensitivity of the option component.

The duration of a callable bond, like the duration of its noncallable counterpart, is ascertained by observing the behavior of the bond's price as market yields change. A callable bond's price is less sensitive to shifts in yield than the price of a similar maturity noncallable issue. The call feature acts as a drag on the callable bond's price, restraining its upward price movement in a bull market and cushioning its downward price movement in a bear market.

Exhibit 6-5 draws the price:yield curves for a callable bond and for a noncallable bond. Effective duration is the slope of the callable bond's price:yield curve at its current market price.[3] The price:yield curve for the callable bond is flatter than the price:yield curve for a noncallable bond of similar maturity. As yields fall, the callable bond's price moves up more slowly than the noncallable bond's price; conversely, as yields rise, the callable bond's price falls more slowly than the noncallable bond's price. Effective duration attempts to capture the inherent price sensitivity of a callable bond. Unfortunately, deriving the price:yield pairings for a callable bond requires option valuation procedures and a simple calculator cannot accomplish the task.

Deriving the price of a callable bond. The price of a callable bond is calculated as the price of an equivalent noncallable bond of similar structure less the value of the call option(s) attached:[4]

---

[3] In actuality, effective duration is a complex average of the slopes of the callable bond's price:yield curve at a series of points along the curve. The concept, however, is made more understandable with this simplification.

[4] The call option value is subtracted because the bondholder implicitly sells the call to the issuer of the bond. If the bondholder has the option (e.g., a put), the option value is added to the option-free bond value.

Exhibit 6-5. The price:yield curves for a callable bond and a noncallable bond of similar maturity.

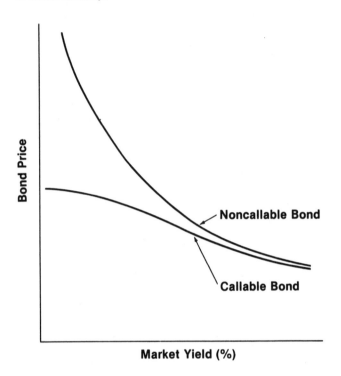

$$\begin{array}{c} \text{callable bond} \\ \text{price} \end{array} = \begin{array}{c} \text{noncallable} \\ \text{bond price} \end{array} - \begin{array}{c} \text{call option} \\ \text{value} \end{array}$$

The value of the call option is subtracted from the noncallable bond's price because the investor is implicitly selling the option (i.e., the right to call) to the issuer of the bond. Rearranging the preceding equation, the noncallable bond's price exceeds the callable bond's price by the value of the call option:

$$\begin{array}{c} \text{noncallable bond} \\ \text{price} \end{array} = \begin{array}{c} \text{callable} \\ \text{bond price} \end{array} + \begin{array}{c} \text{call option} \\ \text{value} \end{array}$$

A noncallable bond is more expensive than a callable issue because an investor values the ability to hold the bond until final maturity without fearing an early redemption (and reinvestment rate risk) in a low interest rate environment. In yield terms, a noncallable bond trades at a lower yield than a callable bond of similar maturity. An investor is willing to give up some yield in order to have the protection against premature retirement of the bond.

With U.S. Treasury bonds yielding 9%, a 10% coupon, 30-year callable industrial bond is priced at par to yield 10% to maturity. The call option is worth approximately 4 points. Therefore, a 10% coupon, 30-year noncallable corporate bond is valued at approximately 104:

$$\begin{matrix} \text{noncallable} \\ \text{bond price} \end{matrix} = \begin{matrix} \text{callable} \\ \text{bond price} \end{matrix} + \begin{matrix} \text{call option} \\ \text{value} \end{matrix}$$

$$= 100 + 4$$

$$= 104$$

The yield corresponding to a 104 price is 9.59%, 41BP lower than the yield on the callable bond. While the mechanics of bond option valuation are beyond the scope of this book, Appendix B discusses the CMS option valuation model for fixed-income securities. This overview provides a basic grasp of option valuation procedures.

The price behavior of a callable bond. As market yields change, the values of both the noncallable bond component and the call option component change. As yields rise, the noncallable bond component's value falls, and as yields fall, the noncallable bond component's value rises. The value of the call option falls as interest rates rise (and refinancing becomes less attractive) and rises as interest rates decline (and refinancing becomes more economical).

With U.S. Treasury bonds yielding 9%, a 10% coupon, 30-year callable industrial bond is priced at par, and the call option is worth approximately 4 points. As U.S. Treasury yields shift up and down 200 BP, the values of the callable bond's components change:

U.S. Treasury Bond Yield (%)	Noncallable Bond Price	Callable Bond Price	Call Option Value
7	127.50	110.50	17.00
9	104.00	100.00	4.00
11	86.50	85.00	1.50

Figures courtesy of Capital Management Sciences.

Because the call option is implicitly sold to the issuer of the bond, the bond's price is constrained by the increasing value of the issuer's option if interest rates fall. Conversely, the depreciating value of the issuer's option in a rising rate environment provides support to the callable bond's price. A callable bond's price:yield curve is flatter than that of its noncallable equivalent (see Exhibit 6–5).

A callable bond's price behavior gravitates between the call date assumption (modified DTC) and the maturity date assumption (modified DTM), depending on the general level of interest rates. The bond's price follows a curve that lies underneath the price:yield curves of a noncallable bond that matures on the call date and a noncallable bond that matures on the final maturity date (see Exhibit 6–6).[5] The callable bond's price approaches the call date bond curve as yields decline and the call becomes increasingly probable. The callable bond's price approaches the maturity date bond curve as yields rise and the call becomes less likely.

The price sensitivity of a callable bond lies between the price sensitivity of an option-free call date bond and the price sensitivity of an option-free maturity date bond. In a low yield environment, the callable bond behaves more like the call date bond, and underperforms the maturity date bond. In a high yield environment, the callable bond acts more like the maturity date bond but suffers a lesser price decline than the maturity date bond.

[5] The callable bond must trade at a price below that of both a noncallable "maturity date" equivalent and a noncallable "call date" equivalent for two reasons. First, despite how high interest rates rise, there is always the possibility that interest rates may subsequently decline, making the call a viable option to exercise. Therefore, the callable bond can never be valued at or above its noncallable "maturity date" equivalent. Second, no matter how much interest rates decline, there is always the possibility that interest rates may subsequently rise, making the call an uneconomic option to exercise. Consequently, the callable bond, versus a noncallable bond that matures on the call date, must sell at a lower price given the potential for its maturity to extend in a rising yield environment.

Exhibit 6-6. The price:yield curves for a callable bond and for two noncallable counterparts: a noncallable bond maturing on the first call date and a noncallable bond maturing on the final maturity date.

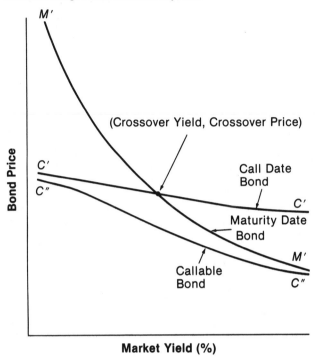

Market Yield (%)

The derivation of effective duration. Effective duration is based on the price behavior of a bond. A callable bond's price behavior is predicted by calculating the prices of the noncallable bond component and the call option component over a wide range of potential interest rate environments. Both the direction of interest rates and the expected future volatility of interest rates affect the probability of early redemption and, therefore, the bond's effective duration.[6]

---

[6] Unless otherwise indicated, all the effective durations presented in this book are provided by Capital Management Sciences (CMS), a Los Angeles firm, which used a 14½% yield volatility assumption for all calculations. This volatility assumption represents the average volatility of long-term U.S. Treasury bonds over the 1970 to 1988 period. There is no directional bias incorporated into the results. Interest rates are assumed to follow a "random walk."

The effective duration calculation considers not only the potential future prices of the callable bond but weights these potential outcomes according to their probabilities of occurrence. Small changes in yield are implicitly more probable than large shifts. As volatility increases, larger shifts in yield earn a higher weighting in the calculation relative to smaller shifts in yield.

Exhibit 6-7. The variability in future interest rates influences the probability of early call.

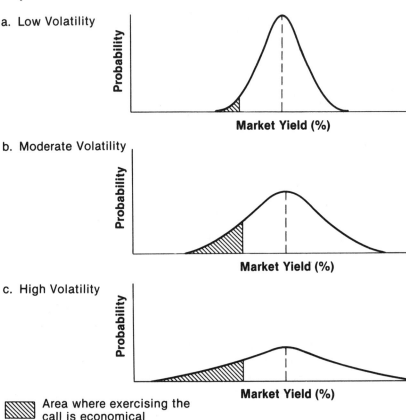

a. Low Volatility

b. Moderate Volatility

c. High Volatility

Area where exercising the call is economical

Mathematical models that derive effective durations assume a "random walk" in interest rates. That is, interest rates are as likely to rise as to fall in the future. The market yield volatility assumption is critical and must be specified. The greater the variability in interest rates, the larger the probability of call and, therefore, the lower the effective duration (see Exhibit 6–7). A low volatility assumption leads to a higher effective duration as the probability of call decreases. Appendix C defines and reviews historical volatility in the bond market.

The Southern Bell Telephone 10¾% due 12/18/25 has an effective duration of 4.82, assuming 14½% volatility in long-term bond yields (see Exhibit 6–8). This bond has a 1.73 modified DTC and a 9.51 modified DTM. A bond's effective duration lies between its modified DTC and its modified DTM. The influences on effective duration are outlined in the next section.

Exhibit 6-8. The durations of the Southern Bell Telephone 10¾% due 12/18/25. The bond is priced at 105.63 on December 30, 1988.

Modified Duration to Call	Modified Duration to Maturity	Effective Duration
1.73	9.51	4.82

The factors that influence a callable bond's duration. The easiest method of assessing a callable bond's price sensitivity is to choose either the modified DTC or the modified DTM, based on a straightforward decision rule. The factors influencing the decision are the market price and the crossover price:

Market Price:Crossover Price Relationship	Duration Measure Selected
Market price > Crossover price	Modified DTC
Market price ≤ Crossover price	Modified DTM

The second approach (calculating a weighted average duration) relies on a subjective estimate of the probability of call. The factors that affect this assessment of a callable bond's duration include:

1. *The modified DTC and the modified DTM.* These values form the lower boundary and the upper boundary, respectively, for the bond's modified duration.

2. *The current market yield environment.* A low yield environment increases the probability of a future call.

3. *The expected trend in interest rates.* A trend to lower rates increases the probability of early redemption.

4. *The expected variability in interest rates.* The greater the degree of variability, the more probable it is that the bond will be redeemed early.

A callable bond's duration has a range between the modified DTC and the modified DTM, with low yields and great variability in yields leading to a high subjective weighting of the probability of call:

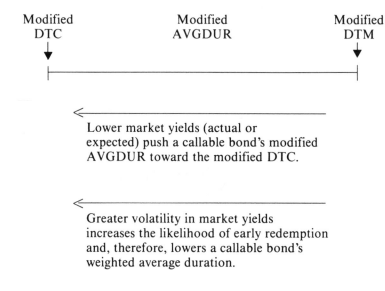

The third, and most advanced, method of calculating a callable bond's duration uses effective duration. This approach is based on option valuation and incorporates several variables:

1. *Call date(s).* An early call date reduces a bond's effective duration.

2. *Maturity date.* A short remaining term to maturity lowers a bond's effective duration.

3. *Call (i.e., strike) price.* A low call price shortens a bond's effective duration.

4. *Market price.* A high market price (i.e., a low market yield) decreases a bond's effective duration.

5. *Market yield volatility.* A high degree of yield volatility reduces a bond's effective duration.

6. *Level of short-term interest rates.* High short-term interest rates increase borrowing costs and increase the value of the call option, thereby lowering a bond's effective duration.

Effective duration is bounded by the modified DTC (lower boundary) and the modified DTM (upper boundary):

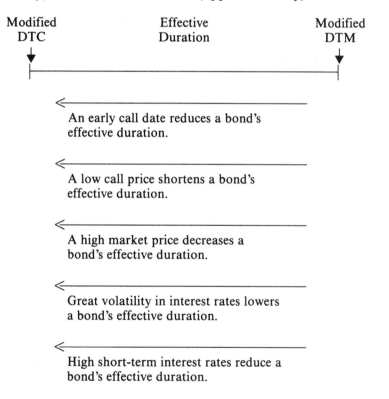

Callable bond illustrations. Most corporate bonds have call provisions. Exhibit 6–9 summarizes the typical structures of new-issue corporate bonds by issuer type (industrial, bank/finance, utility, and telephone). Call provisions come in three forms. A *refunding call* is a provision that allows the issuer to refinance, or refund, the bond at a prespecified price by issuing new, low-cost debt. A *cash call* gives the issuer the right to redeem bonds at a prespecified price by using cash generated from operations, asset sales, and the like. A refinancing cannot be used to implement a cash call. A *sinking fund call* systematically retires a prespecified number of bonds (e.g., 5% of the issue annually) during the issue's life.

Exhibit 6-9. The typical structures of new-issue corporate bonds, categorized by issuer sector.[a]

A. INDUSTRIAL BONDS

    30-year maturity; NR10 at a premium; immediate cash call at a premium; sinking fund in years 11 through 29
    10-year maturity; NC7 at par

B. BANK AND FINANCE BONDS

    12-year maturity; NC7 at par
    10-year maturity; NC7 at par
    10-year maturity; NC5 at par
    7-year maturity; NC5 at par
    5-year maturity; NC3 at par
    4-year maturity; NC2 at par
    3-year maturity; NC2 at par
    1½-year maturity; NC1 at par

C. ELECTRIC UTILITY BONDS

    30-year maturity; NR5 at a premium; immediate cash call at a premium
    10-year maturity; NR5 at a premium; immediate cash call at a premium

D. TELEPHONE UTILITY BONDS

    40-year maturity; NR5 at a premium

[a] "NC" means noncallable; "NR" means nonrefundable. Premium call prices are initially (par + annual coupon) and decline ratably to par over time.

Refunding calls and cash calls are generally made at a premium price (i.e., a price in excess of par) specified in the bond's indenture. This premium call price declines annually until it eventually reaches par value (100.00). Sinking fund calls are typically made at par value. Exhibit 6–10 gives the call schedule for the Anheuser-Busch 10% due 7/1/18. This industrial bond has cash calls, refunding calls, and sinking fund calls.

Exhibit 6–10. The call schedule for the Anheuser-Busch 10% due 7/1/18.[a] The bond has an immediate cash call at 110.00, a refunding call on 7/1/98 at 105.00, and a sinking fund call that starts on 7/1/99 at 100.00 (with an issuer option to double the size of any scheduled sinking fund payment). Cash call and refunding call prices decline ratably as time passes. The cash calls and refunding calls can be exercised at any time after the call protection period expires; the sinking fund calls must be exercised on specific dates (7/1/99, 7/1/00, etc.).

Call Date	Call Price	Call Date	Call Price
7/01/88	110.00	7/01/03	102.50
7/01/89	109.50	7/01/04	102.00
7/01/90	109.00	7/01/05	101.50
7/01/91	108.50	7/01/06	101.00
7/01/92	108.00	7/01/07	100.50
7/01/93	107.50	7/01/08	100.00
7/01/94	107.00	7/01/09	100.00
7/01/95	106.50	7/01/10	100.00
7/01/96	106.00	7/01/11	100.00
7/01/97	105.50	7/01/12	100.00
7/01/98	105.00	7/01/13	100.00
7/01/99	104.50	7/01/14	100.00
7/01/00	104.00	7/01/15	100.00
7/01/01	103.50	7/01/16	100.00
7/01/02	103.00	7/01/17	100.00
		7/01/18	100.00

[a] The sinking fund starts on 7/1/99 and retires 10,000 bonds annually (i.e., 5% of the $200 million issue) through maturity.

Exhibit 6–11 presents the modified durations and the effective durations of a sampling of callable bonds as of December 30, 1988. This table segregates the callable bonds by maturity sector (intermediates and longs) and by issuer sector (U.S. Treasuries, industrials, telephone utilities, electric utilities, yankees, bank and finance bonds, original issue discounts (OIDs), high yield corporates, and municipals). Exhibit 6–11 also provides the specific call provisions of each of the issues listed.

Exhibit 6-11. Effective durations (and specific call provisions) of a sample of callable bonds. Price and duration data as of December 30, 1988. Effective duration calculations courtesy of Capital Management Sciences.

A. Price, yield, and duration data

INTERMEDIATE MATURITY ISSUES

Ratings	Issue Description	Price	YTM(%)	Modified Duration to: Refunding Call	Maturity	Effective Duration
AAA/AAA	International Business Machines (IBM) 9% due 5/1/98	98.00	9.32	4.66	6.10	5.56
AAA/AA+	African Development Bank (ADB) 10% due 11/1/97	101.85	9.68	NA	5.72	5.72
Baa1/BBB+	Commonwealth Edison (CWE) 10⅛% due 5/1/98	99.75	10.16	3.38	5.84	5.47

LONG MATURITY ISSUES

Ratings	Issue Description	Price	YTM(%)	Modified Duration to: Refunding Call	Maturity	Effective Duration
Callable U.S. Treasuries:						
AAA/AAA	U.S. Treasury 14% due 11/15/11	141–20	9.21[a]	7.98	8.66	8.00
AAA/AAA	U.S. Treasury 10⅜% due 11/15/12	110–12	9.20[a]	8.58	9.27	8.62
AAA/AAA	U.S. Treasury 11¾% due 11/15/14	124–04	9.14[a]	8.77	9.34	8.80
Industrials:						
AA3/AA−	Anheuser-Busch (BUD) 10% due 7/1/18	99.50	10.05	5.77	8.97	6.83
A1/A+	Capital Cities Broadcasting (CCB) 11⅝% due 8/15/15	108.75	10.63	4.49	8.39	2.55
A1/A+	Atlantic Richfield Company (ARCO) 10⅞% due 7/15/05	108.75	9.80	NA	7.61	7.61
A1/A+	Atlantic Richfield Company (ARCO) 9⅞% due 3/1/16	100.75	9.79	NA	9.15	9.15
A3/BBB+	Georgia-Pacific (GP) 9½% due 2/15/18	90.50	10.55	5.61	8.77	7.67

LONG MATURITY ISSUES

Ratings	Issue Description	Price	YTM(%)	Modified Duration to: Refunding Call	Modified Duration to: Maturity	Effective Duration
Telephone utilities:						
AAA/AAA	Southern Bell Telephone (SBT) 8⅝% due 9/1/26	88.75	9.75	2.19	9.75	8.15
AAA/AAA	Southern Bell Telephone (SBT) 10¾% due 12/18/25	105.63	10.16	1.73	9.51	4.82
AA3/AA–	Southwestern Bell Telephone (SWBT) 11⅞% due 10/18/21	110.75	10.68	1.57	8.80	4.30
AA3/A+	Pacific Telephone & Telegraph (PAC) 9⅝% due 7/15/18	95.50	10.10	0.00	9.00	7.07
Electric utilities:						
Baa1/BBB+	Commonwealth Edison (CWE) 11⅛% due 5/1/18	102.75	10.81	3.33	8.65	5.93
Baa1/BBB	Texas Utilities Electric (TXU) 12% due 9/1/15	106.25	11.25	1.43	8.05	4.30
Yankees:						
AA2/AA–	British Columbia Hydro (BCH) 15½% due 11/15/11	134.25	9.74[a]	4.96	7.78	5.39
AA3/AA–	Province of Quebec (PQ) 8⅝% due 12/1/26	91.00	9.51	NA	10.21	10.21
Bank and finance:						
A1/AA–	Citicorp (CCI) 10⅞% due 6/15/10	103.00	10.52	1.31	8.38	4.35
Original issue discounts (OIDs):						
AA2/AA	Dupont (DD) 6% due 12/1/01	72.75	9.75	0.00	7.99	7.68
AA3/AA–	General Motors Accept. Corp. (GMAC) 6% due 4/1/11	65.50	9.85	0.00	9.61	9.26
High yield corporates:						
Ba3/B+	Gulf States Utilities (GSU) 12⅜% due 9/1/15	101.25	12.21	1.39	7.53	5.66
B3/CCC+	Federated Dept. Stores (FDS) 16% due 11/1/00	90.25	18.00	3.10	4.82	4.80
Municipals:						
A/A	New Jersey Turnpike (NJT) 7.20% due 1/1/18	95.63	7.58	3.27	11.35	7.94

[a]The issue is trading on a YTC basis; therefore, the YTC is shown rather than the YTM.

Exhibit 6-11. (cont.)

B. Specific Call Provisions

INTERMEDIATE MATURITY ISSUES

International Business Machines (IBM) 9% due 5/1/98; 100.00 refunding call on 5/1/95.

African Development Bank (ADB) 10% due 11/1/97; noncallable for life.

Commonwealth Edison (CWE) 10⅛% due 5/1/98; 109.53 current cash call; 102.72 refund call on 5/1/93.

LONG MATURITY ISSUES

Callable U.S. Treasuries:

U.S. Treasury (UST) 14% due 11/15/11; 100.00 refunding call on 11/15/06.
U.S. Treasury (UST) 10⅜% due 11/15/12; 100.00 refunding call on 11/15/07.
U.S. Treasury (UST) 11¾% due 11/15/14; 100.00 refunding call on 11/15/09.

Industrials:

Anheuser-Busch (BUD) 10% due 7/1/18; 110.00 current cash call; 105.00 refunding call 7/1/98.
Capital Cities Broadcasting (CCB) 11⅝% due 8/15/15; 109.54 current cash call; 105 refunding call on 8/15/95.
Atlantic Richfield Company (ARCO) 10⅞% due 7/15/05; noncallable for life.
Atlantic Richfield Company (ARCO) 9⅞% due 3/1/16; noncallable for life.
Georgia-Pacific (GP) 9½% due 2/15/18; 107.65 current cash call; 103.83 refunding call 2/14/98.

Telephone utilities:

Southern Bell Telephone (SBT) 8⅝% due 9/1/26; 104.69 refunding call on 9/1/91.
Southern Bell Telephone (SBT) 10¾% due 12/18/25; 108.40 refunding call on 12/18/90.
Southwestern Bell Telephone (SWBT) 11⅞% due 10/18/21; 109.96 refunding call on 10/18/90.
Pacific Telephone and Telegraph (PAC) 9⅝% due 7/15/18; 107.28 current refunding call.

Electric utilities:

Commonwealth Edison (CWE) 11⅛% due 5/1/18; 110.25 current cash call; 107.69 refund call on 5/1/93
Texas Utilities Electric (TXU) 12% due 9/1/15; 109.65 cash call; 108.52 refunding call 9/1/90.

Yankees:

British Columbia Hydro (BCH) 15½% due 11/15/11; 106.64 refunding call on 11/15/96.
Province of Quebec (PQ) 8⅝% due 12/1/26; noncallable for life.

Bank and finance:

Citicorp (CCI) 10⅞% due 6/15/10; 106.53 refunding call on 6/15/90.

Original issue discounts:

Dupont (DD) 6% due 12/1/01; 100.00 current refunding call.
General Motors Acceptance Corporation (GMAC) 6% due 4/1/11; 100.00 current refunding call

High yield corporates:

Gulf States Utilities (GSU) 12⅜% due 9/1/15; 110.72 current cash call; 109.70 refund call on 9/1/90.
Federated Department Stores (FDS) 16% due 11/1/00; 106.00 refunding call on 11/1/93.

Municipals:

New Jersey Turnpike 7.20% due 1/1/18; 103.00 refunding call on 1/1/93.

Individual issuer sectors carry different durations. For example, in the long maturity sector, municipal bonds have higher modified durations than do U.S. Treasury bonds which, in turn, have higher modified durations than do high yield corporate bonds:

Issue	Issuer Sector	YTM(%)	Modified Duration
New Jersey Turnpike 7.20% due 1/1/18	Municipal	7.58	11.35
U.S. Treasury 9% due 11/15/18	U.S. Treasury	9.00	10.20
Gulf States Utilities 12⅜% due 9/1/15	High yield	12.21	7.53

The combination of a low coupon and a low yield allows the municipal sector to provide longer modified durations than U.S. Treasuries or high yield corporates (the restrictive call features on municipal bonds, however, can create lower effective durations). For the same reason OIDs typically offer higher durations than do new-issue corporates of similar maturity.

The effective duration of a long maturity bond can be strongly influenced by its call provision(s). For example, the Southern Bell Telephone 10¾% due 12/18/25 is refundable at 108.40 in approximately 2 years (12/18/90). The bond's effective duration of 4.81 years is appreciably less than the bond's modified duration to maturity of 9.51 years. The proximity of the call date contributes to the duration reduction. A discount bond, such as the Southern Bell Telephone 8⅝% due 9/21/26, is less influenced by its underlying call provisions. The effective duration of this bond (8.14) is only modestly lower than its modified DTM (9.75). A noncallable issue, such as the Province of Quebec 8⅝% due 12/1/26, has an effective duration that equals its modified DTM (10.21) because the bond lacks any early redemption features.

Exhibit 6–12 calculates the effective durations of a series of generic corporate bonds. The effective durations of Exhibits 6–11 and 6–12 support several conclusions. First, a sizable difference between the earliest call date and the final maturity date can force substantial reductions in duration. A new-issue 40-year telephone

Exhibit 6-12. The effective durations of new corporate bonds of traditional structures. Each bond is priced at par to yield 10% to maturity. U.S. Treasury bond yields are assumed at 9% across the entire maturity spectrum.

	Modified Duration		
Issue Structure [a]	*To Refunding Call*	*To Maturity*	*Effective Duration*
A. INDUSTRIAL BONDS			
30-year/NR10 at 105.00/			
immediate cash call at 110.00	6.25	9.46	6.69
10-year/NC7 at 100.00	4.95	6.22	5.78
B. BANK AND FINANCE BONDS			
12-year/NC7 at 100.00	4.95	6.89	6.03
10-year/NC7 at 100.00	4.95	6.22	5.78
10-year/NC5 at 100.00	3.86	6.22	5.16
7-year/NC5 at 100.00	3.86	4.94	4.54
5-year/NC3 at 100.00	2.54	3.85	3.21
4-year/NC2 at 100.00	1.77	3.22	2.38
3-year/NC2 at 100.00	1.77	2.54	2.14
1½-year/NC1 at 100.00	0.93	1.36	1.31
C. ELECTRIC UTILITY BONDS			
30-year/NR5 at 107.50/			
immediate cash call at 110.00	3.86	9.46	6.69
10-year/NR5 at 105.00/			
immediate cash call at 110.00	3.86	6.22	5.53
D. TELEPHONE UTILITY BONDS			
40-year/NR5 at 109.82	3.86	9.79	7.89

[a] Abbreviations: "NR" means nonrefundable; "NC" means noncallable. For example, "30-year/NR5 at 107.50" means a 30-year maturity bond that is nonrefundable for 5 years, at which time it is refundable at 107.50.

utility bond has a 7.89 effective duration, almost 2 years less than its 9.79 modified DTM. A new-issue 10-year bank and finance bond (noncallable for 7 years) has a 5.78 effective duration, approximately 6 months less than its 6.22 modified DTM.

Second, impending (or immediate) calls exert a strong influence on a bond's duration. For example, the Capital Cities Broadcasting (CCB) 11⅝% due 8/15/15 has a current cash call at 109.54 and was priced at 108.75 on December 30, 1988. The bond's effective duration is only 2.55 years, significantly below the bond's 8.39 modified DTM. A new-issue 30-year utility bond has an immediate cash call and a refunding call in 5 years. This bond's effective duration is only 6.69 years, approximately 2¾ years less than the bond's 9.46 modified DTM.

Third, the market price:call price relationship strongly influences a bond's effective duration. Higher market prices lead to lower effective durations because of the greater probability of call. For example, the Southwestern Bell Telephone 11⅞% due 10/18/21 (refundable at 109.96 on 10/18/90) was priced at 110.75 on December 30, 1988. The bond's effective duration is only 4.30 years. The British Columbia Hydro 15½% due 11/15/11 is priced at 134.25 on December 30, 1988, well above its refunding call price of 106.64. As a result, the bond's effective duration is only 5.39 years, markedly below its modified DTM of 7.78 years. Lower call prices are responsible for smaller effective durations because of the higher probability of call. A longer period of call protection tames this influence. Finally, greater market volatility leads to lower effective durations. Exhibits 6–13 through 6–23 isolate these effects using generic examples.

Exhibit 6–13. Effective durations for new-issue, 10% coupon corporate bonds priced at par. Each issue is callable at 105.00 in 5 years. U.S. Treasury bond yields are at 9% across the maturity spectrum.[a]

	Modified Duration		*Effective*
Issue	*To Call*	*To Maturity*	*Duration*
10-year bond	3.86	6.22	5.91
30-year bond	3.86	9.46	6.76

CALL DATE: MATURITY DATE SPREAD. Wide divergences between a bond's first call date and the bond's final maturity date create great reductions in the bond's effective duration relative to the bond's modified DTM. Exhibit 6–13 calculates the effective durations of a 10-year corporate bond and a 30-year corporate bond. Each bond is callable at 105.00 in 5 years. With only a 5-year divergence between the first call date and the maturity date, the 10-year bond carries a 5.91 effective duration, marginally less than its 6.22 modified duration to maturity. The 30-year bond, on the other hand, has a 25-year difference between its first call date and its final maturity date. Its effective duration is almost 2¾ years lower than its modified DTM (6.76 versus 9.46).

Exhibit 6–14 presents the effective durations of 30-year corporate bonds with a variety of call dates (1 year to 30 years). The greater the call date:maturity date divergence, the larger the reduction in effective duration. An earlier call date forces a more

Exhibit 6–14. Effective durations of new-issue, 10% coupon, 30-year corporate bonds that are priced at par and are callable at 105.00. U.S. Treasury bond yields are 9% across the maturity spectrum. Each bond has a 9.46 modified duration to maturity.

First Call Date (in Years)	Call Date:Maturity Date Divergence (in Years)	Effective Duration	Reduction in Duration Due to the Call Provision
0	30	4.58	−4.88
1	29	4.93	−4.53
2	28	5.47	−3.99
3	27	5.98	−3.48
4	26	6.40	−3.06
5	25	6.76	−2.70
6	24	7.07	−2.39
7	23	7.36	−2.10
8	22	7.60	−1.86
9	21	7.80	−1.66
10	20	7.97	−1.49
15	15	8.66	−0.80
20	10	9.09	−0.37
25	5	9.40	−0.06
30	0	9.46	−0.00

dramatic duration shortening. A 25-year call requires a 0.06-year duration decrease. A 10-year call warrants a 1.49-year duration shortening, and a 1-year call is responsible for a 4.53-year duration decline. Exhibit 6–15 plots the relationship between the call date:maturity date divergence and a bond's effective duration.

IMPENDING CALL DATE. As a bond's first call date approaches, the bond's effective duration falls. Exhibit 6–16 analyzes the duration behavior of a 30-year corporate bond as time passes and its call date nears. The bond is initially callable at 105.00 in 10 years and carries an 8.02 effective duration.

Exhibit 6-15. The relationship between the call date:maturity date divergence and a bond's effective duration (data from Exhibit 6-14).

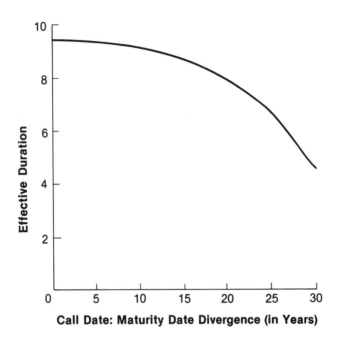

Assuming that U.S. Treasury bond yields remain stable at 9%, the bond's effective duration falls to 6.76 in 5 years, to 5.44 in 8 years, and to 4.48 in 10 years. Exhibit 6-17 plots these findings.

MARKET PRICE. As a bond's market price increases, the bond's effective duration falls. Exhibit 6-18 compares the effective durations of 30-year corporate bonds selling at a variety of prices. High priced bonds have lower effective durations than low priced bonds. A bond priced at 120.00 offers an effective duration of only 5.14 years. A par bond has a 7.10 effective duration, and a bond priced at 80.00 carries an 8.73 effective duration. Exhibit 6-19 graphs these results.

Exhibit 6-16. Effective durations of a new-issue, 10% coupon, 30-year corporate bond priced at par and callable at 105.00 in 10 years. U.S. Treasury bond yields are assumed at 9% across the maturity spectrum.

Evaluation Date	Call Protection Period (in Years)	Effective Duration [a]
At issuance	10	8.02
5 years after issuance	5	6.76
8 years after issuance	2	5.44
10 years after issuance	0	4.48

[a] The decline in effective duration is also affected by the approaching maturity date. The corresponding modified durations to (remaining) maturity are 9.46, 9.12, 8.82, and 8.57, respectively.

Exhibit 6-17. The relationship between a bond's effective duration and its remaining period of call protection (data from Exhibit 6-16).

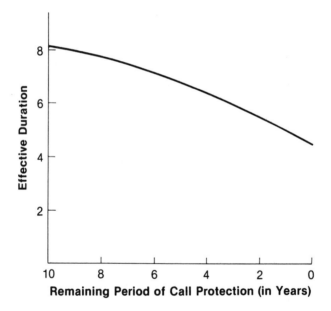

Exhibit 6-18. Effective durations of 30-year corporate bonds that are callable at 105.00 in 5 years. U.S. Treasury bond yields are assumed at 9% across the maturity spectrum.

Bond Price	Effective Duration [a]	Bond Price	Effective Duration [a]
80	8.73	105	6.58
85	8.33	110	6.04
90	8.00	115	5.54
95	7.60	120	5.14
100	7.10		

[a] Each bond has a coupon rate that corresponds to the bond's market price (because U.S. Treasury yields are held constant at 9%). The par bond carries a 10% coupon and yields 100BP more than a U.S. Treasury bond. The remaining bonds reflect the same option-adjusted spread as the par bond. The respective coupon rates are 7.88%, 8.50%, 8.95%, 9.47%, 10.00%, 10.53%, 11.05%, 11.60%, and 12.10% for the lowest priced bond to the highest priced bond.

Exhibit 6-19. The relationship between effective duration and bond prices (data from Exhibit 6-18).

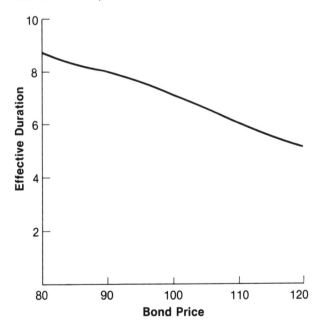

CALL PRICE. A low call price depresses a bond's effective duration. Exhibit 6-20 tallies the effective durations of a new-issue,

40-year corporate bond that is callable in 5 years. Assuming a 112.00 call price, the bond deserves a 7.75 effective duration. For a 106.00 call price, the bond has a 7.10 effective duration. The bond's effective duration falls to 6.48 years if the bond is callable at 100. Exhibit 6–21 summarizes these findings in a graphical format.

Exhibit 6–20. Effective durations of a new-issue, 10% coupon, 40-year corporate bond priced at par and callable in 5 years. A variety of call prices are illustrated. U.S. Treasury bond yields are assumed at 9% across the maturity spectrum.

Call Price	Effective Duration	Call Price	Effective Duration
100	6.48	108	7.32
102	6.66	110	7.55
104	6.89	112	7.75
106	7.10		

Exhibit 6–21. The relationship between a bond's effective duration and call price (data from Exhibit 6–20).

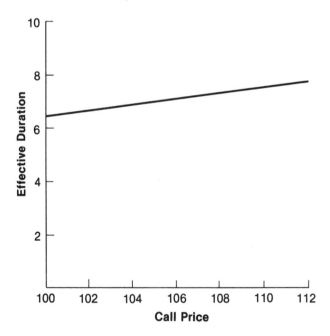

MARKET YIELD VOLATILITY. A higher degree of market yield volatility lowers a bond's effective duration. Exhibit 6–22 derives the effective durations of a new-issue, 30-year corporate bond that is callable at 105.00 in 5 years. At a negligible 2% volatility, the bond has an 8.68 effective duration. With volatility at 10%, the bond's effective duration falls to 7.18 years. For an 18% volatility assumption, the bond's effective duration is only 6.83 years. Exhibit 6–23 plots these findings.

Exhibit 6–22. Effective durations of a new-issue, 10% coupon, 30-year corporate bond priced at par and callable at 105 in 5 years. A variety of volatility assumptions are illustrated. U.S. Treasury bond yields are assumed at 9% across the maturity spectrum.

Yield Volatility Assumption (%)	Effective Duration	Yield Volatility Assumption (%)	Effective Duration
0	9.46	12	7.03
2	8.68	14	6.94
4	8.18	16	6.88
6	7.71	18	6.83
8	7.40	20	6.81
10	7.18		

Sinking fund provisions. Long-term industrial bonds generally have sinking fund provisions that require retirement of a specified number (or percentage) of bonds before final maturity. Long-term utility bonds also have sinking funds, although the provisions are typically smaller than those for industrial issues.[7]

[7] A utility bond typically has a minor sinking fund provision that retires 1% of an issue per annum, commencing at the end of the first year of a bond's life. The sinking fund requirement can be satisfied with cash, bonds (i.e., open-market purchases), or property additions. In many cases, property additions mitigate the need to retire securities. A "funnel" sinking fund provision can be used to direct all the sinking fund requirements toward a single issue (or series of issues), allowing a utility to retire high-coupon bonds at par. In addition, maintenance and replacement (M&R) funds can be used to redeem high-coupon bonds before scheduled refunding dates. Through property release and substitution clauses, a utility can channel the proceeds of property sales (e.g., sale-leaseback transactions) to retire high-coupon debt. In sum, utility issuers typically have a wide range of options available with which to redeem bonds before final maturity.

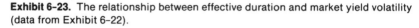

Exhibit 6-23. The relationship between effective duration and market yield volatility (data from Exhibit 6-22).

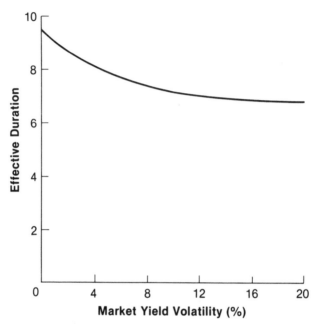

Note: Each of the illustrations for the market price effect, the call price effect, and the market yield volatility effect was based on a long-term bond that is noncallable for 5 years. The impact of each of these effects is magnified if the long-term security is currently callable (e.g., the bond has a cash call provision or the bond has run out of refunding protection).

Bonds that are called for sinking funds are either taken at par (100) or are purchased in the open market at a price below par. Sinking funds shorten the average life and the effective duration of a bond.

For example, a 30-year, 10% coupon noncallable bond bears a modified (and effective) duration of 9.46 years in a 10% yield environment. An identical bond with a 95% sinker (retiring 5% of the issue each year, beginning in the 11th year) carries an effective duration of only 8.82 years (data courtesy of Capital Management Sciences). Sinking fund provisions are most detrimental to bonds trading at a premium to par.[8] Discount bond prices, on the other hand, are supported by mandatory sinking fund requirements.

Putable bonds

The price sensitivity of a putable bond. A put option gives the holder the right to sell or "put" a bond back to the issuer at a prespecified price on a predetermined future date. The put is typically exercised at par value (100). Putable bonds are less prevalent than callable bonds. Exhibit 6–24 summarizes the typical structures of putable bonds. Exhibit 6–25 lists several of the putable bonds issued over the past several years. Exhibit 6–26 compares and contrasts the basic features of putable bonds and callable bonds.

Exhibit 6–24. The typical structures of putable bonds.

30-year maturity; 10-year put at par
30-year maturity; 15-year put at par
30-year maturity; 5-year put at par
20-year maturity; 10-year put at par
10-year maturity; 5-year put at par
7-year maturity; 4-year put at par
5-year maturity; 3-year put at par
4-year maturity; 2-year put at par

A putable bond is attractive because the bond holder (not the issuer) has the discretion to exercise the put option. In a bull market, a putable bond experiences the upside potential of its option-free maturity date equivalent; conversely, in a bear market, a put bond behaves like its option-free put date equivalent. Downside price losses are limited, and upside price gains are significant.

[8] Again, the concept of effective duration is made more understandable with this simplification.

Exhibit 6-25. A sampling of putable bonds.

Issue Size	Issue Date	Ratings	Issue Description	Put Date(s)
300MM	10/23/85	AAA/AAA	Kingdom of Sweden 10¼% due 11/1/15 (11/1/10 call at par)	11/1/95
450MM	8/14/86	AAA/AAA	Imperial Savings 8% due 8/15/11	8/15/94
250MM	6/11/87	A3/A−	Marriott Corp. 9⅜% due 6/15/07	6/15/97
200MM	1/15/88	A1/A+	Province of Manitoba 9⅛% due 1/15/18	1/15/98
100MM	2/5/88	AAA/NR	Centrust Savings Bank 8½% due 2/15/18	2/15/93 2/15/98
250MM	2/18/88	BAA3/BBB−	Consumers Power 8¾% due 2/15/98	2/15/93
250MM	3/23/88	BAA2/BBB	Tenneco 10% due 3/15/08	3/15/98
250MM	4/29/88	A1/AA	Waste Management 8¾% due 5/1/18	5/1/93
350MM	5/9/88	BAA1/A	Philip Morris 9% due 5/15/98	5/15/94
250MM	8/3/88	A2/A	Seagram & Sons, Inc. 9.65% due 8/15/18	8/15/03
300MM	5/15/89	AAA/AAA	Inter-American Development Bank 8⅞% due 5/15/09	5/15/99
200MM	5/25/89	AAA/AAA	Petro-Canada 8.80% due 6/1/19	6/1/04
400MM	6/9/89	AA3/AA−	General Motors Acceptance Corporation 8⅝% due 6/15/99	6/15/94

Exhibit 6-26. A comparison of the basic features of callable bonds and putable bonds.

	Callable Bond	Putable Bond
Option definition	A call option gives the holder the right to buy a bond at a prespecified price at a prespecified future date	A put option gives the holder the right to sell a bond at a prespecified price at a prespecified future date
Option holder	Issuer	Investor
Market availability	Widespread	Limited supply
Option strike price	Typically at a premium	Typically at par
Option exercise	A series of call dates and call prices	A single put date

Exhibit 6–26. (cont.)

	Callable Bond	*Putable Bond*
Option is in-the-money when	Market price is greater than the call price	Market price is less than the put price
Option is at-the-money when	Market price is equal to the call price	Market price is equal to the put price
Option is out-of-the-money when	Market price is less than the call price	Market price is greater than the put price
Yield versus an option-free bond	Higher yield	Lower yield

Exhibit 6–27 illustrates the price:yield relationship for a putable bond. In addition, the graph shows the price:yield curves for a comparable option-free bond that matures on the put date and for a comparable option-free bond that matures on the final maturity date. The effective duration of a put bond attempts to quantify the price sensitivity of the bond by measuring the slope of the put bond's price:yield curve at the current market price.[9] A putable bond requires the use of an option valuation model to project the bond's values in a variety of yield environments.

Assessing the duration of a putable bond. There are three ways to calculate the duration of a putable bond:

1. Calculate the bond's *duration to put* (DTP) and the bond's duration to maturity (DTM).[10] Use the DTP as the bond's representative duration if the bond's market price exceeds

---

[9] The duration to put (DTP) is evaluated using the put date in its derivation. Generally speaking, the put date is a single date, not a series of dates as with a call provision. The duration to maturity (DTM) assumes that the entire issue remains outstanding until the final maturity date.

[10] A more naive approach relies on the put price (typically par) as the differentiation point. At market prices above the put price, the bond is evaluated on a "put date" basis, and the yield to put (YTP) and duration to put (DTP) statistics are used. At market prices at or below the put price, the bond is evaluated on a "maturity date" basis, and the yield to maturity (YTM) and duration to maturity (DTM) figures are used. The most simplistic approach uses the par value (100) as the demarcation point, regardless of the put price.

Exhibit 6-27. The price:yield curves for a putable bond and for two noncallable counterparts: an option-free bond maturing on the put date and an option-free bond maturing on the final maturity date.

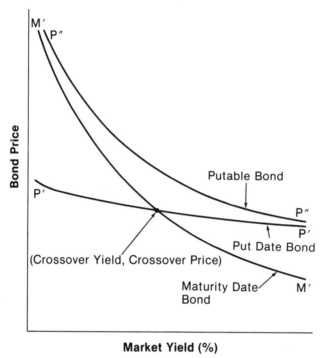

Market Yield (%)

the crossover price; use the DTM if the bond's market price is less than or equal to the crossover price.[11]

2. Calculate a weighted average duration on the basis of a subjective assessment of the probability of put exercise.

3. Calculate an effective or option-adjusted, duration by using an option valuation model.

[11] This is particularly true for callable bonds with sinking funds. For example, a 30-year corporate bond has a 105 refunding call in 10 years (104.50 in the 11th year). The bond has a 95% sinking fund that retires 5% of the issue (at 100) commencing in 11 years. The bond's average refunding price is less than the stated refunding price (105) because the company will exercise its sinking fund rights at par value, not at the refunding price. In essence, the average redemption price is approximately 104.25 in 11 years because 5% of the outstanding bonds can be purchased at par.

A 10% coupon, 30-year bond (with a 10-year put at 100) illustrates each of these approaches.

SELECTING EITHER THE DURATION TO PUT OR THE DURA-TION TO MATURITY. Of the three calculations just listed, the easiest way to assess a putable bond's duration is by choosing either the bond's duration to put (DTP) or the bond's duration to maturity (DTM). These durations are calculated as follows:

$$DTP = \sum_{t=0.5}^{p} \left(\frac{PV(CF_t)}{TPV} \times t \right)$$

$$DTM = \sum_{t=0.5}^{n} \left(\frac{PV(CF_t)}{TPV} \times t \right)$$

where
p = the number of years remaining until the put date
n = the number of years remaining until the final maturity date

The modified versions are derived as follows:

$$\frac{\text{modified}}{\text{DTP}} = \frac{DTP}{\left(1 + \dfrac{YTP}{2} \right)} \qquad \frac{\text{modified}}{\text{DTM}} = \frac{DTM}{\left(1 + \dfrac{YTM}{2} \right)}$$

where
YTP = the yield to put (expressed in decimal form)

YTM = the yield to maturity (expressed in decimal form)

The DTP is shorter than the DTM because the cash flows of the former truncate on the put date. In virtually all cases, the put price is par.

Exhibit 6–28 presents the yields and modified durations of a 10% coupon, 30-year with a 10-year put at par. Based on a market price of 105.00, the bond has two durations:

1. Modified DTP: 6.34
2. Modified DTM: 9.81

Exhibit 6–28. The yields and modified durations of a 10% coupon, 30-year putable bond. The bond has a 10-year put at par and the bond is currently priced at 105. U.S. Treasury bond yields are assumed at 9% across the maturity spectrum.

Holding Period	Yield (%)	Modified Duration
To put date (10 years)	9.22	6.34
To maturity date (30 years)	9.50	9.82

A put option reduces a bond's price sensitivity. The bond's modified duration can be shortened by more than 3 years, from 9.81 to 6.34. The modified DTP is quoted when the bond's market price is below the crossover price; the modified DTM is used when the bond's market price equals or exceeds the crossover price. In this case, the modified DTM (9.81) is chosen since the bond is trading above the crossover price (105.00 > 100.00).

CALCULATING A WEIGHTED AVERAGE DURATION. Under a more advanced approach to assessing the duration of a putable bond, a weighted average duration is calculated by subjectively assigning a probability to the put exercise:

$$\text{weighted average duration (AVGDUR)} = \left[\text{DTP} \times P_p \right] + \left[\text{DTM} \times (1 - P_p) \right]$$

where

P_p = the probability that the put will be exercised (expressed in decimal form)

$1 - P_p$ = the probability that the put will not be exercised (expressed in decimal form)

A modified version is computed by using modified durations in the formula. The probability of put is a subjective estimate and ranges from 0.00 (0% chance) to 1.00 (100% chance).

Exhibit 6–29 calculates the modified durations of a 30-year bond (with a 10-year put at par) in a variety of yield environments. Exhibit 6–30 summarizes the weighted average modified durations of the putable bond for several interest rate environments and also shows the subjective probability of put assigned at each yield level. In an environment of 11% U.S. Treasury yields, the bond has a 6.26 weighted average modified duration:

$$\frac{\text{modified}}{\text{(AVGDUR)}} = \left[\frac{\text{modified}}{\text{DTP}} \times P_p\right] + \left[\frac{\text{modified}}{\text{DTM}} \times (1-P_p)\right]$$

$$= (5.99 \times 0.90) + (8.71 \times 0.10)$$

$$= 5.39 + 0.87$$

$$= 6.26$$

In this case, the investor assigns a 90% probability to the put exercise, thereby warranting a higher weighting to the modified DTP.

Exhibit 6–29. The modified durations of a 10% coupon, 30-year putable bond in a variety of yield environments. The bond is currently priced at 105.00 and has a 10-year put at par. U.S. Treasury bond yields are assumed a 9% across the maturity spectrum.

U.S. Treasury Yield (%)	Bond Price [a]	Modified Duration	
		To Put Date (10 Years)	To Maturity Date (30 Years)
6	140.37	6.95	11.98
7	126.16	6.73	11.18
8	114.56	6.53	10.47
9	105.00	6.34	9.82
10	96.98	6.16	9.24
11	90.13	5.99	8.71
12	84.22	5.84	8.23

[a]Price data courtesy of Capital Management Sciences.

Exhibit 6-30. The weighted average durations of a 10% coupon, 30-year putable bond in a variety of yield environments. Price and duration data from Exhibit 6-29.

U.S. Treasury Yield (%)	Bond Price	Probability of Put (Pp)	Weighted Average Duration [a]
6	140.37	0.10	11.48
7	126.16	0.30	9.85
8	114.56	0.40	8.89
9	105.00	0.50	8.08
10	96.98	0.75	6.93
11	90.13	0.90	6.26
12	84.22	1.00	5.84

[a]Calculated as the DTP (probability of put) + DTM (1 - probability of put).

CALCULATING THE EFFECTIVE DURATION OF A PUTABLE BOND. Effective duration attempts to capture the price sensitivity of a putable bond by assessing the slope of the price:yield curve at the bond's current market price. Exhibit 6-27 (see page 106) plotted a typical price:yield curve for a putable bond with a long-term maturity and an intermediate-term put date. A putable bond is a combination of an option-free bond and a long position in a put option. The price of a putable bond is calculated as the sum of the price of an option-free bond plus the value of the put option:

$$\text{putable bond price} = \text{option-free bond price} + \text{put option value}$$

A putable bond costs more than an option-free bond of similar maturity. The incremental value stems from the bondholder's right to sell the bond back to the issuer at par at an advantageous point in time. In yield terms, a putable bond trades at a lower yield than a similar maturity, option-free security.

With U.S. Treasury bonds yielding 9%, a 10% coupon, 30-year option-free corporate bond is priced at par to yield 10% to maturity. A 10% coupon, 30-year corporate bond (with a 10-year put at par) is valued at 103.50 if the put option is worth 3½ points:

$$\frac{\text{putable}}{\text{bond price}} = \frac{\text{option-free}}{\text{bond price}} + \frac{\text{put option}}{\text{value}}$$

$$= \quad 100.00 + 3.50$$

$$= \quad 103.50$$

The putable bond's yield is 9.64%, 36BP lower than the 10% yield on the option-free equivalent.

Several factors affect a putable bond's effective duration:

1. *Put date.* An early put date reduces a bond's effective duration.
2. *Maturity date.* A short remaining term to maturity lowers a bond's effective duration.
3. *Put (i.e., strike) price.* A high put price shortens a bond's effective duration.
4. *Market price.* A low market price (i.e., a high market yield) decreases a bond's effective duration.
5. *Market yield volatility.* A high degree of market yield volatility reduces a bond's effective duration.
6. *Level of short-term interest rates.* Low short-term interest rates decrease borrowing costs and increase the value of the put option, thereby lowering a bond's effective duration.

A putable bond's effective duration falls within the boundaries of the modified DTP (lower boundary) and the modified DTM (upper boundary).

The price behavior of a putable bond. As market yields shift, the values of the option-free bond component and the put option component change. As yields rise, the option-free bond component's value falls; conversely, as yields fall, the option-free bond component's value rises. The value of the put option component varies directly with interest rates. As interest rates rise, the put option increases in value as it goes further "into the money"; as interest rates fall, the put option loses value as it moves further "out of the money." A putable bond's price decline is cushioned dramatically in a bear market, whereas the bond's price advance is modestly tamed in a bull market.

Exhibit 6–31 summarizes the put option values and total returns for a 30-year bond (with a 10-year put at par) as interest rates fluctuate around current levels. The put option is currently valued at 4.31 points. If yields rise 200BP, the put option value increases to 5.76 points. If yields fall 200BP, the value of the put declines to 2.57 points. The putable bond posts sizable gains in a bull market (e.g., 33.64% return if yields fall 300BP) and suffers modest losses in a bear market (e.g., –19.83% return if yields rise 300BP).

Exhibit 6–31. The put option values and total returns for a 30-year bond with a 10-year put at par. The bond is currently priced at 105. U.S. Treasury bond yields are assumed to be initially at 9% across the maturity spectrum. U.S. Treasury bond yields are shifted in parallel up and down a maximum of 300BP.

U.S. Treasury Bond Yield Change (in BP)	Total Return (%)	Put Option Value
–300	33.64	1.73
–250	26.56	2.14
–200	20.16	2.57
–150	14.38	3.01
–100	9.13	3.45
– 50	4.35	3.89
0	0.00	4.31
+ 50	– 3.99	4.72
+100	– 7.66	5.10
+150	–11.05	5.44
+200	–14.19	5.76
+250	–17.11	6.05
+300	–19.83	6.30

On a graph, the putable bond's price:yield curve lies above both the price:yield curve of its option-free put date equivalent and the price:yield curve of its option-free maturity date equivalent (refer back to Exhibit 6–27). The putable bond's price gravitates between the put date assumption (modified DTP) and the maturity date assumption (modified DTM), depending on the general level of interest rates. The putable bond's price approaches the put date bond curve as yields rise, and the put exercise becomes increasingly probable. As yields fall, the putable bond's price approaches the maturity date bond curve, and the probability of put diminishes.

The price sensitivity of a putable bond lies between the price sensitivity of the option-free put date bond and the option-free maturity date bond. In a bull market, the putable bond's price rises almost as quickly as the maturity date bond. In a bear market, the putable bond acts progressively more like a put date bond by experiencing price declines that are less severe than those of the maturity date bond. The putable bondholder has the best of both worlds: substantial upside potential with limited downside losses. The price for this attractive combination is reflected in the value of the put option, which is incorporated implicitly into the price of the putable bond.

A case study: Province of Manitoba 9⅛% put bond due 1/15/18. Exhibits 6–32 and 6–33 analyze the Province of Manitoba 9⅛% due 1/15/18 (1/15/98 put at par). As of December 30, 1988, the bond was priced at 98 and had a 5.79 modified DTP. The bond's 8.01 effective duration is over 2 years longer than the modified DTP. The Manitoba bond's modified DTM is 9.57 years, and its crossover price is 100.

A putable bond's effective duration lengthens as interest rates fall and shortens as interest rates rise. In this case, the bond's effective duration is currently 8.01. The duration increases to 8.93, 9.93, and 11.03 as yields fall 100BP, 200BP, and 300BP,

Exhibit 6-32. The yields and durations of the Province of Manitoba 9⅛% due 1/15/18. The bond is putable at par on 1/15/98 and the bond is priced at 98 on December 30, 1988.

Holding Period	Yield (%)	Modified Duration
To put date (1/15/98)	9.46	5.79
To maturity date (1/15/18)	9.33	9.57

Effective duration: 8.10

Exhibit 6-33. The prices, effective durations, and put option values for the Province of Manitoba 9⅛% due 1/15/18 as market yields fluctuate. [a]

U.S. Treasury Bond Yield Change (in BP)	Manitoba Bond Price	Effective Duration	Put Option Value
−300	131.20	11.03	3.78
−250	124.17	10.47	3.98
−200	117.84	9.93	4.25
−150	112.13	9.41	4.55
−100	106.97	8.93	4.88
− 50	102.28	8.48	5.22
0	98.00	8.10	5.55
+ 50	94.07	7.72	5.87
+100	90.45	7.39	6.16
+150	87.11	7.09	6.43
+200	84.00	6.82	6.66
+250	81.12	6.56	6.87
+300	78.43	6.33	7.04

[a] Issue data from Exhibit 6-32 and calculations courtesy of Capital Management Sciences.

respectively. The duration declines to 7.39, 6.82, and 6.33 as yields rise 100BP, 200BP, and 300BP, respectively.

The value of the put option is strongly influenced by the market yield level. When U.S. Treasury bond yields are at 9%, the put is worth 5.55 points. The option's value falls to 4.88 points, 4.25 points, and 3.78 points as U.S. Treasury bond yields drop to 8%, 7%, and 6%, respectively. The option's value increases to 6.16 points, 6.66 points, and 7.04 points as U.S. Treasury bond yields rise to 10%, 11%, and 12%, respectively.

The advantages and limitations of effective duration

Effective duration has several attractive features. First, effective duration is a better measure of the price sensitivity of a callable (or putable) bond than modified duration because the latter assumes a straight-line price:yield relationship. A callable bond's price:yield function is particularly curvlinear. Second, effective duration is superior to a "gut feel" approach to how a callable (or putable) bond "should" trade because it values a bond's implicit options on a consistent basis. In addition, effective duration is an improvement over a discrete selection of modified duration based on the bond's market price in relation to the bond's crossover price because it quantifies the average price sensitivity of the callable bond for both "up" and "down" markets. Effective duration intends to provide an objective measure of bond risk. Finally, by considering a bond's implicit option provisions, effective duration allows for comparisons between individual callable bonds, between callable bonds and noncallable bonds, and between putable bonds and callable bonds (or option-free equivalents).

Effective duration has its limitations, however. First, effective duration is based on a series of mathematical assumptions. An incorrect judgment of market yield volatility or a sizable market movement (to either higher or lower yields) renders the effective duration less accurate. Second, effective duration can shift dramatically as market conditions change (e.g., higher rates, lower rates, more volatile rates, or less volatile rates) and as time passes (e.g., declining call price, shorter call protection period, or shorter remaining term to maturity). Assessing a bond's sensitivity to changes in these factors is important.

Third, the variability in a bond's price is affected by several realities in the marketplace that effective duration fails to capture:

1. Excessive demand for noncallable bonds and for long duration bonds.
2. A high demand for incremental yield, regardless of call provisions.
3. An investor preference for discount bonds (and the relative supply of discount bonds available in the marketplace).
4. Supply of new issues.
5. The general sentiment regarding the future trend in interest rates (bullish, bearish, or neutral). Effective duration is always based on a "random walk" (nondirectional) assumption.
6. Individual issue characteristics. For example, a utility bond may trade at a market price exceeding the cash call price if the utility is involved in a large capital spending program.

An industrial bond's price, on the other hand, may have difficulty surpassing the cash call price because the underlying company is profitable and has the ability to exercise the cash call.

No quantitative measure, including effective duration, can incorporate all of the "real world" factors that influence a bond's price behavior. Judgment is required of the professional investor.

Finally, there is no universal agreement on the appropriate model for deriving effective duration. The option-free component of a bond is easy to analyze. It is the option component (put, call, or sinking fund) that presents difficulty when you consider the following points:

1. Does the option valuation model apply to American options as well as to European options?
2. Bond option models are based on stock option models. Adjustments must be made for the unique features of a bond vis-à-vis a stock: a specific lifespan that declines as time passes, options with long lives (e.g., several years), volatility that changes over time (e.g., as a bond's maturity nears, price volatility declines but yield volatility increases), limits on the bond's maximum price (yields cannot fall below 0%), and the like.
3. To what degree does the option valuation model incorporate a tendency of interest rates to regress to a mean over time?
4. Does the option valuation model handle multiple options (e.g., sinking fund, calls, or puts)? Many long maturity corporate bonds carry a series of options, not simply a single one.
5. How does the option valuation model assess volatility? History has shown that different maturity sectors have different degrees of yield volatility. Different issuer sectors (e.g., low quality versus high quality, industrial versus U.S. Treasury) have unique volatilities. Does the model handle the volatility variable in a rigorous manner, or is it oversimplified?

Despite its limitations, effective duration is a useful tool for grasping the "true" price sensitivity of a callable (or putable) bond.

Advances in bond option valuation models will render effective duration more accurate and will make for greater consensus among practitioners and academics. Independent professional judgment will still be required to incorporate all of the real-world effects into an investment purchase or sale decision.

Effective duration of mortgage-backed securities and asset-backed securities

This section analyzes the effective durations of a variety of mortgage-backed securities (MBS) and asset-backed securities (ABS):

1. Mortgage-backed securities
   A. Mortgage passthroughs
      i) 30-year passthroughs
      ii) 15-year passthroughs
   B. Derivative mortgage products
      i) Collateralized mortgage obligations (CMOs)
      ii) Stripped MBS (interest-only strips and principal-only strips)
2. Asset-backed securities
   A. Certificates for automobile receivables (CARS)
   B. Certificates for amortizing revolving debts (CARDS)

Mortgage-backed securities and asset-backed securities differ from corporate bonds in several respects:

1. MBS and ABS typically generate cash flows on a monthly or quarterly basis (versus semiannually for corporate bonds).
2. MBS and ABS are immediately callable at par through prepayment provisions (versus a premium call price for many corporate bonds). In addition, MBS and ABS are subject to partial calls (rather than the all-or-none call exercise that is generally used by corporations).
3. MBS and ABS offer the highest credit quality ("AAA" rated) versus an average "A" rating for investment-grade corporate bonds.

4. MBS and ABS make principal repayments across the life of the security (most corporate bonds return the entire principal amount in a lump sum at final maturity). Therefore, the effective durations of MBS and ABS are lower than their similar maturity corporate counterparts.

5. The cash flows of MBS or ABS must be predicted based on prepayment expectations. Corporate bond cash flows are stated and fixed.

The effective durations of MBS and ABS are discussed in turn.

Mortgage-backed securities

Mortgage-backed securities come in two forms. *Mortgage passthroughs* (GNMAs, FHLMCs, FNMAs, and whole loans) are pools of mortgages that "pass through" the cash flows of the underlying mortgages (net of a servicing fee) to the holder of the mortgage passthrough. These cash flows are typically made on a monthly basis and include both principal and interest. *Derivative mortgage products* are repackaged pieces of a mortgage passthrough (hence the term *derivative*). For example, a mortgage passthrough can be segregated into interest payments (interest-only STRIPS) and principal payments (principal-only STRIPS). Through creative "slicing and dicing," the range of potential derivative mortgage products is endless. The size of the market for derivative products has exploded in recent years as new products have enticed larger numbers of investors into the mortgage-backed securities market.

Mortgage passthroughs. Single-family, fixed-rate home mortgages are originated with either a 15-year or 30-year term.[12] The latter is the traditional choice for many home buyers, although the former has gained popularity in the past few years. Mortgages are packaged into large pools by three government-sponsored agencies: the Government National Mortgage Association

---

[12] The focus of the MBS discussion is on fixed-rate mortgage passthroughs. In addition, floating-rate mortgage passthroughs (using adjustable-rate mortgages as collateral) and floating-rate CMOs are available in the marketplace.

Exhibit 6-34. A comparison of the call provisions of a 30-year corporate bond and a 30-year mortgage passthrough.

Provision	30-Year Corporate Bond	30-Year Mortgage Passthrough
Call price	At a premium to par	At par
Call protection period	5 to 10 years protection from refunding call	None
Call exercise	All or none	Partial calls (i.e, prepayments)
Sinking fund schedule	10 years protection from sinking fund calls	Scheduled principal repayments commence immediately
Sinking fund price	At par (or at a market price below par if an open market sinker)[a]	At par

[a] For electric utility bonds, sinking fund requirements are sometimes satisfied at a premium price.

(GNMA), the Federal Home Loan Mortgage Corporation (FHLMC), and the Federal National Mortgage Association (FNMA). Mortgages pooled by private entities are termed whole loans. Exhibit 6–34 compares the call provisions of a 30-year mortgage passthrough to the call provisions of a 30-year corporate bond.

The effective duration of a mortgage passthrough is a function of its underlying cash flows. The cash flows of a mortgage passthrough arise from (1) interest payments, (2) scheduled principal payments, and (3) unscheduled principal payments (i.e., prepayments). The *interest payments* are calculated using the stated interest rate and the outstanding principal amount. *Scheduled principal payments* are analogous to sinking fund payments on a corporate bond. *Unscheduled principal payments*, or *prepayments*, occur as the result of refinancing activity, foreclosures, home sales, and so on. The scheduled principal payments (and related interest payments) are known in advance. The wild card in the cash flow pattern of a mortgage passthrough is prepayments.

Prepayments are partial redemptions at par value. The value of an MBS is predicated on a forecast of future prepayments. This prepayment expection is derived through the analysis of a combination of historical prepayment experience observed on outstanding mortgage pools (e.g., Federal Housing Administration and Veterans Administration statistics) and factors including the age of the mortgages, the coupon rate(s) on the mortgages, the type of mortgage (e.g., GNMA-backed versus FNMA-backed), the geographical source of the mortgages (e.g., Florida versus Missouri), the behavior of interest rates since the mortgages were originated (e.g., prior refinancing opportunities), seasonality, and predictions of the future direction of interest rates, housing activity, shape of the yield curve, and the like. The prepayment assumption is a critical underpinning to the expected future cash flows of a mortgage passthrough. The cash flows of a mortgage derivative product are also affected by the prepayment assumption.

The effective duration of a mortgage passthrough security is influenced by several factors:

1. *The type of mortgage collateral* (GNMAs, FHLMCs, FNMAs, or whole loans).

2. *The remaining term to maturity of the mortgage passthrough.* A short remaining term to maturity warrants a low effective duration.

3. *The coupon rate(s) of the mortgage passthrough.* A high coupon passthrough has a low effective duration.

4. *The prepayment rate assumption.* A high prepayment rate leads to a low effective duration.

5. *The current market yield environment.* A low yield environment finds a high prepayment rate and a low effective duration.[13]

6. *The expected trend in interest rates.* A trend to lower interest rates increases prepayments and lowers the effective duration.

7. *Market yield volatility.* The greater the volatility in market yields, the more the effective duration is reduced.

Exhibit 6–35 analyzes the price, yield, effective duration, and prepayment statistics for a variety of 30-year GNMAs, FHLMCs, and FNMAs. This table also provides the prepayment rates for each passthrough, as expressed in a % PSA (Public Securities Association). Exhibit 6–36 summarizes the price, yield, effective duration, and prepayment statistics for 15-year mortgage passthroughs. These tables support several conclusions.

---

[13] The general relationship between duration and market yield is an inverse one: as the yield falls, the duration lengthens. This relationship arises because of the (relatively) higher present value weights assigned to longer maturity cash flows when interest rates decline. For bonds with fixed cash flows, such as noncallable bonds, duration and market yield vary inversely. For callable bonds, however, the future cash flows of the investment are altered (sometimes dramatically) when interest rates decline and early redemption provisions take effect. As a result, the present value-weighted average maturity of the investment's cash flows falls and its effective duration declines. Consequently, a direct (rather than inverse) relationship between duration and market yield emerges. The impact of a change in the present value factors (biasing the long-term cash flows to carry more weight) is not powerful enough to overcome the impact of a material shortening in the time to receipt of the investment's cash flows.

Exhibit 6-35. The price, yield, average life, effective duration, and prepayment statistics for a series of 30-year GNMAs, FHLMCs, and FNMAs as of April 10, 1989.[a]

Coupon	Age (in years)	Price	Approx. PSA %	CBE Yield %	Avg. Life (in Years)	Effective Duration[c]	March 1989 PSA %
			Based on Approximate PSA[b]				
GNMA							
8[d]	2.0	86–12	80	10.49	11.7	6.7	49
8[e]	12.0	89–18	90	10.30	7.9	5.4	97
8½[d]	2.0	89–03	86	10.56	11.4	6.4	71
8½[e]	10.5	91–20	96	10.33	8.3	5.4	86
9[d]	2.0	91–23	91	10.61	11.3	6.1	70
9[e]	10.0	92–28	104	10.61	8.3	5.3	86
9½[d]	0.0	94–08	94	10.60	12.4	5.9	99
9½[e]	9.5	95–30	111	10.47	8.3	4.9	102
10[d]	0.0	96–29	107	10.69	11.8	5.4	126
10½[d]	0.0	99–15	127	10.75	10.9	4.7	198
11[e]	5.5	101–18	159	10.79	7.9	3.7	171
12[e]	5.0	104–21	249	10.82	5.7	2.6	282
FHLMC							
8[d]	2.0	87–19	121	10.41	9.5	5.5	89
8[e]	13.0	89–28	135	10.35	6.6	4.5	134
8½[d]	2.0	89–21	127	10.54	9.3	5.3	98
8½[e]	13.0	92–04	145	10.33	6.6	4.4	133
9[d]	2.0	91–31	138	10.61	9.0	5.1	88
9[e]	11.5	93–28	160	10.41	6.6	4.2	158
9½[d]	0.0	94–06	148	10.59	9.8	5.0	151
9½[e]	11.0	95–20	170	10.50	6.5	4.0	167
10[d]	0.0	96–11	163	10.70	9.3	4.5	167
10½[d]	0.0	98–14	171	10.79	9.0	4.1	156
11[e]	9.0	100–10	243	10.77	5.5	3.1	240
12[e]	8.0	102–27	311	10.86	4.6	2.4	274
FNMA							
8[d]	2.0	88–00	120	10.42	9.5	5.5	115
8[e]	13.0	90–08	134	10.43	6.4	4.4	103
8½[d]	2.0	90–04	137	10.64	8.7	5.3	124
8½[e]	12.0	92–16	150	10.33	6.8	4.4	120
9[d]	2.0	92–10	140	10.68	8.7	5.0	131
9[e]	11.0	94–08	158	10.44	6.7	4.2	118
9½[d]	0.0	94–21	145	10.60	9.8	5.0	126
9½[e]	11.0	96–00	174	10.54	6.5	4.0	134
10[d]	0.0	96–29	158	10.70	9.3	4.6	125

Exhibit 6-35. (cont.)

Coupon	Age (in years)	Price	Based on Approximate PSA[b] Approx. PSA %	CBE Yield %	Avg. Life (in Years)	Effective Duration[c]	March 1989 PSA %
FNMA							
10½[d]	0.0	98–29	175	10.81	8.8	4.0	167
11[e]	9.0	100–25	222	10.81	5.3	3.0	237
12[e]	6.0	103–04	315	10.98	4.6	2.4	278

[a]Data courtesy of the First Boston Corporation.

[b]Prepayment projections are based on the First Boston model. The PSA prepayment rate is shown is an approximation for the varying monthly paydowns forecast by the model.

[c]Effective durartions are calculated using a 10% volatility assumption.

[d]New securities: Pools containing mortgages not more than 2.5 years old.
[e]Seasoned securities: Pools containing mortgages more than 2.5 years old.

Exhibit 6-36. The price, yield, average life, effective duration, and prepayment statistics for a series of 15-year GNMAs, FHLMCs, and FNMAs as of April 10, 1989.[a]

Coupon	Age (in years)	Price	Based on Approximate PSA[b] Approx. PSA %	CBE Yield %	Avg. Life (in Years)	Effective Duration[c]	March 1989 PSA %
GNMA Midget							
8	2.5	90–23	67	10.36	6.1	4.5	61
8½[d]	1.0	92–20	78	10.26	6.8	4.6	72
9	1.0	94–24	94	10.32	6.6	4.4	85
9½	1.0	96–26	112	10.37	6.4	4.1	159
10	1.0	99–08	134	10.30	6.0	3.7	174
10½	2.5	100–18	169	10.44	4.9	3.2	165
11	3.5	102–17	210	10.27	4.2	2.7	166
FHLMC Gnome							
8	2.5	90–15	99	10.36	5.7	4.3	89
8½	2.5	92–08	110	10.44	5.6	4.1	98
9	1.0	93–31	118	10.40	6.2	4.2	70
9½	1.0	95–23	133	10.47	6.2	4.0	102
10	1.0	97–15	149	10.55	6.0	3.7	167
10½	3.5	99–09	166	10.56	4.7	3.3	207
11	3.5	101–13	190	10.39	4.5	3.2	240

Exhibit 6-36. (cont'd.)

| Coupon | Age (in years) | Price | Based on Approximate PSA[b] | | | | |
			Approx. PSA %	CBE Yield %	Avg. Life (in Years)	Effective Duration[c]	March 1989 PSA %
FNMA 15–Year							
8	2.0	90–28	83	10.26	6.1	4.4	115
8½	1.0	92–12	98	10.34	6.5	4.5	129
9	1.0	94–06	113	10.46	6.3	4.3	127
9½	1.0	96–05	130	10.51	6.1	4.0	129
10	1.0	97–30	149	10.58	5.8	3.6	133
10½	2.5	99–23	166	10.61	5.0	3.4	138
11	3.5	101–25	190	10.42	4.4	3.2	212

Treasury Yield Curve (4/10/89)

1 Year	9.74%
2 Year	9.57
3 Year	9.53
3 Year	9.50
5 Year	9.42
7 Year	9.36
10 Year	9.27

[a]Data courtesy of the First Boston Corporation.

[b]Prepayment projections are based on the First Boston model. The PSA prepayment rate as shown is an approximation for the varying monthly paydowns forecast by the model.

[c]Effective durrations are calculated using a 10% volatility assumption.

First, 30-year passthroughs carry longer durations than similar coupon 15-year passthroughs. New-issue GNMA 10s have a 5.40 effective duration versus the 3.70 effective duration of GNMA Midget 10s. Second, GNMAs prepay at a slower rate than FHLMCs and FNMAs, and therefore GNMAs deserve higher effective durations. During March 1989, GNMA 11s prepaid at 171% PSA; FHLMC 11s and FNMA 11s recorded prepayment rates of 240% PSA and 237% PSA, respectively. The GNMA 11s have a 3.70 effective duration versus 3.10 and 3.00 effective durations for the FHLMC 11s and the FNMA 11s, respectively.

Third, new issues have higher effective durations than seasoned issues. New GNMA 8s have a 6.70 effective duration whereas seasoned GNMA 8s offer only a 5.40 effective duration. Fourth, discount coupon passthroughs have higher effective durations than premium coupon passthroughs. Seasoned FNMA 9s offer a 4.20 effective duration versus a 2.40 effective duration for FNMA 12s.

Derivative mortgage products

TRADITIONAL CMOs. A derivative mortgage product is a repackaged version of a mortgage passthrough. A derivative product is collateralized by a mortgage passthrough or by a series of mortgage passthroughs. The bulk of the derivative product market is comprised of *collateralized mortgage obligations (CMOs)*. A CMO is structured in several pieces, or *tranches*.

	Average Life (For Illustration Only)
Class A	2.3 years
Class B	4.2 years
Class C	7.1 years
Class D	21.2 years

The cash flows of each tranche differ, such that each subsequent tranche has a longer average life and effective duration. Each tranche has a coupon rate assigned to it at issuance. If the CMO is issued in a positive yield curve environment, the short maturity tranches bear lower coupons than do the long maturity tranches; the opposite holds true in an inverted yield curve environment.

As the underlying mortgage passthrough pays principal and interest, the cash flows are distributed on a quarterly or semiannual basis to the CMO holders. All principal cash flows (scheduled and unscheduled) generated by the underlying mortgage passthrough(s) are funneled to the Class *A* holders until their par amount is fully repaid. After the Class *A* holders are paid off, the Class *B* holders receive all of the principal payments. After the Class *B* holders are fully paid, Class *C* holders are assigned the principal payments.

Finally, Class D holders begin to receive principal and interest cash flows after the initial three classes (A, B, and C) have been retired. Interest payments are made on each class throughout the life of that specific class. The interest amount is based on the outstanding par amount of the particular class and the coupon rate assigned to that class. In some cases, the Class D tranche is structured as a deferred interest bond (i.e., a Z bond), that sells at a deep discount to par and has a long effective duration.

Collateralized mortgage obligations have several attractions: First, each CMO deal is unique. Although a three- or four-class structure may be the norm, the underlying collateral (e.g., GNMA, FNMA, FHLMC, or a combination of these), the coupon rate(s) of the underlying collateral (e.g., a uniform coupon, a combination of coupons, premium coupons, discount coupons, or current coupons) the average age (and age distribution) of the underlying collateral, and the relative sizes of the individual tranches all serve to differentiate individual CMOs.

Second, each CMO tranche experiences less variability in cash flow than the underlying mortgage passthrough. Fluctuations in prepayment rates have less impact on an individual CMO tranche (particularly a tranche of short average life) than on the mortgage passthrough itself. The sequential structure of the principal payment distribution schedule reduces the cash flow variability within a given class.

Finally, individual CMO tranches appeal to different types of investors. Classes of a short average life are sought by banks, savings and loans, short-term bond mutual funds, and bearish investors. Classes of intermediate average life attract insurance companies (for guaranteed investment contracts), yield buyers and middle-of-the-road investors. Classes of long average life draw the attention of pension funds, bond mutual funds, insurance companies, and bullish investors. Relative value investors and total return investors find CMOs attractive for their yield and credit quality. Exhibit 6–37 summarizes the descriptive characteristics of a traditional CMO.

PAC CMOs AND TAC CMOs. One of the major attractions of CMOs is the superior predictability of future cash flows. Investor desire for a more stable cash flow pattern has led to the creation

Exhibit 6–37. The descriptive characteristics for a traditional CMO.[a]

Issue Name:	Collateralized Mortgage Securities Corporation, Series A
Issue Size:	$300 Million
Issue Date:	February 14, 1985
Collateral:	100% FNMA 12s
Payment Frequency:	Quarterly

Description of Tranches:

Class A-1:	10.375% due 10/1/94; 2.1 year average life
Class A-2:	11.750% due 10/1/00; 7.1 year average life
Class A-3:	12.000% due 4/1/01; 10.5 year average life
Class A-4:	11.875% due 4/1/15; 19.9 year average life

[a]Data courtesy of the First Boston Corporation.

of two CMO products that reduce cash flow uncertainty more than a traditional CMO: *planned amortization class (PAC) CMOs and targeted amortization class (TAC) CMOs.* Most newly issued CMOs now include PAC or TAC classes. A PAC CMO is an individual tranche within a CMO deal; the non-PAC tranches of the deal are termed *PAC support bonds.*[14] The PAC CMO is special because the future cash flows are fixed and certain over a wide range of prepayment rates. A prepayment speed in the middle of that "protected" range is assumed when the CMO deal is initially priced. Outside that specific range, the PAC CMO's average life and effective duration shift modestly as the future stream of cash flows changes. By creating the prepayment protection for the PAC bonds, the PAC support bonds are subject to additional cash flow uncertainty.

Exhibit 6–38 summarizes the effective durations of several PAC CMOs. Exhibit 6–39 shows the effective duration behavior of a typical PAC CMO as the prepayment rate changes. The protected range is wide and covers both increases and decreases in prepayment speed vis-à-vis the pricing speed. Exhibit 6-40 demonstrates the average life variability of a sampling of PAC CMOs.

[14]In some instances, more than one PAC or TAC CMO tranche is found in a single CMO deal.

Exhibit 6-38. The price, yield, average life, and effective duration statistics for several PAC CMOs.

Issue Description	Price	Yield (%)	Average Life (in Years)	Effective Duration
GS2D3[a]	95–29	10.46	4.21	3.1
FH28G	91–22	10.30	10.69	6.5
GS3C4	92–18	10.46	4.41	5.5

[a]Data as of April, 1989, and courtesy of Goldman, Sachs & Co.

Issue Description	Price	Yield (%)	Average Life (in Years)	Effective Duration
CMSC882-2[a]	95–05	10.20	4.75	3.4
CMSC884-2	94–31	10.20	4.75	3.4
MLTRS25-2	94–25	10.18	5.06	3.6
GMC3L-5	94–25	10.22	9.96	6.2
FHR10-4	98–30	10.25	10.08	6.1

[a]Data as of April 24, 1989 and courtesy of the First Boston Corporation.

Exhibit 6-39. The effective duration of a PAC CMO as prepayment rates change.

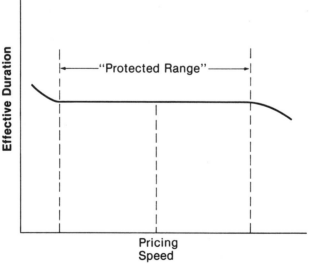

Exhibit 6-40. The average life variability of a sampling of PAC CMO tranches (issue data per Exhibit 6-38 and courtesy of the First Boston Corporation).

Market Yield	Average Life (in years)				
Change (in BP)	CMSC882-2	CMSC884-2	MLTRS25-2	GMC3L-5	FHRI0-4
-300	3.50	3.63	2.48	2.64	5.39
-200	4.39	4.38	4.62	3.57	9.08
-100	4.39	4.38	4.62	3.57	9.08
0	4.39	4.38	4.62	3.57	9.08
+100	4.39	4.38	4.62	3.57	9.08
+200	4.39	4.38	4.62	3.57	9.08
+300	4.41	4.38	4.62	3.65	9.08

A TAC CMO, like a PAC CMO, is an individual tranche within a CMO deal. The non-TAC tranches of the deal are termed *TAC support bonds.* Unlike a PAC CMO, a TAC CMO has cash flow certainty only if the actual prepayment rate exceeds the prepayment rate used in pricing the CMO. If the prepayment rate is slower than the assumed rate, cash flows are deferred further into the future and the PAC CMO's average life and effective duration lengthen. A TAC CMO offers a modest degree of call protection in the event that interest rates decline and prepayments accelerate.

Exhibit 6-41 presents the effective durations of several TAC CMOs. Exhibit 6-42 illustrates the effective duration behavior of a TAC CMO as the prepayment rate changes. The TAC CMO's effective duration is stable for prepayment rates at or modestly above the pricing speed. Slowdowns in prepayments allow the effective duration to extend as with a standard CMO.

Exhibit 6-41. The price, yield, average life, and effective duration statistics for several TAC CMOs.[a]

Issue Description	Price	Yield (%)	Average Life (in Years)	Effective Duration
FN8914G	97–14	10.50	12.20	6.6
FH18B	97–03	10.51	7.62	4.7
FH31F	79–05	10.26	17.78	8.2

[a]Data as of April 11, 1989 and courtesy of Goldman, Sachs & Co.

Exhibit 6–42. The effective duration of a TAC CMO as prepayment rates change.

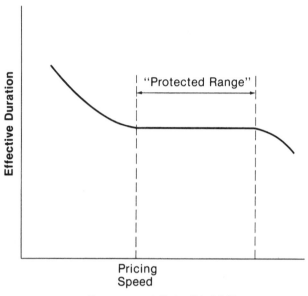

Pricing
Speed

Prepayment Rate (% PSA)

COLLATERALIZED MORTGAGE OBLIGATIONS: A RECAP.
Collateralized mortgage obligations provide a greater degree of
cash flow stability than mortgage passthrough securities. This cash
flow predictability comes at a price: The incremental yield offered
by a CMO tranche is less than the incremental yield offered by
a mortgage passthrough. If this were not the case, the incentive
to repackage the mortgage passthrough into a CMO would not
exist.[15] Planned amortization class CMOs, which offer the greatest
degree of cash flow certainty, trade at the narrowest yield spreads
to U.S. Treasuries. Targeted amortization class CMOs are priced
at slightly wider yield spreads to U.S. Treasuries, because of the
greater cash flow variability of the former. Traditional CMOs
trade at even wider yield spreads than TAC CMOs for similar

[15] The shape of the yield curve is also an important influence on CMO creation
and issuance. A positively sloped yield curve provides an incentive to issue CMOs because
short maturity tranches can be sold at lower yields than the yield of the underlying
passthroughs. An inverted yield curve takes away this incentive.

reasons. In terms of yield spread, the aforementioned investments might trade as follows:

Investment	Yield Spread to U.S. Treasuries
PAC CMO	+ 60BP
TAC CMO	+ 75BP
Traditional CMO	+ 90BP
Mortgage passthrough	+125BP

STRIPPED MBS. Another form of derivative mortgage product is a *stripped MBS*. Mortgage-backed securities strips come in two forms: *interest-only (IO) strips* and *principal-only (PO) strips*. Mortgage-backed strips are collateralized by mortgage passthroughs. The owner of an IO strip receives the interest payments generated by the underlying passthrough collateral. The owner of a PO strip is entitled to the principal payments made on the underlying mortgages. Neither IOs nor POs bear periodic coupons.

The price of an IO strip is based on the present value of an expected stream of cash flows from interest. The size and number of interest payments are the key variables; these values are not known in advance and must be projected. The price of a PO strip is based on the present value of an expected stream of principal payments. The total amount of principal is known in advance; however, the timing of the principal payments is uncertain because of the prepayment variable.

The buyer of an IO strip hopes that the underlying mortgage passthroughs pay down slowly over time so that cash flows from interest are larger and continue for a longer period (recall that the periodic interest payment is based on the amount of principal outstanding). The buyer of a PO strip desires a speedy paydown of principal because the PO strip sells at a deep discount and is paid off at par value.

The prepayment rate is the most critical variable to investors in MBS strips. Fluctuations in prepayment rates (as a result of interest rate gyrations and other factors) can have dramatic impacts on the market values of MBS strips. An IO strip is a bearish instrument. A rise in interest rates increases the value of an IO strip substantially as prepayment rates fall and interest payments from the underlying mortgages decline more slowly than originally anticipated. The price of an IO strip moves in the same direction as interest rates; therefore, an IO strip has a negative duration.

Exhibit 6–43 shows the effective durations of several IO strips. The IO strips have durations ranging from –4.68 to –10.49. Exhibit 6–44 plots the expected total returns of the FNMA Trust 1 IO strip (–6.77 effective duration). The IO's returns are volatile and vary directly with interest rate moves.

Exhibit 6–43. The price, yield, and effective duration statistics for a series of IO strips. [a]

Issue Description	Underlying Collateral	WAC [b] (%)	Price	Yield (%)	Effective Duration
FNMA Trust 54	FNMA 8s	8.88	39–24	12.05	–4.68
FNMA Trust 28	FNMA 8½s	9.25	41–01	11.69	–5.67
FNMA Trust 1	FNMA 9s	9.69	40–31	11.81	–6.77
FNMA Trust 21	FNMA 9½s	10.25	42–16	11.63	–8.67
FNMA Trust 29	FNMA 10s	10.75	42–17	11.75	–10.49

[a]Data as of March 22, 1989, and courtesy of Goldman, Sachs & Co.
[b]Weighted average coupon.

A PO strip has a large effective duration and is an extremely bullish investment. A decline in interest rates quickens the rate of principal repayment, which enhances the present value of the PO strip. Exhibit 6–45 summarizes the effective durations of several PO strips having durations from 13.50 to 14.50. Exhibit 6–46 plots the expected total returns of the FNMA Trust 1 PO strip (13.87 effective duration). The PO's returns are significantly affected by changes in interest rates and bear an inverse relationship to the market yield level.

Exhibit 6-44. The expected 1-year total returns of the FNMA Trust 1 IO strip for a variety of interest rate environments.[a]

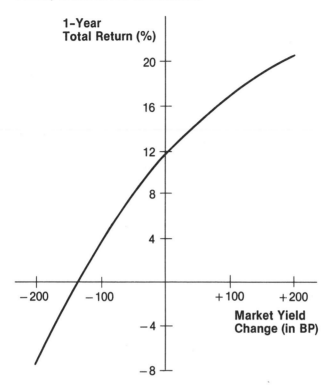

[a]Issue data from Exhibit 6–43 and calculations courtesy of Goldman, Sachs & Co.

Exhibit 6-45. The price, yield, and effective duration statistics for a series of PO strips.[a]

Issue Description	Underlying Collateral	WAC[b] (%)	Price	Yield (%)	Effective Duration
FNMA Trust 54	FNMA 8s	8.88	48–31	8.97	14.50
FNMA Trust 28	FNMA 8½s	9.25	48–07	10.06	14.52
FNMA Trust 1	FNMA 9s	9.69	50–16	10.26	13.87
FNMA Trust 21	FNMA 9½s	10.25	51–09	10.44	14.56
FNMA Trust 29	FNMA 10s	10.75	53–16	10.44	14.56

[a]Data as of March 22, 1989, and courtesy of Goldman, Sachs & Co.

[b]Weighted average coupon.

Exhibit 6-46. The expected 1-year total returns of the FNMA Trust 1 PO strip for a variety of interest rate environments.[a]

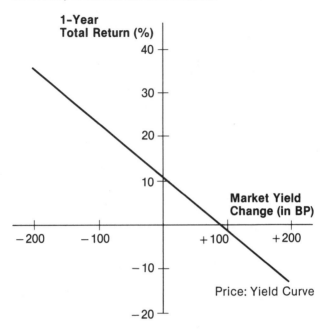

[a] Issue data from Exhibit 6-45 and calculations courtesy of Goldman, Sachs & Co.

The coupon rate of the underlying collateral is a critical influence on the duration of the IO and PO strips.[16] The price volatility of IO strips and PO strips can be severe. Investor caution is warranted.

Asset-backed securities

The securitization of assets has expanded dramatically during the 1980s. The mortgage-backed securities market is a prime

[16] The structure of the deal is also important. In some instances, synthetic passthroughs are created and serve as the collateral. For example, a GNMA 10% passthrough can be repackaged and sold as a combination of synthetic GNMA 7% coupon passthroughs and synthetic GNMA 13% coupon passthroughs. These synthetics, in turn, serve as the collateral for two sets of IO and PO srip holders: one set for the 7% coupon synthetic and one set for the 13% coupon issue.

illustration. The mortgage passthrough market has grown from $60 billion as of January 1, 1980, to $610 billion as of January 1, 1989 (as represented by the market value of the mortgage component of the Salomon Brothers' Broad Investment Grade Bond Index).

In 1985, the securitization of automobile loan receivables and credit card receivables marked the birth of the asset-backed securities market. This market had exploded to $23.5 billion (par amount) in size as of December 30, 1988. Of the $23.5 billion outstanding, approximately $12.3 billion (52%) was automobile loan receivables, $9.1 billion (39%) was credit card receivables, and $2.1 billion (9%) was other receivables (backed by unsecured consumer loans, mobile home loans, equipment leases, and pleasure boat loans). New issuance in 1988 totaled $14.8 billion, a 50% increase over 1987 issuance. (Data courtesy of Goldman, Sachs & Co.)

Most asset-backed securities are short-lived, carrying average maturities (and durations) of only 2 to 2½ years. The following two sections discuss the effective durations of the two major types of asset-backed securities, automobile loan receivables (CARS) and credit card receivables (CARDS).

Certificates for automobile receivables (CARS). Certificates for automobile receivables are collateralized by automobile loans. They are packaged and sold by automobile finance companies (e.g., General Motors Acceptance Corporation and Chrysler Finance Corporation), large banks (e.g., Chemical Bank, Marine Midland Bank, Western Financial Savings Bank, and Bank of America), and brokerage firms (e.g., Salomon Brothers Inc., Goldman, Sachs & Co., the First Boston Corporation). These certificates typically have a letter of credit (LOC) or a loan loss protection arrangement from the packager and generally receive "AAA" or "AA" credit ratings. Automobile loans have 5-year maximum terms and make monthly payments of principal and interest. Certificates for automobile receivables often have 5-year final maturities and make either monthly or quarterly payments that include both principal and interest. They have average lives of approximately 2 years and effective durations of slightly less than 2 years.

Exhibit 6–47 summarizes the average lives of several CARS issues. Although a few CARS have multiple tranches, the typical CARS is based on a single tranche. The cash flows from automobile loans are predictable and stable. The influence of interest rate fluctuations on prepayment rates is minimal. Therefore, the variability in the average life or effective duration of a CARS is not significant.

Exhibit 6–47. The average lives of a few representative CARS issues (as of issuance date). The effective duration of a specific issue is slightly lower than its average life.[a]

Issuance Date	Issue Size ($)	Ratings	Issue Description	Average Life (in Years)
8/20/86	725MM	AA1/AA	GMAC 1986–E Grantor Trust 6.90% Asset-backed Certificates due 8/15/91	2.1
10/07/88	226MM	AAA/AAA	Marine Midland 1988–2 CARS Trust 8.85% due 10/15/93	1.8
10/14/86	4,000MM	AAA/AAA	Asset-Backed Securities Corporation Asset-Backed Obligations, Series 1:	
			Class 1–A: 2,095MM 6.25% due 10/15/88	1.1
			Class 2–A: 585MM 6.90% due 4/15/89	2.2
			Class 3–A: 1,320MM 6.95% due 10/15/90	3.0

[a]Data courtesy of Goldman, Sachs & Co.

Certificates for amortizing revolving debts (CARDS). These certificates are usually issued by large banks that are involved in major credit card programs. They are often collateralized by VISA or MasterCard receivables, although other credit card issuers have recently entered the market (e.g., Montgomery Ward and

Sears). A typical CARDS is a single tranche deal that pays monthly interest. It generally has a 5-year final maturity and receives cash flows on a monthly basis. Principal paydowns do not occur until 2 to 3 years after the issuance date of the deal. A 2½-year average life is common for CARDS. They have minimal cash flow variability, and their average lives remain stable as interest rates fluctuate. They are often rated "AAA" due to letters of credit. Exhibit 6-48 presents the average lives of several representative CARDS deals.

Exhibit 6-48. The average lives of a few representative CARDS issues (as of issuance date). The effective duration of a specific issue is slightly lower than its average life.[a]

Issuance Date	Issue Size ($)	Ratings	Issue Description	Average Life (in Years)
9/07/88	500MM	AAA/AAA	Sears Credit Account Trust 1988B 9.05% Credit Account Pass-through Certificates due 9/15/93	2.5
9/16/88	400MM	AAA/AAA	First Chicago Master Trust CARDS, Series C 9% due 9/15/92	2.4
9/29/88	500MM	AAA/AAA	Chemical Bank Credit Card Trust 1988–B 9.25% due 11/15/93	2.0

[a]Data courtesy of Goldman, Sachs & Co.

Summary

Effective duration is a measure of the price sensitivity of a bond. For an option-free bond (e.g., a noncallable bond), effective duration and modified duration are synonymous. For a callable bond, effective duration is bounded by the modified DTC and the modified DTM. For a putable bond, effective duration is bounded by the modified DTP and the modified DTM.

A callable bond is an implicit combination of a long position in a noncallable bond and a short position in a call option(s). A call option gives the holder the right to redeem the bond before final maturity at a prespecified price on a prespecified future date. Calls come in three forms: cash calls, refunding calls, and sinking fund calls. The price of a callable bond is less volatile than the price of its noncallable counterpart.

The duration of a callable bond is assessed in one of three ways: (1) selecting either the bond's DTC or the bond's DTM; (2) calculating a weighted average duration; or (3) calculating an effective (option-adjusted) duration. An effective duration is based on the combination of the price sensitivity of a noncallable equivalent and the price sensitivity of the call option(s). An option valuation model derives the price sensitivity of the call option(s). Effective duration is affected by the call date(s), the call price(s), the maturity date, the market price, the market yield volatility assumption, and the level of short-term interest rates.

A putable bond is an implicit combination of a long position in an option-free bond and a long position in a put option(s). A put option gives the holder the right to sell a bond at a prespecified price on a prespecified date. The price of a putable bond is less volatile than the price of its option-free equivalent because the investor holds the put option.

The duration of a putable bond is assessed in one of three ways: (1) selecting either the bond's DTP or the bond's DTM; (2) calculating a weighted average duration; or (3) calculating an effective (option-adjusted) duration. An effective duration is based on the combination of the price sensitivity of an option-free equivalent and the price sensitivity of the put option(s). An option valuation model derives the price sensitivity of the put option(s). Effective duration is affected by the put date(s), the put price(s), the maturity date, the market price, the market yield volatility assumption, and the level of short-term interest rates.

As a result of their option features, callable bonds trade at lower prices and higher yields than do comparable noncallable bonds. Putable bonds trade at higher prices and lower yields than comparable option-free bonds. Both callable bonds and putable bonds have less price volatility than their modified DTMs suggest.

Mortgage-backed securities come in two forms: mortgage passthroughs and derivative mortgage products. Mortgage passthroughs include 15-year and 30-year passthroughs. Derivative mortgage products include CMOs and stripped MBS. The effective duration of an MBS is influenced by the security structure, the coupon rate, the underlying mortgage collateral, the prepayment rate assumption, the market yield level (and expected future trend), and the market yield volatility assumption. The effective durations of MBS range from large negative values (e.g., for IO strips) to large positive values (e.g., for PO strips).

Asset-backed securities come in two primary types: CARS and CARDS. The effective duration of an ABS is affected by the underlying collateral, the coupon rate, the principal repayment schedule (and the assumed rate of prepayment), the market yield level (and expected future trend), and the market yield volatility assumption. Asset-backed securities typically have short average lives and low effective durations.

Another Method of Assessing the Duration of a Callable (or Putable) Bond

Callable bonds

In the same way that a callable bond's price can be separated into two components (bond value and option value), a callable bond's duration is a function of the durations of the two components. The noncallable bond component's duration is represented by the modified duration to maturity. An option valuation model assesses the duration, or price sensitivity, of the call option component. The effective duration of a callable bond is the weighted average of the modified durations of the component parts, where market values serve as the weights:

$$
\begin{pmatrix} \text{effective} \\ \text{duration} \\ \text{of a callable} \\ \text{bond} \end{pmatrix} = \begin{pmatrix} \text{modified duration} \\ \text{of a noncallable} \times W_b \\ \text{bond} \end{pmatrix} + \begin{pmatrix} \text{modified duration} \\ \text{of the} \times W_c \\ \text{call option} \end{pmatrix}
$$

where

W_b = the market value weight of the bond component (expressed in decimal form); this value exceeds 1.00.

W_p = 1 – W_b = the market value weight of the call option component (expressed in decimal form); this value is less than 0.00.

The sum of the market value weights (W_b + W_c) must equal 1.00.

An option is extemely price sensitive and, therefore, has a large duration. A callable bond's price sensitivity is reduced by the implicit short position in the call option. The duration of a callable bond is lower than that of an equivalent noncallable security. For example, a 30-year callable bond is priced at par (100.00). An equivalent noncallable issue sells for 105.00 and the call option is valued at 5 points:

$$\begin{matrix} \text{callable bond} \\ \text{price} \end{matrix} = \begin{matrix} \text{noncallable} \\ \text{bond price} \end{matrix} - \begin{matrix} \text{call option} \\ \text{value} \end{matrix}$$

$$100.00 = 105.00 - 5$$

If the noncallable bond has a modified duration of 10.00 and the call option has a modified duration of 70.00, the callable bond has an effective duration of 7.00:

$$\begin{matrix} \text{effective duration} \\ \text{of} \\ \text{callable bond} \end{matrix} = \left(10.00 \times \frac{105.00}{100.00} \right) + \left(70.00 \times \frac{-5.00}{100.00} \right)$$

$$= (10.00 \times 1.0500) + (70.00 \times (-0.0500))$$

$$= 10.50 - 3.50$$

$$= 7.00$$

The call option is responsible for a 3.00-year reduction in duration, from 10.00 years to 7.00 years.

Putable bonds

A putable bond's duration is a function of the durations of its two components: the option-free bond and the put option. The option-free bond's duration is assessed by the bond's modified duration to maturity. An option valuation model derives the price sensitivity of the put option. The effective duration of a putable bond is the weighted average of the modified durations of the two components, where market values serve as the weights:

$$
\begin{array}{l} \text{effective} \\ \text{duration} \\ \text{of a putable} \\ \text{bond} \end{array} = \left(\begin{array}{c} \text{modified duration} \\ \text{of an option-free} \times W_b \\ \text{bond} \end{array} \right) + \left(\begin{array}{c} \text{modified duration} \\ \text{of the} \times W_p \\ \text{put option} \end{array} \right)
$$

where

W_b = the market value weight of the bond component (expressed in decimal form); this value is between 0.00 and 1.00.

W_p = $1 - W_b$ = the market value weight of the put option component (expressed in decimal form); this value is between 0.00 and 1.00.

The sum of the market value weights ($W_b + W_p$) must equal 1.00.

A put option is extremely price sensitive. A put option has a large negative duration because its value moves in the same direction as interest rates. When yields rise, the value of the put option increases; conversely, when yields fall, the value of the put option decreases. A putable bond's price sensitivity is reduced by the long position in the put option. The duration of a putable bond is lower than that of an equivalent option-free security.

For example, a 30-year option-free bond is priced at par (100.00). A 30-year bond with a 10-year put (at par) is priced at 103.50 because the put option is worth 3½ points:

$$\frac{\text{putable bond}}{\text{price}} = \frac{\text{option-free}}{\text{bond price}} + \frac{\text{put option}}{\text{value}}$$

$$103.50 = 100.00 + 3.50$$

If the option-free bond has a modified duration of 10.00 and the put option has a modified duration of –40.00, the putable bond carries an effective duration of 8.31.

$$\frac{\text{effective duration}}{\text{of}}_{\text{callable bond}} = \left(10.00 \times \frac{100.00}{103.50}\right) + \left(-40.00 \times \frac{3.50}{103.50}\right)$$

$$= (10.00 \times 0.9662) + (-40.00 \times 0.0338)$$

$$= 9.66 - 1.35$$

$$= 8.31$$

The put option forces a 1.69-year reduction in duration, from 10.00 years to 8.31 years.

The CMS Option Valuation Method for Fixed-Income Securities*

Introduction

Traditionally, analysis of fixed-income securities focused on the creditworthiness of the debtor, and the required risk premium over U.S. Treasury yields for issues of comparable maturity. Subsequently, more sophisticated analysis was concerned with an understanding of the term structure of interest rates, and how changes in interest rates affect the prices and holding period returns of fixed-income securities having varying maturities and coupon rates.

As of mid-1989, chronic volatility of interest rates had led to a heightened awareness of options and optionlike provisions in bond indentures. These calls, puts, warrants to extend, payment-in-kind (PIK) provisions, and the like are all mechanisms for issuers and holders of fixed-income securities to explicitly manage the implicit risks they bear associated with unanticipated interest rate

---

*This appendix is courtesy of Capital Management Sciences. This article was written by Daniel D. Foley, a vice president at CMS, in July 1989.

fluctuations. As a result of their contractual inclusion in the bond indenture agreements, the traded securities must be viewed and analyzed as a bundle of debtlike and optionlike instruments.

Today, the astute fixed-income securities analyst or portfolio manager has an appreciation for interest rate risks, a conceptual understanding of the effects of interest rate changes on the component securities bundled into a "bond," and a set of analytical tools for expressing those effects as precisely as possible, to assist in decision making.

An historical perspective

While the increase in interest rate volatility was the impetus for the increasing incidence of option provisions in bond indentures, the expanding body of theory and experience in option pricing models has provided the framework for analysis and valuation of the effects of those provisions.

When Fischer Black and Myron Scholes derived their original option pricing model in the early 1970s, their accomplishment was significant for at least two reasons. From a theoretical perspective, their key insight was that a perfectly hedged position can be formed and maintained by holding an appropriate mix of long and short positions in an option and its underlying security, and that such a position, being riskless, must yield the short-term riskless rate. This insight enabled them to specify the first complete analytical framework for the price relationship between an option and its underlying security.

For the practitioner, a fortunate outcome of the Black-Scholes analysis was that their solution to the complicated differential equation describing the option valuation process, while formidable-looking, was nevertheless a single mathematical equation easily solvable using a personal computer or hand-held calculator. This accounts in large part for the continuing popularity of the original Black-Scholes formulation, despite its known weaknesses.

A significant cost of the Black-Scholes breakthrough and "closed form" pricing formula was a reliance on an unrealistically stringent set of assumptions regarding the functioning of securities markets. For example, short-term borrowing and lending rates

were assumed to be fixed and equal; the variability of returns
on the underlying asset was assumed to be constant; trading costs,
margin requirements, taxes and short-sale restrictions were
assumed to be nonexistent; trading was assumed to be continuous
and the paths of prices were assumed to be smooth. For
theoreticians and practitioners alike, therefore, a key issue was
whether and how to relax these assumptions, along with the
implications of doing so. Consequently, much additional work
has been done, on both a theoretical and empirical level, to extend
the original Black-Scholes analysis under relaxed or restated
assumptions.

The new bond math

It is readily observable that long bonds are more sensitive to
changes in interest rates than short bonds. The calculation of
duration, now well accepted by fixed-income professionals,
captures this concept with more mathematical precision.
Essentially, duration is a weighted average time to maturity of
the bond, with the periodic coupon and principal payments serving
as the weights. Duration, calculated in this way, serves not only
as a standardized measure of a bond's longevity, but also (as
intuition would suggest) is a primary measure of the sensitivity
of a bond's price to changes in interest rates.

Furthermore, the value of duration itself changes when
interest rates change. The observed acceleration in price changes
with falling interest rates is obtained by the calculation of a second
measure of price sensitivity, called convexity. Graphically, duration
is the slope of the price/yield curve; convexity measures the degree
of "curvature" of that curve.

The key objective in analyzing a bond, whether it contains
embedded options or not, is to determine its value in the market,
and how that value can be expected to change with the passage
of time and/or with specified yield curve shifts and changes in
spread relationships. This is necessary, for example, for a
meaningful analysis of swap opportunities, or for simulating a
portfolio's future performance either in absolute terms or versus
a benchmark index.

The presence of options complicates the analysis, because the options have their own changing characteristics with respect to changing interest rates. Consequently, the presence of embedded options will always modify, and occasionally overwhelm, the price, yield, duration and convexity of the underlying "straight" bond. For this reason, modified measures must be calculated, usually referred to as effective or option-adjusted price, yield, duration, convexity, and so on. These critical measures for a bond incorporate separate effects from quality and sector yield spreads over Treasuries, and embedded option characteristics.

The holder of a callable bond owns a security consisting of a long position in the underlying straight bond and a short position in the call option. The presence of the call option is advantageous to the issuer, and it is correspondingly disadvantageous to the bondholder, who must deliver the underlying bond should the issuer choose to exercise its option. Consequently, the callable bond is a less desirable investment under some set of conditions (sufficiently low interest rates, resulting in the bond being called away) and will therefore trade in the market at a lower price (higher yield) than an identical bond without the call provision. In the same way, an embedded put option providing benefits to the bondholder will result in the putable bond trading at a price premium (lower yield) in comparison with a bond lacking the put provision.

Exercise by the issuer or the holder of the call or put option rights will cut short the life of the bond. Hence, the mere presence of embedded call or put options, but especially an increasing likelihood of either being exercised, will reduce the (effective) duration of the bond. As an option becomes virtually certain to be exercised, the bond will have a very short remaining life expectancy, and the range of possible return outcomes from holding the bond will fall within a tight band. Accordingly, the usefulness of (effective) duration as a measure of both a bond's life and interest rate sensitivity, continues intact, even in the presence of embedded options.

The value of an option accelerates as it moves deeper into the money. This dramatic curvature of an option's price curve with respect to the price of the underlying security causes the embedded option within a callable or putable bond to eventually dominate the price sensitivity of the bond for large moves in interest rates. A call provision causes the bond's price/yield curve to flatten as interest rates fall, since the call "caps" the price appreciation otherwise available to the holder of the bond in a bull market. Similarly, because a put provision in the bond indenture serves to protect the holder of the bond in a bear market, the presence of the put will flatten the bond's price/yield curve as interest rates rise.

The analysis of fixed-income securities with embedded options proceeds in a building-block fashion, both conceptually and in practical terms. First, the term structure of "risk-free" interest rates is ascertained by market observation of prices/yields on Treasury securities of varying maturities. Next, quality and sector credit spreads are layered onto the Treasury yield curve, again utilizing cross-sectional market observations. Finally, the values and price-sensitivities of debt options are modeled utilizing an option pricing framework. The critical measures (price, yield, duration, convexity) for the bond thereby incorporate the combined effects of time, credit risk, and option characteristics.

Modified Black-Scholes vs. binomial method

Black and Scholes' derivation of their original option pricing formula utilized advanced techniques for the solution of a stochastic second-order partial differential equation. This level of mathematical sophistication is of course unusual among financial economists, business school students, and finance professionals. Consequently, refinements and extensions to Black and Scholes' breakthrough accomplishments have proceeded along two related but separate paths.

The first approach is that taken by researchers and practitioners familiar with advanced calculus applications. For these individuals, who often have backgrounds in the physical sciences or engineering, modifying the functional coefficients or boundary conditions for a differential equation to accommodate less stringent (more realistic) assumptions than Black and Scholes is a straightforward procedure.

It is a mathmatical fact of life that a restated, improved formulation of the Black-Scholes differential equation does not have an analytical solution that can be written out as a single equation like the famous Black-Scholes option pricing formula. Therefore, a numerical integration technique must be utilized to solve for the option's value, convexity, and other factors for a given set of model input variables. Once again, this is a familiar process for an individual with a background in advanced calculus applications.

The second, competing approach to improving upon the original Black-Scholes analysis is the "binomial" calculation method. This approach utilizes a binomial lattice structure (reminiscent of a decision tree) to model the "states of nature" that interest rates may obtain over the life of an option. The values of the option at each "node" of the lattice corresponding to the maturity date of the underlying bond are first calculated, given the boundary condition that the underlying bond will trade at par on that date. Through a process of "backward iteration," option values at earlier nodes in the lattice can be calculated. Stepping this calculation process back to the present time gives an approximation of the current value of the option, where the accuracy of the approximation is dependent on the time step size used.

Weaknesses of the binomial method

The binomial approach is an effective teaching device for presenting option valuation topics in a classroom setting, utilizing a minimum of mathematical sophistication. Unfortunately, when this method is applied to real-world problems, the computational burden is significant, even for a high-speed personal computer. This is caused by the geometric growth in the number of lattice nodes or calculation points that results when the time to expiration of the option is divided into small enough steps to obtain meaningful accuracy in the backward calculation of "today's" option value.

In contrast, a differential equation formulation of the option valuation process inherently operates in "continuous time" and therefore does not face a geometically growing computational burden with smaller time step sizes.

When comparing the relative merits of the differential equation versus binomial approaches to valuing debt options, it is important to recognize that the two approaches are merely alternative ways of looking at the same problem. It can be shown that either method, skillfully applied to a given set of input data, will yield the same result to a close approximation.

But it is important to understand that the binomial methodology approximates the differential equation result, not the reverse. The differential equation is the exact specification of the pricing process in continuous time, and the binomial calculation strives to achieve a satisfactory approximation to it. So the burden of proof lies with proponents of the binomial method to demonstrate sufficient accuracy of their results for practical applications. In contrast, the differential equation approach *is* the standard of comparison.

The accuracy of the binomial method improves as the time to maturity of the bond is divided into smaller and smaller time intervals, corresponding to the spacing between successive layers of the binomial lattice. Unfortunately, the computational burden increases correspondingly, so that additional accuracy in a computed result is achieved at a large and possibly unreasonable cost. When a large number of securities must be evaluated using this methodology, the computational time delays may well become onerous, leading to a search for computational shortcuts giving quicker results at an indeterminate cost in accuracy. This should be a matter of concern for portfolio managers making investment decisions based on computerized binomial analysis methods.

The CMS option valuation model

The Capital Management Sciences option valuation model was created by CMS executive vice president David Silvern. The CMS model utilizes a modified Black-Scholes framework incorporating several factors that are key to an accurate representation of the pricing process for options on fixed-income securities. These factors are all departures from the assumptions used by Black and Scholes in their derivation of the pricing formula for options on common stocks, including:

- Incorporation of a bond's periodic coupon payments, if any;
- Utilization of interest rates as the random variable in the option pricing framework, rather than the price of the underlying security;
- Recognition of the changing nature of short-term interest rates; and
- Specification of a changing variance of interest rates with time, as a function of the duration of the underlying bond.

Incorporating these modifications in the Black-Scholes framework involves making appropriate changes to the functional coefficients in the Black-Scholes differential equation and to the accompanying boundary conditions constraining its solution.

Because, as already noted, the modified Black-Scholes model has no closed form analytical solution, a numerical integration technique is utilized to compute the solution to the differential equation.

The solution process computes the price/yield curve for the bond, over a ±300 basis points interval centered on the bond's present yield to maturity. The slope of the tangent to this curve at today's price and yield is the bond's effective (option-adjusted) duration. The bond's convexity is computed as the average of the two differences between this tangent line and the price curve at ±100 basis points from today's yield.

The solution process commences at the maturity date of the bond, and works its way in monthly increments back to the present time. At each step, the price/yield curve of the bond is computed, taking into account the optimal exercise of any embedded options, as well as the changing nature with time of functional inputs such as the variance rate of the bond's yield.

The solution algorithm is extremely efficient, permitting the complete recalculation of the price/yield curve when simulating the behavior over time of a single bond, a proposed swap, or an entire portfolio. This of course gives exact results, and should be contrasted with utilizing a binomial algorithm, whereby one may have to "make do" with a rough approximation or partial recalculation rather than taking the unacceptably long time to recalculate the entire binomial lattice for a range of simulation inputs.

Because the CMS valuation model steps backward in time from a horizon date to the present, one might think that the computational requirements would be very similar to the binomial approach. But this is not the case.

While the choice of time interval for the solution step size does affect the computational requirements for the CMS model, the effect is only proportional to the step size, rather than geometrical as with the binomial approach. This is because the number of calculations performed by the CMS model is the same for each individual time interval. In contrast, as noted, the triangular shape of the binomial lattice results in dramatic growth in the total number of calculation nodes as the number of lattice levels increases.

A major benefit of the efficiency of the CMS model is that a portfolio manager can change a bond's market price and instantly recalculate duration, convexity, and the value of embedded options. A binomial-based system will often not permit such price changes, because the recalculations would be unacceptably slow.

A binomial-based system can be expected to do only two things quickly: use a large step size to compute inaccurate results; and retrieve precalculated data for a rigidly specified base scenario. So the user of a binomial system may be faced with either performing analysis quickly with inaccurate or irrelevant data, or more accurately but with a tedious delay. Neither alternative should be acceptable to an investment manager, given the availability of the CMS model.

Summary

Understanding the price behavior of bonds over a range of interest rate changes is key to making informed investment decisions in today's volatile interest rate environment. Proper analysis of embedded options is crucial to this understanding, and yields "effective" or "option-adjusted" measures of duration and convexity. While these summary measures are important for a static analysis of price and yield changes, it is necessary to recalculate the entire price curve under varying interest rates to accurately simulate future returns. The analytical framework that

CMS uses, based on modifications to the Black-Scholes differential equation and its boundary conditions, excels at this. In contrast, the competing approach, the binomial method of option analysis, is easy to understand but computationally expensive for a usable degree of accuracy.

Bond Market Volatility

Introduction

Volatility has an important influence on effective duration. Volatility is simply the variablity in a bond's price (or yield). Volatility is expressed in either implied or historical terms. *Implied volatility* is derived from the observed prices of fixed-income options. An option valuation model is used to calculate implied volatility. Implied volatility reflects investors' expectations regarding future levels of volatility. *Historical or actual volatility* is based on the observed variation in a bond's price (or yield) over a specific historical period (e.g., a week, a month, or a year). Historical volatility is calculated as the standard deviation of the percentage changes in a bond's price (or yield). This standard deviation is typically stated on an annualized basis. Exhibit 6–49 provides a sample calculation of historical volatility.

Historical yield volatility

Short-term bond yields are more volatile than long-term bond yields. Exhibit 6–50 illustrates the actual yield volatility

Exhibit 6-49. A sample calculation of historical price volatility for a bond over a 10-day period. The volatility is translated into an annualized figure as shown.

End of Day	Bond Price	Price Change (in %)
0	100.00	
1	99.50	-0.5000
2	98.40	-1.1055
3	100.50	2.1341
4	100.50	0.0000
5	100.80	0.2985
6	101.25	0.4464
7	102.00	0.7407
8	102.25	0.2451
9	101.50	-0.7335
10	101.40	-0.0985

Standard deviation of daily percentage of price changes: 0.7268%
Annualized price volatility: 11.58%[a]

[a] Calculated as the standard deviation times an annualized factor ($\sqrt{254}$) based on 254 trading days per year.

of 91-day U.S. Treasury bills, 5-year U.S. Treasury notes, and 30-year U.S. Treasury bonds from 1977 through 1988 on an annual basis. The yield volatility of a 3-month T-bill averaged 26.62% over the 12-year period, versus only 16.66% for a 5-year T-note and 14.37% for a 30-year T-bond. Furthermore, in every year except 1986, the yield volatility of a 3-month T-bill exceeded that of both a 5-year note and a 30-year bond, often by a sizable margin.

Historical price volatility

Long-term bonds have greater price volatility than short-term bonds. Exhibit 6-51 analyzes the price volatility of a series of U.S. Treasury notes and bonds from 1980 through 1988. The price volatility of a 30-year U.S. Treasury bond averaged 15.14% over the 9-year period, versus only 6.84% for a 5-year note and 3.48% for a 2-year note. The incremental price volatility of issues of long maturity is evident in each of the 9 years.

Exhibit 6-50. Historical yield volatility of a 91-day U.S. Treasury bill, a 5-year U.S. Treasury note, and a 30-year U.S. Treasury bond over the 1977-1988 period, by year.[a]

Year	91-Day T-Bill (%)	5-Year Note (%)	30-Year Bond (%)
1977	17.86	11.80	5.51
1978	29.36	8.59	5.84
1979	28.29	13.77	9.25
1980	46.60	31.88	20.49
1981	41.73	23.39	18.77
1982	43.03	20.82	30.78
1983	15.34	12.73	10.94
1984	16.43	12.07	11.75
1985	16.00	14.41	12.36
1986	14.54	19.70	18.64
1987	34.34	18.73	16.50
1988	15.86	12.01	11.64
Average			
1977-1988	26.62	16.66	14.37

[a] Data courtesy of the First Boston Corporation.

Interpreting and using volatility statistics

Historical volatility often serves as a basis for projecting future volatility. Recent volatility data (e.g., the past 3 years) may deserve a higher weighting in forming an expectation regarding future variations in bond yields and bond prices. Volatility measures are stated in the form of a standard deviation. In addition, these statistics are shown as a percentage change. For normally distributed data, a standard deviation is useful in capturing the likely range in price (or yield) over a specific period. A range of 1 standard deviation captures approximately 68% of the values, a range of 2 standard deviations covers approximately 95% of the values, and a range of 3 standard deviations includes approximately 99% of the potential data points.

Exhibit 6-51. Historical yield volatility of a 2-year U.S. Treasury note, a 5-year U.S. Treasury note, and a 30-year U.S. Treasury bond over the 1980–1988 period, by year.[a]

Year	2-Year Note (%)	5-Year Note (%)	30-Year Bond (%)
1980	8.65	12.22	21.35
1981	5.76	10.65	27.50
1982	4.45	8.19	14.65
1983	2.36	4.72	10.40
1984	2.42	4.96	10.62
1985	2.39	5.37	10.51
1986	2.05	5.64	14.62
1987	1.98	6.07	15.77
1988	1.29	3.74	10.80
Average			
1980–1988	3.48	6.84	15.14

[a]Data courtesy of the First Boston Corporation

The historical volatility statistics summarized in this appendix are based on annualized data. Assume that an investor wants to assess the likely price and yield behavior of a 30-year U.S. Treasury bond for the forthcoming year. The investor decides that a 14% yield volatility assumption and a 16% price volatility assumption are appropriate for this bond. The 30-year U.S. Treasury bond (9% due 11/15/18) is currently priced at par to yield 9% to maturity. The end-of-year price and yield for the 30-year bond are likely to fall within the following bounds:

	14% yield volatility assumption		
Standard Deviations	Bond Yield Range	Low Bound, High Bound	Probability (in %)
1	9.00% ±1.26%	(7.74%, 10.26%)	68
2	9.00% ±2.52%	(6.48%, 11.52%)	95
3	9.00% ±3.78%	(5.22%, 12.78%)	99

	16% yield volatility assumption		
Standard Deviations	Bond Price Range	Low Bound, High Bound	Probability (in %)
1	100.00 ±16.00	(84.00, 116.00)	68
2	100.00 ±32.00	(68.00, 132.00)	95
3	100.00 ±48.00	(52.00, 148.00)	99

CHAPTER 7

Portfolio Duration

Introduction

Chapters 1 through 6 discussed the duration of an individual security. This chapter defines and illustrates the duration of a portfolio of bonds. The Appendix presents the calculations necessary to derive the internal rate of return of a bond portfolio. Chapter 8 will apply duration to bond portfolio management.

Calculating a portfolio duration

A portfolio of bonds, like an individual security, is a series of future cash flows. A *portfolio's duration* is the weighted average maturity of the portfolio's cash flows, where the present values of the cash flows serve as the weights. The Macaulay's duration of a portfolio is calculated as follows:

$$\text{portfolio duration} \atop \text{(in years)} = \sum_{t=0.50}^{n} \left(\frac{\text{PV(CF}_t)}{\text{TPV}} \times t \right)$$

where

PV(CF$_t$) = the present value of the cash flow received in year t. The portfolio's internal rate of return is used to calculate the present value.

CF$_t$ = the nominal cash flow received in year t

TPV = the total present value of all of the portfolio's future cash flows (i.e., the portfolio's current market value including accrued interest)

t = the number of years remaining until the receipt of cash flow CF$_t$

n = the number of years remaining until receipt of the portfolio's final cash flow

This formulation is identical to that for a single bond (see Chapter 2). In applying the formula to a portfolio, however, two subtle differences emerge.

First, a portfolio's cash flows are "lumpier" than an individual bond's cash flows. A bond provides a level stream of coupon cash flows before final maturity and a lump sum return of principal at final maturity. A portfolio, on the other hand, is a collection of various coupons with varying maturities. Second, the portfolio's internal rate of return (IRR) is the discount rate applied to the portfolio's future cash flows (this chapter's Appendix summarizes the calculations for deriving an IRR). The portfolio's IRR differs from the portfolio's average yield to maturity (YTM). On the other hand, an individual bond's IRR and the bond's YTM are synonymous.

An illustration

Exhibit 7-1 displays a portfolio of U.S. Treasury bonds and corporate bonds. Based on May 15, 1988, prices, the portfolio has a market value of $100 million.[1] Through the arduous task

---

[1] You may notice that all the bonds in the portfolio make coupon payments on a May 15 to November 15 cycle. A May 15, 1988, settlement date is used to simplify the illustration of a portfolio duration derivation (no partial period discounting is necessary). In actuality, prices reflect May 16, 1988, data because May 15, 1988, was a Sunday.

of trial and error, the portfolio's IRR is calculated as 9.52% (the portfolio's average YTM is 8.94%). This figure serves as the basis for the present value (PV) factors of Exhibit 7–2. A portfolio's cash flows are hardly uniform. Exhibit 7–2 illustrates this fact by listing the portfolio's cash flows on both a nominal basis and a present value basis. The portfolio has a duration of 3.51 years (see Exhibit 7–2):

$$\text{portfolio duration} = \sum_{t=0.50}^{10} \left(\frac{\text{PV(CF}_t)}{\text{TPV}} \times t \right)$$

$$= \left(\frac{4,659,000}{100,000,000} \times 0.5 \right) + \left(\frac{22,672,000}{100,000,000} \times 1.0 \right) + \cdots$$

$$+ \left(\frac{4,123,000}{100,000,000} \times 10.0 \right)$$

$$= 3.51$$

Exhibit 7-1. A portfolio of U.S. Treasury bonds and corporate bonds (data as of May 15, 1988). The portfolio's average YTM is 8.94%.

Par Amount ($000)	Issue Description	Price	YTM(%)	Macaulay's Duration	Modified Duration	Market Value $000	Portfolio Market Value (%)
20,000	U.S. Treasury 11¾% Due 5/15/89	104.00	7.52	0.97	0.93	$ 20,800	0.2080
23,750	U.S. Treasury 8% Due 11/15/90	100.00	8.00	2.32	2.23	23,750	0.2375
15,000	Associates Corp. 9% Due 5/15/91	100.00	9.00	2.70	2.58	15,000	0.1500
30,000	Philadelphia Electric 10⅞% Due 11/15/95	101.50	10.58	5.33	5.06	30,450	0.3045
10,000	U.S. Treasury 9% Due 5/15/98	100.00	9.00	6.80	6.51	10,000	0.1000
						$100,000	

Exhibit 7-2. Calculation of the duration of a portfolio of bonds (portfolio from Exhibit 7-1). The present value factors reflect a portfolio IRR of 9.52%.

(1) t (Years)	(2) Cash Flow (in $000)	(3) PV Factor	(4) = (2) × (3) PV (CF$_t$)	(5) = (4) / Price Weighting Factor	(6) = (1) × (5) PV-Weighted t
0.5	$ 4,881	0.9546	$ 4,659	0.0466	0.0233
1.0	24,881	0.9112	22,672	0.2267	0.2267
1.5	3,706	0.8698	3,223	0.0322	0.0483
2.0	3,706	0.8303	3,077	0.0308	0.0616
2.5	27,456	0.7925	21,759	0.2176	0.5440
3.0	17,756	0.7565	13,432	0.1343	0.4029
3.5	2,081	0.7222	1,503	0.0150	0.0525
4.0	2,081	0.6893	1,434	0.0143	0.0572
4.5	2,081	0.6580	1,369	0.0137	0.0617
5.0	2,081	0.6281	1,307	0.0131	0.0655
5.5	2,081	0.5996	1,248	0.0125	0.0688
6.0	2,081	0.5723	1,191	0.0119	0.0714
6.5	2,081	0.5463	1,137	0.0114	0.0741
7.0	2,081	0.5215	1,085	0.0109	0.0763
7.5	32,081	0.4978	15,970	0.1597	1.1978
8.0	450	0.4752	214	0.0021	0.0168
8.5	450	0.4536	204	0.0020	0.0170
9.0	450	0.4330	195	0.0020	0.0180
9.5	450	0.4133	186	0.0019	0.0181
10.0	10,450	0.3945	4,123	0.0412	0.4120
			$100,000	1.0000	3.5140

Portfolio value (in $000) — Macaulay's duration

Calculating the modified duration of a portfolio

A *portfolio's modified duration* is an adjusted version of the portfolio's duration:

$$\text{portfolio modified duration} = \frac{\text{portfolio duration}}{1 + \dfrac{\text{portfolio IRR}}{2}}$$

The portfolio's modified duration can be used as an estimate of the portfolio's price sensitivity to changes in interest rates. For example, the modified duration of the portfolio of Exhibits 7–1 and 7–2 is 3.35 years:

$$\begin{aligned}\text{portfolio} \atop \text{modified duration} \;&=\; \frac{3.51}{1 + \dfrac{0.0952}{2}}\\[2em]&=\; \frac{3.51}{1.0476}\\[1em]&=\; 3.35\end{aligned}$$

For every 100BP shift in yields, the portfolio's value is expected to change by 3.35%:

$$\begin{aligned}\text{percentage change} \atop \text{in portfolio value} \;=\; -\left(\begin{array}{c}\text{portfolio}\\\text{modified}\\\text{duration}\end{array}\right) \times \left(\begin{array}{c}\text{basis point change}\\\text{in portfolio IRR}\\\hline 100\end{array}\right)\end{aligned}$$

The only difference between this formula and that for a single bond is that the basis point change in IRR is used instead of the basis point shift in the average YTM.

Estimating a portfolio's duration and modified duration

Portfolio duration is typically estimated by using the weighted average duration of the securities comprising the portfolio:

$$\text{portfolio duration} \;=\; \sum_{i=1}^{N} (D_i \times w_i)$$

where

D_i = the duration of the ith security

w_i = the market value weight of the ith security (expressed in decimal form)

N = the number of securities in the portfolio

For example, the portfolio of earlier illustrations bears a duration of approximately 3.46 years (data from Exhibit 7–1):

$$\text{portfolio duration} = \sum_{i=1}^{5} (D_i \times w_i)$$

$$= 0.97(0.2080) + 2.32(0.2375) + 2.70(0.1500)$$
$$+ 5.33(0.3045) + 6.80(0.1000)$$

$$= 3.46$$

The actual duration was calculated as 3.51 years; the estimate of 3.46 is reasonably close.

The modified duration of a portfolio can be estimated in two ways. The first way is to use the weighted average of the modified durations of the securities comprising the portfolio:

$$\text{portfolio modified duration} = \sum_{i=1}^{N} (\text{moddur}_i \times w_i)$$

where
moddur_i = the modified duration of the ith security

w_i = the market value weight of the ith security (expressed in decimal form)

The portfolio of earlier analyses has a modified duration of approximately 3.50 years (data from Exhibit 7-1):

$$\text{portfolio modified duration} = \sum_{i=1}^{5} (\text{moddur}_i \times w_i)$$

$$= 0.93(0.2080) + 2.23(0.2375) + 2.58(0.1500)$$
$$+ 5.06(0.3045) + 6.51(0.1000)$$

$$= 3.30$$

This figure compares to the actual modified duration of 3.35 years.

The portfolio modified duration can also be estimated by the portfolio duration as adjusted by the portfolio's average YTM:

$$\text{portfolio modified duration} = \frac{\text{portfolio duration}}{1 + \dfrac{\text{portfolio average YTM}}{2}}$$

The portfolio in Exhibit 7-1 carries a modified duration of approximately 3.31 years as shown below. (The actual figure is 3.35 years.)

$$\text{portfolio modified duration} = \frac{3.46}{1 + \dfrac{0.0894}{2}}$$

$$= \frac{3.46}{1.0447}$$

$$= 3.31$$

The arduous nature of the precise calculation and the ready availability of individual bond durations and yields are the primary reasons why estimated figures are commonly used. The examples show that the estimates are reasonably accurate. The illustrations presented in subsequent chapters rely on estimates.

Calculating the effective duration of a portfolio

The effective, or option-adjusted, duration of a portfolio is represented by the weighted average of the effective durations of the underlying securities:

$$\text{portfolio effective duration} = \sum_{i=1}^{N} (\text{effdur}_i \times w_i)$$

where

effdur$_i$ = the effective duration of the ith security

w_i = the market value weight of the ith security (expressed in decimal form)

In deriving the effective durations of the component securities, a consistent set of assumptions (e.g., volatility estimate) is critical to the usefulness of the portfolio average.

An illustration

Exhibit 7–3 presents a 15-bond portfolio that includes U.S. Treasury bonds, STRIPS, federal agency bonds, corporate bonds, and mortgage passthroughs. The portfolio has a modified duration of 4.77 years and an effective duration of 3.99 years. In each case, the portfolio duration is a market value-weighted average of the durations of the underlying portfolio members. Call features reduce a portfolio's duration. In this case, the duration reduction is 0.78 years, from 4.77 (modified) to 3.99 (effective).

Summary

A bond portfolio is a series of promised future cash flows. The Macaulay's duration for a bond portfolio is derived in the same manner as that for a single bond. A portfolio's duration is the weighted average maturity of the portfolio's cash flows, where the present values of the cash flows serve as the weights. The portfolio's IRR is the discount rate that derives the present values (see Appendix to this chapter). Portfolio duration can be estimated as the weighted average of the durations of the portfolio members.

A portfolio's modified duration is a revised version of the Macaulay's duration for the portfolio. The modified duration can be estimated as the weighted average of the modified durations of the portfolio members. A portfolio's modified duration is a measure of the price sensitivity of the portfolio to changes in interest rates. A portfolio with a 4.00 modified duration experiences

Exhibit 7-3. A portfolio of U.S. Treasury bonds, STRIPS, federal agency bonds, corporate bonds, and mortgage passthroughs (courtesy of Capital Management Sciences).

Par Value ($000)	CUSIP	Issuer	Quality	Coupon (%)	Maturity	12/30/88 Price	Market Value ($000)	Percentage of Portfolio	YTM/C^a (%)	Modified Duration	Effective Duration
750	912810BT	U.S. Treasury Bonds	TSY	8.250	5/15/90	99.013	750	7.7	9.016	1.26	1.26
875	912827PS	U.S. Treasury Notes	TSY	10.750	7/15/90	102.142	937	9.6	9.221	1.33	1.33
750	313388NY	Federal Home Loan Banks	AGY	10.300	9/25/90	101.358	781	8.0	9.415	1.52	1.52
750	912827QJ	U.S. Treasury Notes	TSY	11.750	1/15/91	104.612	825	8.4	9.215	1.71	1.71
500	912827VA	U.S. Treasury Notes	TSY	7.875	6/30/91	97.078	505	5.2	9.210	2.21	2.21
300	313311KH	Federal Farm Credit Banks	AGY	10.600	10/21/91	102.643	314	3.2	9.494	2.35	2.35
1150	053528AS	AVCO Financial Services	A	9.125	3/01/98	95.055	1128	11.5	9.957	5.84	5.12
950	912833FZ	U.S. Treasury STRIPS	TSY	0.000	11/15/06	20.557	195	2.0	9.049	17.10	17.10
650	14141AU	Carolina Power & Light	A	8.500	10/1/07	85.492	569	5.8	10.251	8.35	7.62
763	GN120009	GNMA	AGY	12.000	6/15/09	105.826	811	8.3	10.453	3.29	2.29
950	912833KD	U.S. Treasury STRIPS	TSY	0.000	11/15/14	10.609	101	1.0	8.861	24.78	24.78
523	GN090015	GNMA	AGY	9.000	6/15/15	93.828	493	5.0	10.374	5.35	5.56
750	742718AG	Proctor & Gamble Co.	AAA	10.625	11/15/15	102.453	778	7.9	10.302	8.88	5.54
821	FH105016	FHLMC	AGY	10.500	6/15/16	99.727	822	8.4	10.789	4.73	4.26
750	694308CT	Pacific Gas & Electric	A	11.250	11/1/18	103.336	789	8.1	10.864	8.64	5.17

Par Value ($000)	Market Value ($000)	Annual Income ($000)	Average Quality	Average Coupon (%)	Average Maturity (Years)	Current Yield (%)	YTM/C (%)	Modified Duration	Effective Duration
11232	9799	942	AAA	8.38	10.80	9.83	9.88	4.77	3.99

^a YTM/C: The Yield to Maturity (YTM) is used for noncallable bonds. The Discounted Cash Flow (DCF) yield is used for mortgage-backed securities. The Yield to Call (YTC) is used for callable bonds trading on a YTC basis.

approximately a 4% change in value for every 100BP change in market yield.

A portfolio's effective duration is calculated as a weighted average of the effective durations of the underlying securities. For a portfolio containing callable bonds or putable bonds, effective duration serves as a better proxy for the portfolio's price sensitivity than either the Macaulay's duration or the modified duration. Chapter 8 concludes the duration part of the book by applying the concepts of Chapters 1 through 7 to management strategy for bond portfolios.

Calculating an Internal Rate of Return

Calculating the IRR of a semiannual-pay bond

The IRR of a semiannual-pay bond is derived from the familiar formula:

$$\text{market value of the bond} = \sum_{t=1}^{n} \frac{CF_t}{\left(1 + \dfrac{IRR}{2}\right)^t}$$

where

CF_t = the nominal cash flow received in period t

IRR = the annual internal rate of return of the bond (expressed in decimal form); also termed the yield to maturity (YTM)

t = the time (in semiannual periods) remaining until receipt of cash flow CF_t

n = the time (in semiannual periods) remaining until receipt of the final cash flow (i.e., the principal repayment); the total number of cash flows to be received

The IRR is solved through an arduous process of trial and error; financial calculators and software programs simplify this task.

The foregoing formula assumes that the bond makes a coupon payment every 6 months and that the bond is analyzed on a coupon payment date. To calculate the IRR of a bond analyzed between coupon payment dates, the following formula is appropriate:

$$\text{market value of the bond} = \sum_{t=1}^{n} \frac{CF_t}{\left(1 + \dfrac{IRR}{2}\right)^{t-f}}$$

where
n = the total number of cash flows to be received

$t - f$ = the time (in semiannual periods) remaining until receipt of cash flow CF_t

f = the fraction of a semiannual period that has passed since the most recent coupon payment

This formula simply adjusts for the fact that the first coupon period is shorter than a full 6-month interval. The market value of the bond includes accrued interest. The IRR is again solved through a trial-and-error procedure.

Calculating the IRR of an annual-pay bond

With a few minor modifications, the internal rate of return of an annual-pay bond (e.g., a Eurodollar bond) is derived in the same manner as a semiannual-pay bond.

On a coupon payment date:

$$\text{market value of the bond} = \sum_{t=1}^{n} \frac{CF_t}{(1 + IRR)^t}$$

where
CF_t = the nominal cash flow received in year t

IRR = the annual IRR on the bond (expressed in decimal form); also termed the annually compounded YTM

t = the time (in years) remaining until receipt of cash flow CF_t

n = the time (in years) remaining until receipt of the final cash flow (i.e., the principal repayment); the total number of cash flows to be received

Between coupon payment dates:

$$\text{market value of the bond} = \sum_{t=1}^{n} \frac{CF_t}{(1 + IRR)^{t-f}}$$

where

n = the total number of cash flows to be received

$t-f$ = the time (in years) remaining until receipt of cash flow CF_t

f = the fraction of a year that has passed since the most recent coupon payment

The market value of the bond, as always, includes accrued interest.

Calculating the IRR of a bond portfolio

The IRR for a portfolio of bonds is calculated by viewing the cash flows of the portfolio as though they come from a single bond:

$$\text{market value of the porfolio} = \sum_{t=1}^{n} \frac{CF_t}{\left(1 + \dfrac{IRR}{2}\right)^{t}}$$

where

CF_t = the total nominal cash flow received in period t

IRR = the annual internal rate of return of the bond portfolio (expressed in decimal form); also termed the discounted cash flow (DCF) yield

n = the time (in semiannual periods) remaining until receipt of the portfolio's final cash flow

This formula applies to a portfolio of semiannual-pay bonds whose coupon payment dates coincide; the portfolio is analyzed on a coupon payment date. A more general formula is as follows:

$$\begin{array}{c}\text{market value}\\\text{of the}\\\text{porfolio}\end{array} = \sum_{\substack{i=1,n\\t=a,m}} \frac{CF_i}{\left(1 + \dfrac{IRR}{2}\right)^t}$$

where

CF_i = the ith cash flow generated by the portfolio (i.e., the total nominal cash flow received on a particular date)

n = the total number of cash flows generated by the portfolio (cash flows received on the same date are recognized as a large single cash flow)

t = the time (in semiannual periods) until receipt of a specific cash flow

a = the time (in semiannual periods or fractions thereof) until receipt of the first cash flow

m = the time (in number of semiannual periods) until receipt of the portfolio's final cash flow

The market value of the portfolio includes accrued interest.

CHAPTER 8

Duration and Bond Portfolio Management Strategy

Introduction

This chapter concludes the duration section of the book by applying the concept of duration to both passive bond and active bond management strategies. The chapter discusses three passive bond management techniques and three active bond management strategies. The chapter Appendix assesses the impact of bond swaps on a bond portfolio and illustrates the mechanics of duration-weighted swaps.

Passive bond management

Passive management strategies are of three basic types: cash flow matching, bond immunization, and bond indexation. As its name suggests, a passive management approach minimizes the amount of activity (i.e., turnover) in a bond portfolio. Passive strategies are used by long-term pension plans to match a long-term liability stream and by investors who are dissatisfied with the return performance of their active bond managers.

Cash flow matching.

Description of the approach. A *cash flow matching,* or *dedication, strategy* entails creating and maintaining a bond portfolio that has a cash flow structure that exactly (or very closely) matches the cash flow structure of a stream of future liabilities, or obligations. Zero-coupon bonds are useful in this matching process.

Illustrations. For example, a $10 million obligation due in 5 years can be "dedicated" by purchasing a $10 million 5-year STRIPS. Exhibit 8-1 illustrates the cash flow match graphically. A dedicated portfolio has an average duration equal to the average duration of the liability stream.

Exhibit 8-1. A dedication strategy requires a matching of cash flow requirements with cash flow receipts. This timeline illustrates the dedication of a 5-year, $10 million liability.

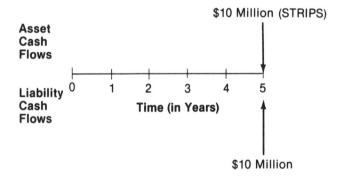

Advantages and limitations. The dedication strategy has several advantages:

1. The concept of a cash flow match is easy to understand.
2. A cash flow match eliminates market (i.e., interest rate) risk and reinvestment risk.
3. There is a minimal amount of maintenance required on a dedicated portfolio (e.g., no rebalancings and no reinvestments).

The dedication strategy does, however, have its limitations. First, a perfect cash flow match can be costly (or even impossible) to implement. The availability of bonds in the specific maturities desired may be limited. Second, if the liability stream is long-term (e.g., with requirements extending beyond 30 years), a cash flow match is difficult to execute because U.S. Treasury bonds and STRIPS mature in 30 years or less. Third, the liability stream may be subject to change. A reestimation of future cash outlays eliminates the cash flow match. Fourth, the dedicated portfolio is exposed to market risk and reinvestment risk if a perfect cash flow match cannot be executed. Finally, the dedicated portfolio is subject to credit risk and call risk if high-yielding mortgage-backed securities or corporate bonds are used to reduce the cost of the dedication.

Bond immunization

Description of the approach. A *bond immunization strategy* is an offshoot of the cash flow matching concept. This strategy requires a matching of the portfolio duration to the average duration of the liability stream. Given parallel yield shifts and periodic rebalancings, the match between asset duration and liability duration "immunizes" the portfolio from general shifts in interest rates. A duration match differs from a cash flow match because there is a variety of bond combinations that can create the duration match. For example, a $10 million, 5-year liability is immunized by equal dollar investments in 3-year STRIPS, 4-year STRIPS, 5-year STRIPS, 6-year STRIPS, and 7-year STRIPS. Exhibit 8-2 shows this immunization in a timeline format. Alternatively, a 7-year U.S. Treasury bond with a 5.00-year duration can be used as the sole portfolio holding.

Illustrations. Exhibit 8-3 lists the future liabilities of a hypothetical pension fund. The average duration of these future cash flows is 17.21 years, not unusual for a long-term pension fund. Exhibit 8-4 presents a bond portfolio designed to meet the cash flow requirements of the retirement plan while immunizing against general shifts in interest rates. The recently enacted Financial Accounting Standards Board (FASB) Statement No.

Exhibit 8-2. A bond immunization strategy requires a duration, not a cash flow, match. In this case, the $10 million liability is due in 5 years; the immunized bond portfolio is a series of STRIPS carrying an average duration of 5.00 years.

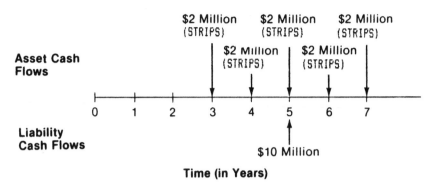

87 requires an annual marking-to-market of pension fund liabilities that is based on current interest rate levels. Traditionally, pension fund assets were reported on the basis of a current market value, whereas pension fund liabilities were valued using an actuarial interest rate that rarely changed. A mismatch of the durations of the pension fund assets and the pension fund liabilities now creates fluctuations in a corporation's net income. Consequently, bond immunization is an attractive investment approach for some pension plans. Given the typically long durations of pension fund liabilities, a bond portfolio of long duration is desirable. Bond dedication and bond immunization have increased the demand for long-term STRIPS owing to the lack of alternative investments of long duration.

Advantages and limitations. A bond immunization strategy has several attractive features. First, an immunization is cheaper to implement than a cash flow match. Second, there is more flexibility in the selection of individual issues to satisfy the immunization. The immunized portfolio can be structured to take advantage of undervalued sectors or undervalued securities in the bond market. Third, the immunized portfolio experiences market fluctuations identical to those of the underlying liability stream (assuming parallel yield shifts). The duration match protects the asset:liability structure from general movements in interest rates.

Exhibit 8-3. The liability stream of a hypothetical pension fund (as of December 31, 1988).

Payment Date	Cash Flow Requirement (in Millions)	Payment Date	Cash Flow Requirement (in Millions)
12/31/89	$ 10	12/31/14	250
12/31/90	10	12/31/15	250
12/31/91	10	12/31/16	250
12/31/92	10	12/31/17	250
12/31/93	10	12/31/18	250
12/31/94	50	12/31/19	100
12/31/95	50	12/31/20	100
12/31/96	50	12/31/21	100
12/31/97	50	12/31/22	100
12/31/98	50	12/31/23	100
12/31/99	200	12/31/24	100
12/31/00	200	12/31/25	100
12/31/01	200	12/31/26	100
12/31/02	200	12/31/27	100
12/31/03	200	12/31/28	100
12/31/04	200	12/31/29	20
12/31/05	200	12/31/30	20
12/31/06	200	12/31/31	20
12/31/07	200	12/31/32	20
12/31/08	200	12/31/33	20
12/31/09	250	12/31/34	20
12/31/10	250	12/31/35	20
12/31/11	250	12/31/36	20
12/31/12	250	12/31/37	20
12/31/13	250	12/31/38	20

The immunization approach does have its drawbacks. First, an immunized bond portfolio requires periodic rebalancings to maintain the duration match. Second, additional rebalancing is necessary if the liability stream is altered. Third, an immunized bond portfolio can be adversely affected by nonparallel yield shifts. Given the frequency of changes in yield curve shapes, quality spread relationships, coupon spread relationships, and the like, nonparallel moves are a real threat, especially for a long duration immunization.

Exhibit 8–4. An immunized bond portfolio (and related cash flow schedule) for a hypothetical pension fund. [a]

Portfolio Analysis Report
Securities Analysis

Time Frame 12/31/88 — 12/31/38

Reinvestment Rate 5.00%

Par Amount ($000)	Issuer	Coupon (%)	Maturity	12/31/88 Market Price	Yield (%)	Duration	IRR (%)	Average Life (Years)	Market Value Including Accrued Interest
40,000	STRIPS	0.000	11/15/94	59.096	9.16	5.873	9.15	5.87	$23,638,452
39,700	STRIPS	0.000	11/15/95	54.069	9.15	6.872	9.14	6.87	21,465,339
39,800	STRIPS	0.000	11/15/96	49.479	9.14	7.874	9.13	7.87	19,692,528
39,700	STRIPS	0.000	11/15/97	45.364	9.11	8.873	9.10	8.87	18,009,441
39,800	STRIPS	0.000	11/15/98	41.576	9.09	9.873	9.08	9.87	16,547,159
87,700	STRIPS	0.000	8/15/99	38.927	9.08	10.620	9.08	10.62	34,138,660
100,000	STRIPS	0.000	11/15/99	38.079	9.08	10.872	9.07	10.87	38,078,995
87,700	STRIPS	0.000	8/15/00	35.698	9.06	11.622	9.06	11.62	31,307,425
100,000	STRIPS	0.000	11/15/00	34.923	9.06	11.874	9.05	11.87	34,922,638
87,700	STRIPS	0.000	8/15/01	32.750	9.04	12.621	9.04	12.62	28,721,991
100,000	STRIPS	0.000	11/15/01	32.040	9.04	12.873	9.03	12.87	32,040,176
90,500	STRIPS	0.000	8/15/02	30.057	9.02	13.621	9.02	13.62	27,201,771
97,200	STRIPS	0.000	11/15/02	29.407	9.02	13.873	9.01	13.87	28,583,498
87,700	STRIPS	0.000	8/15/03	27.673	8.98	14.620	8.98	14.62	24,269,653
100,000	STRIPS	0.000	11/15/03	27.000	9.00	14.872	8.99	14.87	27,000,351
88,500	STRIPS	0.000	8/15/04	25.271	9.00	15.622	9.00	15.62	22,364,494
99,200	STRIPS	0.000	11/15/04	24.725	9.00	15.874	8.99	15.87	24,527,236
91,800	STRIPS	0.000	8/15/05	23.178	8.99	16.621	8.99	16.62	21,277,314
96,000	STRIPS	0.000	11/15/05	22.678	8.99	16.873	8.98	16.87	21,770,918
87,700	STRIPS	0.000	8/15/06	21.263	8.98	17.621	8.98	17.62	18,647,277

a The author would like to thank Kathy Burke, a Vice President in Portfolio Strategies at the First Boston Corporation, for preparing this exhibit.

Exhibit 8–4. (cont.)

Par Amount ($000)	Issuer	Coupon (%)	Maturity	12/31/88 Market Price	Yield (%)	Duration	IRR (%)	Average Life (Years)	Market Value Including Accrued Interest
99,900	STRIPS	0.000	11/15/06	20.805	8.98	17.873	8.97	17.87	20,783,700
87,700	STRIPS	0.000	8/15/07	19.544	8.96	18.620	8.96	18.62	17,140,134
99,900	STRIPS	0.000	11/15/07	19.124	8.96	18.872	8.95	18.87	19,104,793
94,600	STRIPS	0.000	8/15/08	18.005	8.93	19.622	8.93	19.62	17,032,821
93,100	STRIPS	0.000	11/15/08	17.619	8.93	19.874	8.92	19.87	16,403,576
36,300	STRIPS	0.000	5/15/09	16.932	8.91	20.370	8.91	20.37	6,146,368
100,000	STRIPS	0.000	8/15/09	16.564	8.91	20.621	8.91	20.62	16,564,148
100,000	STRIPS	0.000	11/15/09	16.210	8.91	20.873	8.90	20.87	16,209,991
58,600	STRIPS	0.000	2/15/10	15.987	8.87	21.125	8.86	21.13	9,368,091
100,000	STRIPS	0.000	5/15/10	15.646	8.87	21.369	8.87	21.37	15,646,188
99,700	STRIPS	0.000	8/15/10	15.339	8.86	21.621	8.86	21.62	15,293,324
100,000	STRIPS	0.000	11/15/10	15.013	8.86	21.873	8.85	21.87	15,013,160
100,000	STRIPS	0.000	2/15/11	14.689	8.86	22.125	8.85	22.12	14,688,636
100,000	STRIPS	0.000	5/15/11	14.376	8.86	22.368	8.86	22.37	14,376,290
100,000	STRIPS	0.000	8/15/11	14.066	8.86	22.620	8.86	22.62	14,065,533
100,000	STRIPS	0.000	11/15/11	13.766	8.86	22.872	8.85	22.87	13,766,438
100,000	STRIPS	0.000	2/15/12	13.529	8.84	23.124	8.83	23.12	13,528,649
100,000	STRIPS	0.000	5/15/12	13.242	8.84	23.370	8.83	23.37	13,241,599
100,000	STRIPS	0.000	8/15/12	12.985	8.83	23.622	8.82	23.62	12,985,339
100,000	STRIPS	0.000	11/15/12	12.710	8.83	23.874	8.82	23.87	12,710,118
100,000	STRIPS	0.000	2/15/13	12.436	8.83	24.126	8.82	24.13	12,436,277

Exhibit 8–4. (cont.)

Par Amount ($000)	Issuer	Coupon (%)	Maturity	12/31/88 Market Price	Yield (%)	Duration	IRR (%)	Average Life (Years)	Market Value Including Accrued Interest
100,000	STRIPS	0.000	5/15/13	12.173	8.83	24.370	8.83	24.37	$12,172,694
100,000	STRIPS	0.000	8/15/13	11.910	8.83	24.621	8.83	24.62	11,910,432
100,000	STRIPS	0.000	11/15/13	11.658	8.83	24.873	8.82	24.87	11,657,993
100,000	STRIPS	0.000	2/15/14	11.434	8.82	25.125	8.81	25.13	11,434,303
100,000	STRIPS	0.000	5/15/14	11.192	8.82	25.369	8.82	25.37	11,192,222
100,000	STRIPS	0.000	8/15/14	10.978	8.81	25.621	8.81	25.62	10,978,260
100,000	STRIPS	0.000	11/15/14	10.746	8.81	25.873	8.80	25.87	10,746,090
100,000	STRIPS	0.000	2/15/15	10.568	8.79	26.125	8.78	26.12	10,567,828
100,000	STRIPS	0.000	5/15/15	10.345	8.79	26.368	8.79	26.37	10,344,829
100,000	STRIPS	0.000	8/15/15	10.149	8.78	26.620	8.78	26.62	10,148,777
100,000	STRIPS	0.000	11/15/15	9.960	8.77	26.872	8.76	26.87	9,960,465
25,100	U.S. Treasury	9.875	11/15/15	108.313	9.04	10.238	9.04	26.87	27,501,526
100,000	STRIPS	0.000	5/15/16	9.542	8.77	27.370	8.76	27.37	9,542,047
50,000	U.S. Treasury	7.250	5/15/16	82.094	9.02	10.788	9.02	27.37	41,507,635
100,000	STRIPS	0.000	11/15/16	9.215	8.74	27.874	8.73	27.87	9,214,730
49,500	U.S. Treasury	7.500	11/15/16	84.594	9.02	10.771	9.01	27.87	42,345,784
$4,995,100									$1,071,936,105

Note: The portfolio's IRR is 8.93%. Market prices reflect the "ask" price.

Exhibit 8-4. (cont.)

Porfolio Analysis Report
Cash Flow Analysis

Time Frame 12/31/88 — 12/31/38

Reinvestment Rate 5.00%

Period Ending	Costs & Proceeds (+)	Accrued Interest (+)	Principal (+)	Coupon Income (+)	Reinvestment Income (+)	Liability Payments (−)	Ending Balance (=)
12/31/88							$1,071,936,105
12/31/89	−$1,070,688,752	−$1,247.353		$9,816,125	$ 185,780	$ 10,000,000	1,905
12/31/90				9,816,125	185,877	10,000,000	3,907
12/31/91				9,816,125	185,978	10,000,000	6,010
12/31/92				9,816,125	186,085	10,000,000	8,220
12/31/93				9,816,125	186,196	10,000,000	10,541
12/31/94			$ 40,000,000	9,816,125	436,046	50,000,000	262,712
12/31/95			39,700,000	9,816,125	446,939	50,000,000	225,776
12/31/96			39,800,000	9,816,125	445,725	50,000,000	287,626
12/31/97			39,700,000	9,816,125	448,200	50,000,000	251,951
12/31/98			39,800,000	9,816,125	447,019	50,000,000	315,095
12/31/99			187,700,000	9,816,125	2,478,951	200,000,000	310,171
12/31/00			187,700,000	9,816,125	2,478,746	200,000,000	305,041
12/31/01			187,700,000	9,816,125	2,478,442	200,000,000	299,608
12/31/02			187,700,000	9,816,125	2,513,457	200,000,000	329,190
12/31/03			187,700,000	9,816,125	2,479,664	200,000,000	324,980
12/31/04			187,700,000	9,816,125	2,489,580	200,000,000	330,685
12/31/05			187,800,000	9,816,125	2,532,040	200,000,000	478,850
12/31/06			187,600,000	9,816,125	2,486,616	200,000,000	381,591
12/31/07			187,600,000	9,816,125	2,481,693	200,000,000	279,409
12/31/08			187,700,000	9,816,125	2,564,150	200,000,000	359,684
12/31/09			236,300,000	9,816,125	3,860,424	250,000,000	336,233
12/31/10			358,300,000	9,816,125	8,451,690	250,000,000	126,904,047
12/31/11			400,000,000	9,816,125	16,690,842	250,000,000	303,411,014

Exhibit 8-4. (cont.)

Period Ending	Costs & Proceeds	Accrued Interest (+)	Principal (+)	Coupon Income (+)	Reinvestment Income (−)	Liability Payments (=)	Ending Balance
12/31/12			400,000,000	9,816,125	25,683,768	250,000,000	488,910,907
12/31/13			400,000,000	9,816,125	35,017,439	250,000,000	683,744,471
12/31/14			400,000,000	9,816,125	44,880,888	250,000,000	888,441,484
12/31/15			425,100,000	9,816,125	55,400,381	250,000,000	1,128,757,990
12/31/16			299,500,000	5,525,000	63,106,075	250,000,000	1,246,889,065
12/31/17					63,123,759	250,000,000	1,060,012,824
12/31/18					53,663,149	250,000,000	863,675,973
12/31/19					43,723,596	250,000,000	807,399,569
12/31/20					40,989,384	100,000,000	748,388,954
12/31/21					37,887,191	100,000,000	686,276,144
12/31/22					34,742,730	100,000,000	621,018,874
12/31/23					31,439,081	100,000,000	552,457,955
12/31/24					28,046,722	100,000,000	480,504,677
12/31/25					24,325,549	100,000,000	404,830,226
12/31/26					20,494,530	100,000,000	325,324,756
12/31/27					16,469,566	100,000,000	241,794,322
12/31/28					12,275,211	100,000,000	154,569,533
12/31/29					7,799,770	20,000,000	141,869,304
12/31/30					7,182,133	20,000,000	129,051,437
12/31/31					6,533,229	20,000,000	115,584,666
12/31/32					5,867,905	20,000,000	101,452,571
12/31/33					5,136,036	20,000,000	86,588,608
12/31/34					4,383,548	20,000,000	70,972,156
12/31/35					3,592,965	20,000,000	54,565,122
12/31/36					2,770,116	20,000,000	37,335,238
12/31/37					1,890,096	20,000,000	19,225,334
12/31/38					973,283	20,000,000	198,617

In addition, an immunized bond portfolio has a modest degree of market risk and reinvestment risk. Such a portfolio also has credit risk and call risk if mortgage-backed securities or corporate bonds are held in the portfolio. Finally, the immunization strategy is difficult to implement if the liability stream has a long duration. The lack of noncallable bonds of long maturity can pose a problem.

Bond indexation

Description of the approach. A bond indexation strategy involves structuring and maintaining a bond portfolio similar to that of a bond index (e.g., the Shearson Lehman Hutton Government/Corporate Bond Index). Exhibit 8-5 gives a list of bond indexes and their durations (Macaulay's and effective) as of December 31, 1988. The duration of the portfolio is targeted to that of the benchmark, but unlike immunization, the target is typically a moving one. A bond index continues to "buy" new issues that fit its criteria for inclusion. A liability stream, on the other hand, eventually dissolves.

In addition to establishing the duration match, the bond indexer attempts to match other risk characteristics such as the maturity distribution, the duration distribution, the issuer sector distribution, the quality sector distribution, the coupon sector distribution, and the call risk and credit risk of the underlying bond index.

Illustrations. Capital Management Sciences has identified four risk measures that in combination capture most of the sources of return variability:

1. *Parallel duration:* the portfolio's average effective (option-adjusted) duration.

2 *Nonparallel duration:* the portfolio's sensitivity to nonparallel shifts in the U.S. Treasury yield curve.

3 *Quality spread duration:* the portfolio's sensitivity to changes in quality spreads.

4 *Passthrough spread duration:* the portfolio's sensitivity to changes in mortgage passthrough spreads.

Exhibit 8-5. A sample of bond index durations.[a]

Shearson Lehman Hutton Bond Index	Macaulay's Duration	Effective Duration
1- to 3-year Government Bond Index	1.75	1.75
Intermediate Gov./Corporate Bond Index	3.35	3.27
Government/Corporate Bond Index	5.15	4.77
Long-Term Treasury Bond Index	9.37	9.14

[a] Data as of December 31, 1988 and courtesy of Shearson Lehman Hutton Inc.

When all four of these portfolio risk statistics are matched to those of the bond index, the indexed portfolio's return is likely to resemble the return behavior of the underlying index. Exhibit 8-6 uses the CMS technology to create and analyze an indexed portfolio.

Exhibit 8-6 presents a $100 million bond index portfolio that is designed to mimic the risk and return characteristics of the Shearson Lehman Hutton Government/Corporate (SLHGC) bond index. The portfolio's average yield to maturity (9.45%), parallel duration (4.73), nonparallel duration (0.67), and quality spread duration (1.07) are virtually identical to the same statistics for the SLHGC bond index. The portfolio's sector distributions are similar to those of the SLHGC bond index, particularly on a duration-weighted basis.

The latter portion of Exhibit 8-6 projects the total returns of the indexed portfolio over a 1-year investment horizon as attributable to coupons and reinvestment ("income effect"), parallel shifts in U.S. Treasury yields ("parallel effect"), nonparallel shifts in the U.S. Treasury yield curve ("nonparallel effect"), and changes in quality spreads ("quality spread effect"). The "total return differences" vis-à-vis the SLHGC bond index are minimal. The "income" portion of return finds the variation from the index within 4 basis points over a 1-year horizon. Using a 10% to 90% confidence interval (a range in which future observations are likely to occur):

1. The parallel effect (i.e., impact of parallel shifts in U.S. Treasury yields) finds return differences of 50BP or less.

2. The nonparallel effect (i.e., effect of nonparallel yield curve shifts) sees return divergences of 5BP or less.

Exhibit 8-6. A comparison of a bond index portfolio designed to mimic the risk and return characteristics of the SLH Government/Corporate bond index (courtesy of Capital Management Sciences). Prices as of December 30, 1988.

Par Amount ($000)	CUSIP	Issuer	Quality	Coupon (%)	Maturity	Price 12/30/88
2000	313586VH	Fed. Nat. Mortgage Assoc.	AGY	8.000	7/10/89	99.137
2000	313388MX	Federal Home Loan Banks	AGY	11.200	1/25/90	101.516
2000	313311KE	Federal Farm Credit Banks	AGY	10.850	2/ 1/90	101.168
2000	202795CZ	Commonwealth Edison	BBB	8.125	4/15/90	97.456
1750	173034DM	Citicorp	A	8.375	5/ 1/90	98.386
2000	912827WH	U.S. Treasury	GOV	8.000	6/30/90	98.328
1000	912827WL	U.S. Treasury	GOV	8.375	7/31/90	98.801
2000	912827SG	U.S. Treasury	GOV	9.875	8/15/90	100.889
2000	912827WP	U.S. Treasury	GOV	8.625	8/31/90	99.078
2000	912827WP	U.S. Treasury	GOV	8.625	8/31/90	99.078
1000	391417BB	Great Western Bank	A	9.250	9/ 8/90	99.313
2000	912827WR	U.S. Treasury	GOV	8.500	9/30/90	98.770
2000	912827QA	U.S. Treasury	GOV	11.500	10/15/90	103.512
2000	912827WU	U.S. Treasury	GOV	8.250	10/31/90	98.388
2000	912827SR	U.S. Treasury	GOV	9.625	11/15/90	100.671
2000	912827VM	U.S. Treasury	GOV	8.000	11/15/90	97.922
1000	161610BB	Chase Manhattan Corp.	BBB	9.250	12/15/90	99.218
2000	912827TJ	U.S. Treasury	GOV	8.125	5/15/91	97.735
2000	912827WM	U.S. Treasury	GOV	8.750	8/15/91	98.889
1000	173034EN	Citicorp	A	9.350	9/ 1/91	99.176
2000	122781AN	Burroughs Corp.	BBB	8.000	9/15/91	94.734
1000	912827VJ	U.S. Treasury	GOV	9.125	9/30/91	99.803
1750	983901AS	Xerox Credit Corp.	A	9.000	11/ 1/91	98.284
2000	912827WV	U.S. Treasury	GOV	8.500	11/15/91	98.270
2000	912827VS	U.S. Treasury	GOV	8.250	12/31/91	97.550
2000	912827WJ	U.S. Treasury	GOV	8.250	6/30/92	97.203
2000	912827WJ	U.S. Treasury	GOV	8.250	6/30/92	97.203
2000	912827UY	U.S. Treasury	GOV	8.250	8/15/92	97.047
2000	912827WS	U.S. Treasury	GOV	8.750	9/30/92	98.575
1500	644239AX	New England Telephone	AA	9.500	10/ 1/92	99.651
2000	912827VG	U.S. Treasury	GOV	8.375	11/15/92	97.303
2000	912827VQ	U.S. Treasury	GOV	8.250	2/15/93	96.739
2000	907770AJ	UNOCAL	BBB	9.750	3/ 1/94	97.111
2000	912827VB	U.S. Treasury	GOV	8.000	7/15/94	94.770
2000	580033AK	McDermott J Ray	BBB	10.250	6/ 1/95	98.618
1000	538021AD	Litton Industries Inc.[a]	BBB	11.500	7/ 1/95	102.594
2000	370424EW	GMAC[b]	AA	8.375	5/ 1/97	96.164
2000	912810DB	U.S. Treasury[a]	GOV	10.375	11/15/12	110.331
2000	912810DN	U.S. Treasury[a]	GOV	11.750	11/15/14	124.081
2000	912810DP	U.S. Treasury	GOV	11.250	2/15/15	121.761
2000	912810DS	U.S. Treasury	GOV	10.625	8/15/15	115.766
2000	912810DT	U.S. Treasury	GOV	9.875	11/15/15	108.208
2000	313586UB	Fed. Nat. Mortgage Assoc.	AGY	10.350	12/10/15	108.016
2000	912810DV	U.S. Treasury	GOV	9.250	2/15/16	101.990
2000	912810DY	U.S. Treasury	GOV	8.750	5/15/17	97.174
2000	912810DZ	U.S. Treasury	GOV	8.875	8/15/17	98.422
1500	362320AK	GTE Corp.	A	10.750	9/15/17	101.328
2000	313586YX	Fed. Nat. Mortgage Assoc.	AGY	8.950	2/12/18	94.328
2000	912810EA	U.S. Treasury	GOV	9.125	5/15/18	100.893
1000	811845AM	Seagram and Sons[b]	A	9.650	8/15/18	97.586
2000	667748AD	Northwest Pipeline Corp.	BBB	10.650	11/15/18	100.724
2000	912810EB	U.S. Treasury	GOV	9.000	11/15/18	99.930
1000	154051AZ	Central Maine Power	BBB	10.250	12/ 1/18	97.580

[a] Bond's yield is quoted on a YTC, not a YTM, basis.

184 [b] Bond's yield is quoted on a YTP, not a YTM, basis.

Exhibit 8-6. (cont.)

Market Value ($000)	% of Portfolio	Yield to Maturity (%)	Duration Years			
			Parallel	Non-Parallel	Quality Spread	Passthrough Spread
2058	2.1	9.706	0.51	0.44	0.19	0.0
2127	2.1	9.658	0.99	0.73	0.37	0.0
2113	2.1	9.673	1.01	0.74	0.37	0.0
1983	2.0	10.257	1.23	0.85	1.23	0.0
1746	1.8	9.674	1.28	0.87	0.96	0.0
1967	2.0	9.219	1.44	0.94	0.00	0.0
1023	1.0	9.197	1.46	0.93	0.00	0.0
2092	2.1	9.259	1.49	0.94	0.00	0.0
2039	2.1	9.220	1.54	0.96	0.00	0.0
2039	2.1	9.220	1.54	0.96	0.00	0.0
1022	1.0	9.684	1.56	0.96	1.17	0.0
2018	2.0	9.262	1.63	0.99	0.00	0.0
2118	2.1	9.307	1.64	0.98	0.00	0.0
1995	2.0	9.213	1.72	1.02	0.00	0.0
2037	2.1	9.215	1.74	1.02	0.00	0.0
1978	2.0	9.222	1.76	1.03	0.00	0.0
996	1.0	9.693	1.83	1.04	1.83	0.0
1975	2.0	9.200	2.18	1.11	0.00	0.0
2043	2.1	9.228	2.32	1.10	0.00	0.0
1023	1.0	9.697	2.35	1.10	1.76	0.0
1941	2.0	10.256	2.41	1.09	2.41	0.0
1021	1.0	9.197	2.44	1.11	0.00	0.0
1746	1.8	9.697	2.53	1.12	1.90	0.0
1987	2.0	9.191	2.58	1.14	0.00	0.0
1951	2.0	9.203	2.71	1.15	0.00	0.0
1944	2.0	9.203	3.10	1.14	0.00	0.0
1944	2.0	9.203	3.10	1.14	0.00	0.0
2003	2.0	9.221	3.10	1.10	0.00	0.0
2015	2.0	9.200	3.20	1.10	0.00	0.0
1530	1.5	9.604	3.17	1.09	1.59	0.0
1967	2.0	9.213	3.35	1.11	0.00	0.0
1997	2.0	9.213	3.46	1.06	0.00	0.0
2007	2.0	10.481	4.03	0.92	4.03	0.0
1969	2.0	9.225	4.38	0.90	0.00	0.0
1989	2.0	10.548	4.81	0.77	4.81	0.0
1083	1.1	10.586	3.71	0.97	3.71	0.0
1951	2.0	9.746	3.13	1.08	1.56	0.0
2233	2.3	9.210	9.01	0.04	0.00	0.0
2511	2.5	9.145	9.20	0.03	0.00	0.0
2520	2.5	9.060	9.75	0.01	0.00	0.0
2395	2.4	9.047	9.89	0.00	0.00	0.0
2189	2.2	9.054	10.23	0.00	0.00	0.0
2172	2.2	9.518	9.94	0.00	3.68	0.0
2109	2.1	9.050	10.13	0.00	0.00	0.0
1965	2.0	9.026	10.56	0.00	0.00	0.0
2035	2.1	9.028	10.33	0.00	0.00	0.0
1567	1.6	10.595	7.89	0.06	5.92	0.0
1955	2.0	9.527	9.98	0.00	3.69	0.0
2041	2.1	9.036	10.57	0.00	0.00	0.0
1021	1.0	9.964	9.62	0.00	7.21	0.0
2041	2.1	10.567	9.37	0.00	9.37	0.0
2021	2.0	9.005	10.65	0.00	0.00	0.0
984	1.0	10.515	9.49	0.00	9.49	0.0

Exhibit 8-6 (cont.)

COMPARE SYSTEM PORTFOLIO SUMMARY

Fundamentals
Portfolio vs. SLHGC Index

	Yield to Maturity (%)	Current Yield (%)	Quality	Coupon (%)	Maturity (Years)
Portfolio Assets	9.454	9.163	AAA	9.270	10.801
SLHGC Index	9.450	9.387	AAA	9.290	9.760
Difference	0.004	-0.224		-0.20	1.041

COMPARE SYSTEM PORTFOLIO SUMMARY REPORT

Four Factor Duration
Portfolio vs. SLHGC Index

	Parallel	Non-Parallel	Quality Spread	Pass-through Spread
Portfolio Assets	4.73	0.67	1.07	0.0
SLHGC Index	4.73	0.67	1.05	0.0
Difference	-0.00	0.00	0.02	0.0

COMPARE SYSTEM PORTFOLIO DISTRIBUTION

Duration (Years)	% of Portfolio	% of Index	Maturity (Years)	% of Portfolio	% of Index
Cash	0	0	Cash	0	0
0–1	4	2	0–1	2	0
1–2	27	18	1–2	30	15
2–3	14	15	2–3	12	12
3–4	17	13	3–4	13	10
4–5	6	11	4–5	2	9
5–6	0	9	5–7	7	11
6–7	0	8	7–10	2	13
7–8	2	6	10–15	0	6
8–9	0	9	15–20	0	6
9–10	18	3	20–25	2	6
10+	12	5	25+	30	12

Issuing Sector

	% of Portfolio	% of Index
Cash	0	0
Government	65	62
Agency	11	11
Passthrough	0	0
Industrial	8	8
Electric/Gas	5	5
Telephone	3	3
Finance	9	8
International	0	3
Other	0	0

Quality

	% of Portfolio	% of Index
Cash	0	0
Government	65	62
Agency	11	11
AAA	0	4
AA	4	8
A	8	9
BBB	13	6
Other	0	0

Coupon

	% of Portfolio	% of Index
Cash	0	0
0–7	0	4
7–9	51	49
9–11	39	26
11–13	10	15
13–15	0	6
15+	0	1

Call Provisions

	% of Portfolio	% of Index
Non (Including Cash)	89	73
With Future Call	9	14
With Current Call	2	13
Price to Call	8	8

Exhibit 8–6 (cont.)

COMPARE System
Duration-Weighted Distribution

Issuing Sector	Portfolio				SLHGC Index		
	Market Value ($000)	% of Portfolio	Parallel Duration (Years)	Contribution to Duration (Years)	% of Portfolio	Parallel Duration (Years)	Contribution to Duration (Years)
Cash	0	0	0.00	0.00	0	0.00	0.00
Government	64,140	65	4.99	3.23	62	4.82	3.00
Agency	10,425	11	4.45	0.47	11	3.34	0.38
Passthrough	0	0	0.00	0.00	0	0.00	0.00
Corporate	24,620	25	4.17	1.04	27	5.13	1.40
Industrials	8,032	8	4.49	0.36	8	5.33	0.43
Electric/Gas	5,008	5	6.17	0.31	5	5.83	0.30
Telephones	3,097	3	5.56	0.17	3	6.75	0.20
Finance	8,483	9	2.19	0.19	8	3.73	0.30
International	0	0	0.00	0.00	3	5.56	0.17
Other	0	0	0.00	0.00	0	0.00	0.00
	99,185			4.73			4.73

Exhibit 8-6 (cont.)

COMPARE System Sensitivity Analysis 1.00-Year Horizon

Portfolio Total Return Components

Interest Rate Change (in BP)	Income Effect (%)	Parallel Effect (%)	Non-Parallel Effect (%)	Quality Spread Effect (%)	Passthrough Spread Effect(%)
-400	9.454	22.427	2.677	4.859	0.0
-350	9.481	19.127	2.333	4.163	0.0
-300	9.509	15.978	1.992	3.497	0.0
-250	9.537	12.976	1.657	2.860	0.0
-200	9.565	10.109[a]	1.320	2.241	0.0
-150	9.593	7.373	0.984[a]	1.640	0.0
-100	9.621	4.776	0.652	1.066[a]	0.0[a]
-50	9.649	2.317	0.324	0.517	0.0
0	9.677	0.0[b]	0.0[b]	0.0[b]	0.0[b]
50	9.705	-2.199	-0.320	-0.502	0.0
100	9.733	-4.258	-0.636	-0.974[a]	0.0[a]
150	9.761	-6.191	-0.948[a]	-1.422	0.0
200	9.789	-7.995[a]	-1.255	-1.844	0.0
250	9.817	-9.670	-1.558	-2.242	0.0
300	9.845	-11.220	-1.858	-2.615	0.0
350	9.873	-12.641	-2.153	-2.963	0.0
400	9.901	-13.936	-2.443	-3.286	0.0

[a] 10% to 90% confidence interval.   [b] Mean interest rate change.

COMPARE System Sensitivity Analysis 1.00-Year Horizon

Portfolio vs. SLHGC Index Total Return Differences

Interest Rate Change (in BP)	Income Effect (%)	Parallel Effect (%)	Non-Parallel Effect (%)	Quality Spread Effect (%)	Passthrough Spread Effect(%)
-400	-0.034	1.959	0.294	0.518	0.0
-350	-0.029	1.500	0.227	0.406	0.0
-300	-0.024	1.102	0.168	0.307	0.0
-250	-0.020	0.765	0.118	0.222	0.0
-200	-0.015	0.489[a]	0.077	0.150	0.0
-150	-0.010	0.275	0.045[a]	0.092	0.0
-100	-0.006	0.122	0.021	0.048[a]	0.0[a]
-50	-0.001	0.030	0.006	0.017	0.0
0	0.004	0.0[b]	0.0[b]	0.0[b]	0.0[b]
50	0.009	0.031	0.002	-0.004	0.0
100	0.013	0.123	0.013	0.007[a]	0.0[a]
150	0.018	0.277	0.033[a]	0.030	0.0
200	0.023	0.491[a]	0.061	0.068	0.0
250	0.027	0.767	0.099	0.118	0.0
300	0.032	1.105	0.144	0.183	0.0
350	0.037	1.503	0.199	0.261	0.0
400	0.042	1.963	0.262	0.353	0.0

[a] 10% to 90% confidence interval.   [b] Mean interest rate change.

Exhibit 8-6 (cont.)

COMPARE System
Tracking Summary

Portfolio vs. SLHGC Index
Table of Expected Return Differences[a]

			Months	
	3	6	9	12
10% C.L.	0.52	0.71	0.87	1.02
25% C.L.	0.35	0.49	0.62	0.74
Mean	0.11	0.18	0.25	0.33
75% C.L.	-0.04	0.02	0.08	0.14
90% C.L.	-0.15	-0.10	-0.04	0.02

[a]C.L. stands for "confidence level."

COMPARE System
Multi-Scenario Report — 1.00-Year Horizon

	Rates Fall	Ending YTM (%)	Rates Unchanged	Ending YTM (%)	Rates Rise	Ending YTM (%)
Change in Long-Term Treasury (in BP)	-100	8.040	0	9.040	100	10.040
Change in Short-Term Treasury (in BP)	-150	7.180	0	8.680	150	10.180
Change in Long-Term BBB Corporate Bond vs. Long Treasury (in BP)	- 25	9.190	0	10.440	25	11.690
Change in Long 8% Passthroughs vs. 10-Year Treasury (in BP)	- 25	8.991	0	10.270	25	11.520

Exhibit 8-6 (cont.)

COMPARE System
Multi-Scenario Report — 1.00-Year Horizon

Effect	Rates Fall			Rates Unchanged			Rates Rise		
		SLHGC			SLHGC			SLHGC	
	Portfolio	Index	Difference	Portfolio	Index	Difference	Portfolio	Index	Difference
Income (%)	9.62	9.63	-0.01	9.68	9.67	0.00	9.73	9.72	0.01
Parallel (%)	4.78	4.65	0.12	0.00	0.00	0.00	-4.26	-4.38	0.12
Non-Parallel (%)	0.33	0.32	0.01	0.00	0.00	0.00	-0.31	-0.32	0.00
Quality Spread (%)	0.25	0.24	0.01	0.00	0.00	0.00	-0.26	-0.26	-0.00
Passthrough Spread (%)	0.00	0.00	0.00	0.00	0.00	0.00	0.00	0.00	0.00
Total Return (%)	14.97	14.84	0.13	9.68	9.67	0.00	4.90	4.76	0.14

3. The quality spread effect (i.e., impact of quality spread changes) creates return discrepancies of 5BP or less.

4. There is no passthrough effect since the portfolio lacks any mortgage-backed securities.

Periodic portfolio rebalancing can reduce these total return differences. A blanket rule of rebalancing the indexed portfolio monthly (or more often if market yields shift markedly) enhances the ability of the portfolio to behave like its index counterpart.

The last page of Exhibit 8–6 shows the 1-year component returns for the indexed portfolio and for the SLHGC bond index in a bull market (rates fall), a flat market (rates unchanged), and a bear market (rates rise). The total return differences are negligible because the average risk and distributional characteristics of the indexed portfolio and the benchmark index are virtually identical.

The size and complexity of the underlying bond index have an impact on the replication of the risk and return features of the index. A less complex index (such as a U.S. Treasury bond index) is much easier to copy than a broad market index (such as the 4,900-member SLHGC bond index or the 4,900-member Salomon Brothers Broad Investment Grade bond index). An index containing callable bonds is more difficult to replicate than an index of noncallable bonds.

Advantages and limitations. Bond indexation has several attractive features:

1. Bond indexation minimizes portfolio turnover and transaction costs.

2. The management fees for bond indexation are lower than those for active bond management.

3. An indexed portfolio is typically well diversified.

4. An indexed portfolio generates total returns that are predictable vis-à-vis the underlying benchmark.

5. The total returns (particularly net of management fees) of a bond index often exceed those of an average active bond manager.

There are limitations to bond indexation, however. First, the bond index may be difficult to replicate. The underlying issues may not be available in the marketplace, particularly if the bond index includes corporate bonds. A sample introduces some degree of mismatch between the indexed portfolio and the underlying benchmark. In addition, the sampling process can be rigorous and quantitatively demanding. Second, rebalancing and reinvesting can be time-consuming and costly. Third, structuring the indexed portfolio can be expensive, particularly if the target index covers a broad range of issuer classes, quality categories, coupon rates, and the like. The smaller the portfolio size (in total dollars), the more costly the initial setup (e.g., odd lot purchases may be required). Fourth, the quantitative requirements of an indexed portfolio can be expensive. An addition to, or distribution from, the portfolio demands a complex rebalancing.

Active bond management

Active management strategies have two primary forms: *risk-controlled bond management* and *risk-altering bond management*. The former purposely neutralizes the market risk of a bond portfolio. The latter intentionally alters the market risk of a bond portfolio to capitalize on an expected shift in the general level of interest rates. Exhibit 8-7 presents issue data (as of December 30, 1988) that serve as reference points for the applications that follow.

Risk-controlled bond management. The risk-controlled approach to active bond portfolio strategy attempts to meet an investment objective(s) while rigorously controlling the general interest rate risk of the portfolio. Using modified duration (or effective duration) as the proxy for market risk, the portfolio duration is targeted to a specific benchmark (e.g., a bond index, a liability stream, or a fixed number).[1] Active swapping is carried out through the use of duration-weighted trades. The Appendix

---

[1] Using effective duration as the market risk proxy is even more desirable because effective duration incorporates the impacts of option features in its derivation.

Exhibit 8-7. Issue data as of December 30, 1988.

Issue Description	Price	YTM (%)	Modified Duration	Effective Duration
U.S. Treasury 7⅞% due 5/15/90	98-10	9.20	1.26	1.26
U.S. Treasury 8⅞% due 11/15/98	98-08	9.15	6.38	6.38
U.S. Treasury 9% due 11/15/18	100-00	9.00	10.20	10.20
STRIPS 0% due 11/15/18	7.853	8.70	28.63	28.63
Texas Utilities Electric 12% due 9/1/15	106.25	11.25	8.05	4.30
Southern Bell Telephone 8⅝% due 9/1/26	88.75	9.75	9.75	8.14

of this chapter details the mechanics of duration-weighted trades. You are encouraged to review the Appendix now to gain a better understanding of the forthcoming examples.

Risk-controlled bond management uses two basic methods to achieve a portfolio's investment objective(s): sector rotation and security selection. Common investment objectives include (1) the maximization of total return, (2) the maximization of current income (i.e., current yield), and (3) the maximization of yield (i.e., yield to maturity). A discussion of each of these objectives follows. A combination of these distinct objectives may be required, making the portfolio management task a more challenging one.

Total return maximization

DESCRIPTION OF THE APPROACH. A *total return maximization* objective demands that a bond portfolio be overweighted in securities and sectors that are undervalued on a relative basis.[2] An expectation of a flattening or inversion of the yield curve warrants an overweighting in a combination of short-maturity bonds and long-maturity bonds at the expense of intermediate-maturity holdings. Anticipation of a large supply of new-issue corporate bonds justifies an underweighting in that sector and an overweighting in an alternative sector such as U.S. Treasury bonds. Finally, a newly issued bond that is not fully understood by investors (e.g., a put bond, a CMO, a foreign currency hedged

---

[2]The weightings can be based on market value, or, perferably, on duration contributions (which considers both the market value weighting and the average duration of the securities and sectors involved).

security) may initially be underpriced and, as a result, may be attractive to a total return maximizer. As the bond's inherent value is recognized by an increasing number of market participants, its price is likely to rise to a fair value. At this point, the fairly valued bond is sold (to lock in the excess return), and the proceeds are reinvested in an undervalued security or market sector.

ILLUSTRATIONS. Exhibit 8-8 presents a bond portfolio that is overweighted in U.S. Treasury bonds, utility bonds, and yankee bonds and underweighted in industrial bonds and bank and finance bonds. The comparative benchmark in this case is the Shearson Lehman Hutton Government/Corporate (SLHGC) bond index. Exhibit 8-9 provides a sector-weighting comparison between the portfolio and the SLHGC bond index, on both a market value weighted basis and a duration contribution basis.[3] The portfolio is structured in anticipation of superior total return performance by the U.S. Treasury bond, utility bond, and yankee bond market sectors. Conversely, the expectation of subpar performance by the industrial bond and the bank and finance bond market sectors explains the underweightings in those sectors. The average market risk of the portfolio, as measured by effective duration, is pegged to that of the underlying benchmark (4.77 effective duration as of December 31, 1988).

On a *market value weighted basis*, the portfolio is overweighted in the U.S. Treasury (+13.02%), utility (+10.79%), and yankee (+2.23%) sectors. The portfolio is underweighted in the federal agency (-10.68%), industrial (-7.63%), and bank and finance (-7.72%) sectors. On a *duration contribution basis*, the portfolio is approximately equally weighted in U.S. Treasury bonds. The portfolio is underweighted in federal agency bonds (-0.41), industrial bonds (-0.42), and bank and finance bonds (-0.33). The portfolio is overexposed to utility bonds (+0.78) and yankee bonds (+0.37).

---

[3] For further discussion of portfolio comparisons that are based on a weighted market value and a duration contribution, consult Chapter 15 ("Bond Portfolio Analysis") of *Yield Curve Analysis: The Fundamentals of Risk and Return* (New York: New York Institute of Finance, 1988).

Exhibit 8-8. A bond portfolio designed to outperform the SLHGC bond index by overweighting in U.S. Treasury bonds, utility bonds, and yankee bonds (sector comparisons provided in Exhibit 8-9). The portfolio has an average market risk identical to that of the SLHGC bond index (4.77 effective duration). Data as of December 30, 1988.

Par Amount ($000)	Issue Description	Price	YTM (%)	Effective Duration	Market Value ($000)	Percentage of Portfolio
29,050	U.S. Treasury 6⅝% due 12/31/90	95–16	9.13	1.76	28,700	0.2870
36,480	U.S. Treasury 11½% due 11/15/95	111–16	9.20	4.77	41,200	0.4120
10,000	Commonwealth Edison 10⅛% due 5/1/98	99.75	10.16	5.47	10,140	0.1014
5,000	U.S. Treasury 9⅜% due 2/15/06	102–20	9.07	8.28	5,300	0.0530
10,000	Southern Bell Telephone 8⅝% due 9/1/26	88.75	9.75	8.14	9,160	0.0916
6,000	Province of Quebec 8⅝% due 12/1/26	91.00	9.50	10.21	5,500	0.0550
					$100,000	

Exhibit 8-9. An issuer sector comparison of the bond portfolio of Exhibit 8-8 vis-à-vis the Shearson Lehman Hutton Government/Corporate (SLHGC) bond index as of December 31, 1988.

Market value weighted basis

	Market Value (%)		
Issuer Sector	Portfolio	SLHGC Index[a]	Difference
U.S. Treasury	75.20	62.18	+13.02
Federal agency	0.00	10.68	−10.68
Industrial	0.00	7.63	− 7.63
Bank and finance	0.00	7.72	− 7.72
Utility	19.30	8.51	+10.79
Yankee	5.50	3.27	+ 2.23
Totals	100.00	100.00	

[a] Index data courtesy of Shearson Lehman Hutton, Inc.

Exhibit 8-9. (cont.)

Duration contribution basis[b]

	Duration Contribution (years)		
Issuer Sector	*Portfolio*	*SLHGC Index*[a]	*Difference*
U.S. Treasury	2.91	2.94	−0.03
Federal agency	0.00	0.41	−0.41
Industrial	0.00	0.42	−0.42
Bank and finance	0.00	0.33	−0.33
Utility	1.30	0.52	+0.78
Yankee	0.56	0.19	+0.37
Totals	4.77	4.77	

[a] Index data courtesy of Shearson Lehman Hutton Inc.

[b] Based on effective duration.

The duration contribution approach considers both the market value and the average duration (in this case, the average effective duration) of each market sector. In this way, the "true" market risk contribution of each sector is ascertained. Each market sector carries a unique average duration:

Issuer Sector	*Average Effective Duration*
U.S. Treasury	4.73
Federal agency	3.86
Industrial	5.53
Bank and finance	4.31
Utility	6.14
Yankee	5.66
SLHGC index	4.77

[a] Data as of December 31, 1988 and courtesy of Shearson Lehman Hutton Inc.

The market sector durations range from 3.86 (federal agency) to 6.14 (utility). The selection of subsectors, or individual issues, within a given sector allows the flexibility to deviate substantially from the average duration of that sector. For example, a long-term noncallable Financing Corporation (FICO) bond (in the federal agency category) has substantially more market risk than the "average" federal agency bond (10.00 effective duration versus

3.96 effective duration). An equivalent market value weighting hides this sizable difference in sector exposure. A market value approach, therefore, can misrepresent the "true" bets that an investor makes in a bond portfolio vis-à-vis the bond index benchmark.

Current income maximization. All other factors held constant, high coupon bonds offer more current yield than low-coupon bonds. For example, Exhibit 8–10 summarizes the price, yield, and duration statistics of two U.S. Treasury bonds. The bonds have an identical maturity (5/15/90) and virtually identical YTMs and modified durations; however, the higher coupon 11⅜% issue provides an additional 306BP in current yield versus its 7⅞% coupon counterpart (11.07% versus 8.01%).

A portfolio with a concentration in high coupon bonds achieves a *current income maximization* objective. As an example, an investor has a current income requirement of 10% and a risk tolerance of 5.00 years effective duration. Exhibits 8–11 and 8–12 present two portfolios that satisfy the investor's risk preference. Portfolio *A* is comprised solely of low coupon U.S. Treasury bonds and offers an average current yield of only 8.14%. Portfolio *B* is filled with high coupon U.S. Treasury bonds and corporate bonds. This portfolio's current yield is an attractive 11.47%. Portfolio *B* meets the investor's 10% current yield bogey while maintaining an average effective duration of 5.00 years. Mutual funds and university endowment funds often have objectives that include current yield maximization.

Exhibit 8-10. A sample of 1½-year U.S. Treasury bonds (data as of December 30, 1988).

Issue Description	*Price*	*YTM (%)*	*Current Yield*	*Modified Duration*	*Effective Duration*
U.S. Treasury 7⅞% due 5/15/90	98-10	9.20	8.01	1.26	1.26
U.S. Treasury 11⅜% due 5/15/90	102-24	9.18	11.07	1.24	1.24

Yield maximization. A *yield* (i.e., *yield to maturity*) *maximization* objective necessitates a portfolio concentrated in high yielding issues such as mortgage-backed securities, callable

Exhibit 8-11. A portfolio of low coupon U.S. Treasury bonds (data as of December 30, 1988). The portfolio has a 5.00 effective duration and an average current yield of 8.14%.

Portfolio A

Par Amount ($000)	Issue Description	Price	Current Yield (%)	Effective Duration	Market Value ($000)	Percentage of Portfolio
20,200	U.S. Treasury 7⅞% due 5/15/90	98-10	8.01	1.26	20,050	0.2005
84,200	U.S. Treasury 7¼% due 11/15/96	89-04	8.14	5.70	75,800	0.7580
5,000	U.S. Treasury 7¼% due 5/15/16	82-04	8.83	10.33	4,150	0.0415
					$100,000	

high coupon corporate bonds, and low quality corporate bonds. U.S. Treasury bonds and federal agency bonds are generally avoided because of their low yields.

Exhibit 8-12. A portfolio of high coupon U.S. Treasury bonds and corporate bonds (data as of December 30, 1988). The portfolio has a 5.00 effective duration and an average current yield of 11.47%.

Portfolio B

Par Amount ($000)	Issue Description	Price	Current Yield (%)	Effective Duration	Market Value ($000)	Percentage of Portfolio
15,000	U.S. Treasury 13⅞% due 8/15/89	102–28	13.49	0.57	16,200	0.1620
14,930	U.S. Treasury 14⅞% due 8/15/91	113–22	13.08	2.10	17,800	0.1780
20,000	British Columbia Hydro 15½%, due 11/15/11	134.25	11.55	5.39	27,240	0.2724
10,000	Texas Utilities Electric 12% due 9/1/15	106.25	11.29	4.30	11,025	0.1103
22,000	U.S. Treasury 11¼% due 2/15/15	121–28	9.23	9.34	27,735	0.2774
					$100,000	

As an illustration, an investor desires a minimum portfolio yield of 10% and an average effective duration of 5.00 years. The U.S. Treasury bond portfolio of Exhibit 8–13 offers an average yield of 9.09%, a far cry from the investor's minimum of 10%. Conversely, the portfolio displayed in Exhibit 8–14 has an average yield of 10.72%, comfortably above the investor's 10% threshold. Each portfolio bears an effective duration of 5.00 years. Incremental call risk and credit risk may be required to achieve the yield objective.

Exhibit 8-13. A portfolio of U.S. Treasury bonds (data as of December 30, 1988). The portfolio has a 5.00 effective duration and an average yield of 9.09%.

Portfolio "Low Yield"

Par Amount ($000)	Issue Description	Price	YTM (%)	Effective Duration	Market Value ($000)	Percentage of Portfolio
78,950	U.S. Treasury 9% due 11/15/93	99–16	9.11	3.77	80,885	0.8089
18,900	U.S. Treasury 9% due 11/15/18	100–00	9.00	10.20	19,115	0.1912
					$100,000	

Risk-controlled bond management: advantages and limitations. Risk-controlled bond management techniques offer several attractions. First, the market risk of the bond portfolio is rigorously controlled. Other risks (e.g., call risk, credit risk, and yield curve risk) are strategically managed. Second, appropriate moves into and out of specific securities and sectors can be used to achieve the portfolio objective(s).

Risk-controlled strategies have drawbacks as well. Portfolio turnover and transaction costs can be high. Poor selection of specific securities and sectors can detract from meeting the investment objective(s). In addition, investment objectives are subject to change. Finally, credit risk and/or call risk may be undertaken in an effort to enhance a portfolio's total return, current yield, or yield to maturity. The reality of these risks may prove to be unpleasant (e.g., reinvestment risk and price depreciation caused by credit deterioration).

Exhibit 8-14. A portfolio of corporate bonds and mortgage backed securities (data as of December 30, 1988). The portfolio has a 5.00 effective duration and an average yield of 10.72%.

Portfolio "High Yield"

Par Amount ($000)	Issue Description	Price	YTM (%)	Effective Duration	Market Value ($000)	Percentage of Portfolio
20,000	GNMA 10% due 6/15/15	98.11	10.59[a]	4.55	19,705	0.1971
43,750	Commonwealth Edison 11⅛% due 5/1/18	102.75	10.81	5.93	45,750	0.4575
25,535	Southwestern Bell 11⅞%, due 10/18/21	110.75	10.68	4.30	28,890	0.2889
5,000	Capital Cities Broadcasting 11⅞% due 8/15/15	108.75	10.63	2.55	5,655	0.0566
					$100,000	

[a]For the GNMA issue, the YTM% is the DCF yield.

Risk-altering bond management

Risk-altering bond management, or interest rate anticipation, is a total return maximizing approach in which a portfolio's duration is adjusted in anticipation of a general movement in interest rates. An expectation of higher interest rates warrants a decrease in portfolio duration and an expectation of lower rates demands an increase in portfolio duration.

Exhibit 8-15 presents a set of contrasting portfolios: a portfolio of 2-year U.S. Treasury bonds (1.76 effective duration) and a portfolio of 30-year U.S. Treasury bonds (10.20 effective duration). The exhibit calculates the 6-month total returns of both portfolios under two alternative scenarios: a 200BP rise in interest rates and a 200BP fall in interest rates. A bearish investor would prefer the 2-year bond portfolio because the downside in a rising interest rate environment is minimal (1.93% return versus -12.71% return). A bullish investor would opt for the 30-year bond portfolio because the upside potential is maximized in long duration bonds (29.03% return versus 7.36% return).

Exhibit 8-15. The durations and total return behaviors of a low duration (2-year U.S. Treasury bond) portfolio and a high duration (30-year U.S. Treasury bond) portfolio. A 6-month holding period is assumed, with U.S. Treasury bond yields either rising 200BP or falling 200BP. (Calculations based on prices as of December 30, 1988).

		6-Month Total Return If Yields	
PORTFOLIO DESCRIPTION 1:	*Effective*		
2-Year U.S. Treasuries	*Duration*	*Rise 200BP*	*Fall 200BP*
U.S. Treasury 6⅞% due 12/31/90	1.76	1.93%	7.36%
PORTFOLIO 2: 30-Year U.S. Treasuries			
U.S. Treasury 9% due 11/15/18	10.20	–12.71%	29.03%

An interest rate anticipation strategy can be executed by swaps into high coupon bonds or low coupon bonds. Duration varies inversely with the coupon rate of interest. A premium bond has a lower duration than a discount bond of similar maturity. Anticipation of higher interest rates warrants swaps into higher coupon issues. For example, a swap from the U.S. Treasury 9% due 11/15/18 into the Texas Utilities Electric (TXU) 12% due 9/1/15 creates a 5.90 drop in effective duration (10.20 – 4.30 = 5.90). An "up-in-coupon" swap reduces a portfolio's average duration. Swaps into lower coupon bonds increase a portfolio's average duration and reflect a bullish market stance.

United States government guaranteed zero coupon bonds (STRIPS) can be used to carry out an interest rate anticipation strategy. They have maturities (and durations) as long as 30 years. A small quantity of long-term STRIPS can markedly increase a portfolio's duration. Assume that a $100 million portfolio has an effective duration of 5.00 years. If $20 million market value of 2-year U.S. Treasury bonds (6⅞% due 12/31/90; 1.76 effective duration) are swapped for $20 million market value of 30-year STRIPS (0% due 11/15/18; 28.63 effective duration), the portfolio's effective duration surges to 10.37 years (data as of December 30, 1988). The trade doubles the portfolio's duration by manipulating only 20% of the portfolio's value.

Interest-only (IO) strips can be used to lower a portfolio's duration because they carry negative effective durations. Assume that a $100 million portfolio bears a 5.00 effective duration. If a 20% position in 30-year U.S. Treasury bonds (9% due 11/15/18;

10.20 effective duration) is swapped for an IO strip with a −5.00 effective duration, the portfolio's effective duration falls to 1.96 years.

There are two primary advantages to this strategy. If the interest rate predictions are correct, the bond portfolio's principal is protected in a down market while the portfolio's capital appreciation potential is maximized in an up market. In addition, if the strategy is executed through the use of U.S. Treasury securities, transaction costs are minimal and credit risk and call risk are avoided.

The interest rate anticipation strategy has several drawbacks. First, portfolio turnover (and transaction costs) can be high. Second, a "wrong call" on interest rates can be costly. Predicting the future direction of interest rates has proved to be a difficult and frustrating endeavor, even for the most seasoned fixed-income professionals. Third, this strategy entails significant shifts in portfolio duration. The accompanying volatility in portfolio market value can be severe. As a result, risk-adjusted returns may be mediocre.[4]

Summary

Duration has important implications for a wide variety of bond portfolio management strategies, which are of two basic types: passive and active. Passive bond management strategies include cash flow matching, bond immunization, and bond indexation. A cash flow matching strategy involves constructing and maintaining a bond portfolio with cash flows that exactly match the cash flows of a set of future liabilities. A bond immunization strategy requires a bond portfolio with a duration that is identical to that of a liability stream. A bond indexation strategy entails creating and maintaining a bond portfolio with structural characteristics similar to those of a bond index. Sophisticated

---

[4] For a discussion of risk-adjusted returns, consult Chapter 11 ("Risk-Adjusted Return") of *Yield Curve Analysis: The Fundamentals of Risk and Return* (New York: New York Institute of Finance, 1988).

software packages, such as those offered by Capital Management Sciences, assist in this matching process.

Active bond management strategies come in two basic types: risk-controlled bond management and interest rate anticipation. These strategies satisfy investment objectives such as total return maximization, current income maximization, and yield maximization. Risk-controlled bond management techniques include sector rotation and security selection. Sector rotation involves concentrating portfolio holdings in market sectors that best achieve the portfolio's investment objective(s). Security selection entails choosing individual portfolio holdings with characteristics that help to meet the underlying objective(s) of the portfolio. The interest rate anticipation strategy makes purposeful adjustments to a portfolio's duration in anticipation of a general shift in market yields. Exhibit 8-16 summarizes the advantages and disadvantages of each of the bond management strategies discussed.

The Appendix of this chapter analyzes the impacts of bond swaps on the risk and return characteristics of a bond portfolio. The Appendix also presents the mechanics of bond swaps. This chapter concludes the duration part of the book. The second part of the book discusses the concept of convexity and applies it to both individual securities and portfolios of securities.

Exhibit 8–16. A summary of the advantages and disadvantages of a variety of passive bond management strategies and active bond management strategies.

PASSIVE MANAGEMENT STRATEGIES

		Advantages	*Disadvantages*
1.	Cash flow matching (or dedication)	Simple concept No interest rate risk No reinvestment rate risk Minimal maintenance requirements (no rebalancing or active swapping)	Can be costly to set up May be subject to credit risk or call risk (if non-U.S. Treasury securities are used to reduce the cost of the dedication) May be subject to market risk and/or reinvestment rate risk if a perfect cash flow match is not feasible Liability stream subject to change, creating a mismatch of asset and liability cash flows, and requiring a restructuring of the dedicated portfolio Liabilities with extended maturities (e.g., in excess of 30 years) can be difficult, if not impossible, to dedicate
2.	Bond immunization	Cheaper to implement than a cash flow match More flexibility in selecting securities (can take advantage of undervalued bonds or market sectors) Duration match protects the portfolio from general shifts in interest rates	Periodic rebalancings required to maintain the duration match Subject to some degree of interest rate risk and reinvestment rate risk May be subject to credit risk or call risk Liability stream subject to change, which requires additional rebalancing efforts Immunized portfolio not protected against nonparallel yield shifts Difficult to implement if the liability stream carries an average duration in excess of 10 years
3.	Bond indexation	Minimizes portfolio turnover and transaction costs Lower management fees than active management Predictable returns vis-à-vis the underlying bond index Portfolio well diversified Performance often superior to that of an average bond manager	Index may be difficult to replicate (and the sampling process is demanding) Rebalancing/reinvesting may be time-consuming and costly Setting up the portfolio can be costly Implementation and maintenance of an indexation strategy often requires advanced quantitative and statistical skills

Exhibit 8-16. (cont.)

ACTIVE MANAGEMENT STRATEGIES

		Advantages	*Disadvantages*
1.	Risk-controlled bond management	Portfolio risk is strictly controlled and monitored Active management can contribute to the achievement of the investment objective(s) without taking interest rate risk	Portfolio turnover and transaction costs can be high Poor judgment on relative values can detract from achieving the stated investment objective(s) The portfolio may be subject to call risk and/or credit risk
2.	Interest rate anticipation	If interest rate predictions are correct, portfolio principal is protected in a down market and portfolio appreciation is maximized in an up market If executed using U.S. Treasuries, transaction costs are minimal, and call risk and credit risk are avoided	Portfolio turnover and transaction costs can be high A "wrong call" on interest rates can be costly The volatility in portfolio value can be severe Typically involves significant shifts in portfolio duration Risk-adjusted returns may be mediocre

The Impacts and Mechanics
of Bond Swaps

The impact of a bond swap on a portfolio's risk and return structure

An interest rate anticipation swap alters a bond portfolio's risk (as assessed by the portfolio's duration) as follows:[1]

$$
\begin{array}{ccc}
\text{change in} & \text{change in} & \text{market} \\
\text{portfolio} \quad = & \text{security} \quad \times & \text{value} \\
\text{duration} & \text{duration} & \text{weighting}
\end{array}
$$

For example, assume that Bond A carries a 1.50 duration and accounts for 12% of the market value of a bond portfolio. If Bond A is swapped for Bond B, which bears a 10.00 duration, the portfolio's duration surges by 1.02 years:

---

[1] The duration measure may be Macaulay's duration, modified duration, or effective duration. It is critical that the security duration and the portfolio duration be of a comparable type. Under a risk-controlled bond investment strategy, there is no net change in portfolio duration because every swap is duration weighted.

$$\begin{array}{ll} \text{change in} \\ \text{portfolio} & = (10.00 - 1.50) \times 0.12 \\ \text{duration} \end{array}$$

$$= 8.50 \times 0.12$$

$$= 1.02$$

A bond swap that entails moving into a lower duration security reduces a portfolio's duration. The impact of a bond swap on portfolio duration is positively related to (1) the magnitude of the change in security duration and (2) the amount of portfolio dollars involved in the swap (i.e., the market value weighting).

A bond swap affects a bond portfolio's total return as follows:

$$\begin{array}{llll} \text{change in} & \text{change in} & & \text{market} \\ \text{portfolio} = & \text{security} & \times & \text{value} \\ \text{return} & \text{return} & & \text{weighting} \end{array}$$

For example, Bond B is expected to generate 300BP (i.e., 3%) more return than Bond A. If 10% of a portfolio is invested in Bond A, a swap into Bond B is expected to enhance the portfolio's return by 30BP:

$$\begin{array}{ll} \text{change in} \\ \text{portfolio} & = (+300BP) \times 0.10 \\ \text{return} \end{array}$$

$$= +30BP$$

The impact on a portfolio's return is positively related to (1) the magnitude of the difference in security returns and (2) the proportion of the portfolio involved in the trade.

The mechanics of duration-weighted bond swaps

A risk-controlled bond management strategy is executed through duration-weighted bond swaps. Duration-weighted swaps maintain the market risk of a portfolio while pursuing investment objectives such as maximizing yield, enhancing current income, or adding total return. Because the duration calculation is based on the market value of a security (or a portfolio of securities), duration-weighted swaps are proceeds trades that rely on market values as the weighting factors. Cash balances are often used to maintain duration equivalence. The successful implementation of a duration-weighted swap finds this equality:[2]

$$\begin{matrix} \text{duration of} \\ \text{"sell" bond} \end{matrix} = \begin{matrix} \text{duration of} \\ \text{"buy" bond} \end{matrix}$$

If more than one bond is sold (or purchased), the market value-weighted average duration of the "sell" bonds (or "buy" bonds) is used. Cash equivalents are considered as a "bond" with a zero duration.

For a duration-weighted swap, the weightings are calculated as follows:[3]

$$\begin{matrix} \text{long maturity} \\ \text{bond allocation} \\ (\%) \end{matrix} = \frac{\text{effective duration of the short maturity bond}}{\text{effective duration of the long maturity bond}} \times 100$$

$$\begin{matrix} \text{cash allocation} \\ (\%) \end{matrix} = 100\% - \text{long maturity bond allocation (\%)}$$

In the case of a duration-weighted maturity extension, a long maturity (i.e., high duration) bond is purchased with a fraction of the proceeds of the sale of a short maturity bond; the remaining balance is invested in cash equivalents. If a bond with a 3.00-year effective duration is sold to buy a bond with an 8.00-year effective duration, 37.50% (i.e., 3.00/8.00) of the sale proceeds

---

[2] The duration measure may be Macaulay's duration, modified duration, or effective duration. Effective duration is the preferred choice.

[3] For this formula, the long maturity bond is assumed to bear a longer duration than the short maturity issue. If this is not the case, then the ratio of the short duration to the long duration serves as the percentage allocation assigned to the long duration bond. A less accurate approach relies on modified durations, rather than effective durations, to derive the weightings.

is invested in the long duration bond and the balance is invested in cash equivalents. The percentages are applied to the market value of the bond(s) sold.

In the case of a duration-weighted maturity contraction, a short maturity (i.e., low duration) bond is purchased with the proceeds of two bonds: a long maturity bond and a cash equivalent. The funding of the short maturity bond purchase is made by using the same weightings as prescribed earlier. If a bond with an effective duration of 8.00 years is liquidated to buy a bond with an effective duration of 3.00 years, 37.50% (i.e., 3.00/8.00) of the purchase is funded with sales of the long maturity bond; the balance (62.50%) is financed with cash equivalents. The percentages are applied to the market value of the bond(s) to be purchased.

An alternative way to ensure duration neutrality in bond swaps is through the use of duration dollars. The duration dollars of the bond(s) sold must equal the duration dollars of the bond(s) purchased:

$$\begin{array}{c} \text{duration dollars} \\ \text{of bond(s) sold} \end{array} = \begin{array}{c} \text{duration dollars} \\ \text{of bond(s) purchased} \end{array}$$

Duration dollars are simply the product of a bond's effective duration and the bond's market value (in dollars).

For example, a $10 million (par value) bond selling at a full price of 82 carries 53.3 million duration dollars if the bond has a 6.50 effective duration:

$$\begin{array}{c} \text{duration dollars} \\ \text{for bond}_i \end{array} = \begin{array}{c} \text{effective duration} \\ \text{of bond}_i \end{array} \times \begin{array}{c} \text{market value} \\ \text{of bond}_i \end{array}$$

$$= 6.50 \times \$8,200,000$$

$$= 53,300,000$$

Any bond or combination of bonds purchased with the proceeds of this issue must offer exactly 53.3 million duration dollars to maintain duration equivalence.

For a combination (or a portfolio) of bonds, the total amount of duration dollars is calculated as:

$$\begin{array}{l}\text{duration dollars} \\ \text{for a combination} \\ \text{of bonds}\end{array} = \sum_{i=1}^{n} \left(\begin{array}{l}\text{effective} \\ \text{duration} \\ \text{of bond}_i\end{array} \times \begin{array}{l}\text{market} \\ \text{value} \\ \text{of bond}_i\end{array} \right)$$

where

n = the total number of bonds involved
i = the ith bond

A duration-weighted swap has no impact on the duration dollar position of a bond portfolio. The duration dollar concept is particularly helpful when a combination of bonds is involved in a duration-weighted swap. Market value percentage weightings can become cumbersome in such an analysis. Duration dollars avoid the necessity of such weightings and generate identical results.

PART II

Convexity

CHAPTER 9

The Concept of Convexity

Introduction

This chapter introduces convexity, a corollary to the duration concept discussed in Chapters 1 through 8. Chapter 10 elaborates on the convexity concept by analyzing the mathematics of convexity. Chapter 11 assesses the factors that affect convexity. Chapter 12 studies the concept of negative convexity, an element commonly found in callable corporate bonds and mortgage-backed securities. The chapter also discusses the factors that influence a callable bond's negative convexity. Chapter 13 analyzes portfolio convexity. Chapter 14 concludes this section of the book with a series of applications of convexity to bond portfolio management strategy.

The price:yield relationship

Bond prices and bond yields are inversely related.[1] That is, as interest rates rise, bond prices fall. Conversely, as interest rates

---

[1] The focus of this chapter is on noncallable bonds. The price:yield relationship for callable bonds is discussed in Chapter 12. Yield refers to yield to maturity.

fall, bond prices rise. The price:yield relationship appears as a cup-shaped curve (see Exhibit 9-1). Mathematically, modified duration is the first derivative of the price:yield function. *Convexity* is the second derivative of the price:yield. function; it is an expression of the rate of change in modified duration as yields shift. In more simple terms, modified duration is the slope of the price:yield curve at a specified point along the curve, and convexity is the gap between the modified duration tangent line and the price:yield curve.

Exhibit 9-1. The typical price:yield relationship for a noncallable bond.

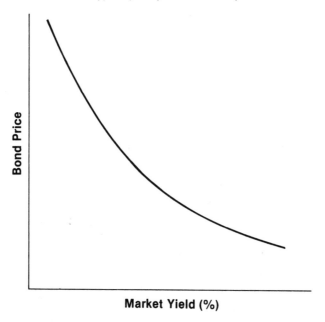

Market Yield (%)

Modified duration is a linear estimate of the nonlinear price:yield relationship. As illustrated in Chapter 5, modified duration can be used as a predictor of bond price change for a given movement in interest rates:

$$\begin{matrix}\text{percentage} \\ \text{change} \\ \text{in bond price}\end{matrix} = -\left(\begin{matrix}\text{modified} \\ \text{duration}\end{matrix}\right) \times \left(\frac{\text{basis point change in yield}}{100}\right)$$

Exhibit 9-2. The modified duration line is an estimate of the price:yield relationship.

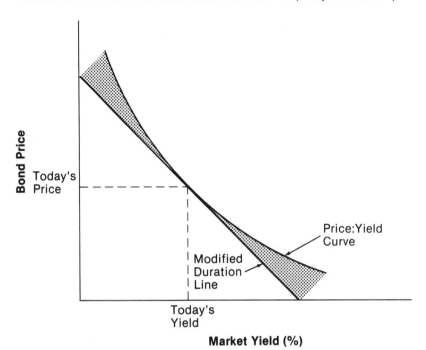

Graphically, modified duration plots a straight line that is tangent to the price:yield curve at a specific price:yield coordinate (see Exhibit 9-2).[2] The prediction error is shown as the shaded area between the modified duration line and the price:yield curve. Bond convexity accounts for this prediction error.

A simple definition of convexity

Convexity can be defined as the difference between the actual bond price and the bond price predicted by the modified duration

---

[2] Recall from Chapter 5 that, in actuality, the slope of such a price:yield curve is: − (modified duration) × the bond's current market price. The bond's price is a full price, including accrued interest.

line.[3] In percentage terms, convexity is the incremental price change not attributable to modified duration:

$$\text{convexity (in \$)} = \begin{array}{l}\text{actual bond} \\ \text{price}\end{array} - \begin{array}{l}\text{predicted bond} \\ \text{price}\end{array}$$

$$\text{convexity (in \%)} = \begin{array}{l}\text{actual \% change} \\ \text{in bond price}\end{array} - \begin{array}{l}\text{predicted \% change} \\ \text{in bond price}\end{array}$$

The term convexity arises from the fact that the price:yield curve is convex to the origin of the graph. This curvature creates the convexity effect.

An illustration of convexity (10-year bond)

Exhibit 9–3 calculates the actual price changes and the modified duration-predicted price changes for a 10-year U.S. Treasury bond over a wide range of yield shifts (±900BP). The "actual-predicted" differences are termed convexity. Notice that (1) all the convexities are positive values, (2) the convexity effect strengthens as the size of the yield change increases, and (3) the convexity effect is not the same for an identical rise and fall in yields (the "falling yields" scenario generates a greater degree of convexity).

For a 300BP decline in yield (to 6%), the 10-year U.S. Treasury bond's price surges 22.32% to 122.32, while the duration-predicted increase is only 19.53%:

---

[3] The higher order derivatives (third, fourth, etc.) of the price:yield function have been lumped into the definition of convexity. In actuality, the second derivative (i.e., convexity) accounts for most, but not all, of the observed price change that remains unexplained by the first derivative (i.e., modified duration). The residual impacts are small and detract from the understanding of the convexity concept. Consequently, theoretical perfection is sacrificed for the sake of brevity and simplicity. Chapter 10's Appendix presents the theoretical definition of convexity.

Convexity can also be defined as the difference between the actual price and the effective duration-predicted price. Later chapters will make this distinction. For a noncallable bond, modified duration and effective duration are synonymous.

$$\begin{array}{ll} \text{percentage change} \\ \text{in bond price} \end{array} = -\left(\begin{array}{l} \text{modified} \\ \text{duration} \end{array}\right) \times \left(\begin{array}{c} \text{basis point change in yield} \\ \hline 100 \end{array}\right)$$

$$= -6.51 \times \left(\frac{-300}{100}\right)$$

$$= -6.51 \times (-3)$$

$$= 19.53$$

There is a positive "surprise" (i.e., convexity) that allows the actual price change to outpace the predicted price change by 2.79%:

$$\begin{array}{ll} \text{convexity} \\ \text{(in \%)} \end{array} = \begin{array}{l} \text{actual percentage} \\ \text{change in bond price} \end{array} - \begin{array}{l} \text{predicted percentage} \\ \text{change in bond price} \end{array}$$

$$= 22.32\% - 19.53\%$$

$$= 2.79\%$$

Exhibit 9-3. The convexity of the U.S. Treasury 9% due 5/15/98 for a variety of yield changes. The bond is priced at par on May 15, 1988 and bears a modified duration of 6.51 years.

YTM (%)	Yield Change (in BP)	Bond Price	Percentage Change in Bond Price		Convexity (in %)
			Actual	*Predicted*	
0.0	−900	190.00	+90.00	+58.59	+31.41
1.0	−800	175.95	+75.95	+52.08	+23.87
2.0	−700	163.16	+63.16	+45.57	+17.59
3.0	−600	151.51	+51.51	+39.06	+12.45
4.0	−500	140.88	+40.88	+32.55	+ 8.33
5.0	−400	131.18	+31.18	+26.04	+ 5.14
6.0	−300	122.32	+22.32	+19.53	+ 2.79
7.0	−200	114.21	+14.21	+13.02	+ 1.19
8.0	−100	106.80	+ 6.80	+ 6.51	+ 0.29
8.9	− 10	100.65	+ 0.65	+ 0.65	0
9.0	0	100.00	0	0	0
9.1	+ 10	99.35	− 0.65	− 0.65	0
10.0	+100	93.77	− 6.23	− 6.51	+ 0.28
11.0	+200	88.05	−11.95	−13.02	+ 1.07
12.0	+300	82.80	−17.20	−19.53	+ 2.33
13.0	+400	77.96	−22.04	−26.04	+ 4.00
14.0	+500	73.51	−26.49	−32.55	+ 6.06
15.0	+600	69.42	−30.58	−39.06	+ 8.48
16.0	+700	65.64	−34.36	−45.57	+11.21
17.0	+800	62.15	−37.85	−52.08	+14.23
18.0	+900	58.92	−41.08	−58.59	+17.51

For a 300BP rise in interest rates (to 12%), the 10-year U.S. Treasury bond's price falls 17.20% to 82.80. The duration-predicted price decline is 19.53%:

$$\text{percentage change in bond price} = -6.51 \times \left(\frac{300}{100}\right)$$

$$= -6.51 \times 3$$

$$= -19.53$$

Modified duration underestimates the actual price by 2.33%:

$$\text{convexity (in \%)} = \text{actual percentage change in bond price} - \text{predicted percentage change in bond price}$$

$$= -17.20\% - (-19.53\%)$$

$$= -17.20\% + 19.53\%$$

$$= 2.33\%$$

Convexity enhances a bond's price performance in both bull and bear markets, albeit not in a uniform manner. Convexity is also called *positive convexity* because of its beneficial effects.

Exhibit 9-4 plots the actual and predicted price behavior of the 10-year U.S. Treasury bond used in prior illustrations. The actual price behavior is captured by the price:yield curve; the modified duration-predicted price behavior is represented by the tangent line. The positive convexity effects are indicated by the shaded area between the tangent line and the price:yield curve. Since the price:yield curve lies above the duration tangent line, the price effects of convexity must be positive.[4] The convexity effect becomes greater with larger changes in yield. Modified duration serves as a good estimate of the actual price:yield

---

[4] Chapter 12 deals with the realities of the negative surprises, or negative convexity, prevalent in callable bonds.

Exhibit 9-4. The actual and predicted price behavior of the U.S. Treasury 10-year bond (data from Exhibit 9-3).

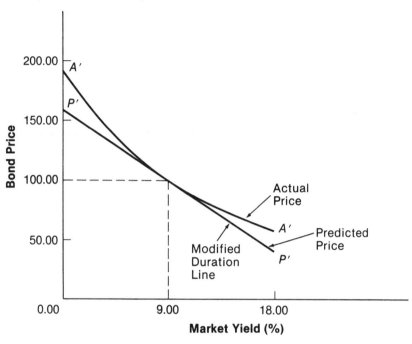

relationship for small changes in yield but loses its predictive accuracy when the yield fluctuates over a wider range.

An illustration of convexity (30-year bond)

Exhibit 9–5 calculates the convexity effects for a 30-year U.S. Treasury bond over a variety of yield changes. The 30-year U.S. Treasury bond has more convexity than the 10-year U.S. Treasury bond used in earlier examples. For example, a 300BP decline in yield creates a 10.36% convexity return (40.96% actual price change less the 30.60% predicted price change) for the 30-year bond versus only a 2.79% convexity return for the 10-year bond (22.32% actual price change less the 19.53% predicted price change). Graphically, this incremental convexity shows up as a more severe curvature in the price:yield relationship (see Exhibit 9–6). (Chapter 11

Exhibit 9-5. The convexity of the U.S. Treasury 9⅛% due 5/15/18 for a variety of yield changes. The bond is priced at par on May 15, 1988 and has a modified duration of 10.20 years.

YTM (%)	Yield Change (In BP)	Bond Price	Percentage Change in Bond Price		Convexity (in %)
			Actual	Predicted	
0.125	−900	364.92	+264.92	+91.80	+173.12
1.125	−800	303.22	+203.22	+81.60	+121.62
2.125	−700	254.69	+154.69	+71.40	+ 83.29
3.125	−600	216.26	+116.26	+61.20	+ 55.06
4.125	−500	185.60	+ 85.60	+51.00	+ 34.60
5.125	−400	160.95	+ 60.95	+40.80	+ 20.15
6.125	−300	140.96	+ 40.96	+30.60	+ 10.36
7.125	−200	124.63	+ 24.63	+20.40	+ 4.23
8.125	−100	111.18	+ 11.18	+10.20	+ 0.98
9.025	− 10	101.03	+ 1.03	+ 1.02	+ 0.01
9.125	0	100.00	0	0	0
9.225	+ 10	98.99	− 1.01	− 1.02	+ 0.01
10.125	+100	90.63	− 9.37	−10.20	+ 0.83
11.125	+200	82.72	−17.28	−20.40	+ 3.12
12.125	+300	75.98	−24.02	−30.60	+ 6.58
13.125	+400	70.20	−29.80	−40.80	+ 11.00
14.125	+500	65.19	−34.81	−51.00	+ 16.19
15.125	+600	60.83	−39.17	−61.20	+ 22.03
16.125	+700	57.00	−43.00	−71.40	+ 28.40
17.125	+800	53.62	−46.38	−81.60	+ 35.22
18.125	+900	50.62	−49.38	−91.80	+ 42.42

explains the rationale behind the greater convexity inherent in long duration bonds).

Convexity as a change in duration

Exhibit 9–7 summarizes the modified durations of the 10-year U.S. Treasury bond and the 30-year U.S. Treasury bond as interest rates fluctuate. The 10-year bond currently has a 6.50 modified duration; the 30-year bond currently claims a 10.20 modified duration.

Exhibit 9-6. The actual and predicted price behavior of the U.S. Treasury 30–year bond (data from Exhibit 9–5).

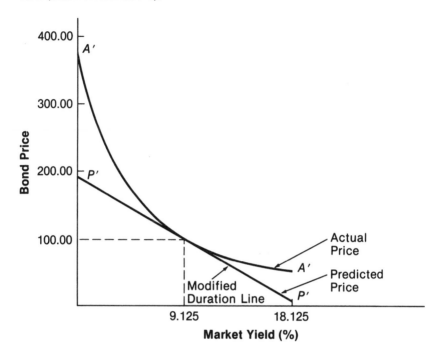

Exhibit 9-7. The duration behavior of a 10-year U.S. Treasury bond and a 30-year U.S. Treasury bond as yields change (issue data from Exhibits 9-4 and 9-5).

Yield Change (in BP)	Modified Duration of:	
	10-Year Bond	30-Year Bond
−400	7.06	13.35
−300	6.92	12.71
−200	6.78	11.86
−100	6.64	10.95
0	6.50	10.20
+100	6.36	9.43
+200	6.23	8.81
+300	6.08	8.16
+400	5.94	7.65

If yields fall 300BP, the 10-year bond's modified duration rises to 6.92 years and the 30-year bond's modified duration surges to 12.71 years. If yields rise 300BP, the 10-year bond's modified duration falls to 6.08 years while the 30-year bond's modified duration collapses to 8.16 years. The duration behavior of each of these bonds reflects duration's natural tendency to lengthen as yields fall and to shorten as yields rise. This phenomenon is magnified in long maturity issues.

If a bond's duration were constant at all levels of yield, convexity would not exist. The natural change in duration creates the convexity effect. This convexity effect is positive: A bond's duration lengthens in a bull market (thereby enhancing the price gains) and shortens in a bear market (thereby taming the price declines). Graphically, a bond's duration tangent line steepens as yields fall and flattens as yields rise.[5] In a world without convexity, the price:yield relationship is linear and is described by the bond's modified duration line, and duration is unaffected by fluctuations in market yield.

Summary

Convexity is the difference between a bond's actual price behavior and its duration-predicted price behavior. Graphically, convexity is the area between a bond's price:yield curve and its modified duration tangent line. Convexity can be expressed in either dollar terms or percentage terms. For a noncallable bond, convexity always has a positive effect; that is, the actual price exceeds the duration-predicted price. Chapter 10 delves into the mathematics of convexity. Chapter 11 follows with a discussion of the factors that affect convexity.

---

[5] These duration behaviors apply only to noncallable bonds. Callable bonds experience bouts of negative convexity, when duration changes in the same direction as interest rates, a most unpleasant phenomenon.

The Mathematics of Convexity

Introduction

This chapter expands on the basic calculations explained in Chapter 9 by introducing convexity factors and price volatility multipliers. It applies the mathematics of convexity to noncallable bonds, both actual and generic, and its Appendix discusses the more complex mathematics of convexity.

The concept of a convexity factor

Convexity can be observed through the curvature of the price:yield relationship away from the modified duration tangent line.[1] A table such as Exhibit 9-3 (see page 217) summarizes a bond's convexity effects for a variety of yield shifts. To allow comparability between securities, a standardized expression of convexity is

---

[1] This chapter's Appendix segregates the second-order derivative of the price:yield relationship from higher-order derivatives. For simplicity, impacts of the higher-order derivatives are incorporated into the convexity factor.

necessary. The convexity should be stated in the same units as modified duration such that the quantities are comparable. A combination of the two figures is then meaningful and can serve as a superior estimate of the price sensitivity of a bond. This is the rationale behind a convexity factor.

Exhibit 10-1 replicates the convexity calculations from Exhibit 9-3 for the 10-year U.S. Treasury bond. Exhibit 10-1 adds a column of convexity factors. Each convexity factor is derived as follows:

$$\frac{\text{convexity}}{\text{factor}} = \frac{\text{convexity (in \%)}}{\text{absolute BP change in yield} / 100}$$

For example, a 300BP decline in yield renders a 0.93 convexity factor for the 10-year U.S. Treasury bond:

$$\begin{aligned} \frac{\text{convexity}}{\text{factor}_{-300BP}} &= \frac{2.79}{\dfrac{300}{100}} \\[2ex] &= \frac{2.79}{3} \\[2ex] &= 0.93 \end{aligned}$$

For the same bond, a 500BP rise in yield leads to a 1.21 convexity factor:

$$\begin{aligned} \frac{\text{convexity}}{\text{factor}_{+500BP}} &= \frac{6.06}{\dfrac{500}{100}} \\[2ex] &= \frac{6.06}{5} \\[2ex] &= 1.21 \end{aligned}$$

Exhibit 10-1. The convexity of the U.S. Treasury 9% due 5/15/98 for a variety of yield changes. The bond is priced at par on May 15, 1988 and has a modified duration of 6.51 years.

YTM (%)	Yield Change (in BP)	Bond Price	Percentage Change in Bond Price		Convexity (in %)	Convexity Factor
			Actual	Predicted		
0.0	−900	190.00	+90.00	+58.59	+31.41	3.49
1.0	−800	175.95	+75.95	+52.08	+23.87	2.98
2.0	−700	163.16	+63.16	+45.57	+17.59	2.51
3.0	−600	151.51	+51.51	+39.06	+12.45	2.08
4.0	−500	140.88	+40.88	+32.55	+ 8.33	1.67
5.0	−400	131.18	+31.18	+26.04	+ 5.14	1.29
6.0	−300	122.32	+22.32	+19.53	+ 2.79	0.93
7.0	−200	114.21	+14.21	+13.02	+ 1.19	0.60
8.0	−100	106.80	+ 6.80	+ 6.51	+ 0.29	0.29
8.9	− 10	100.65	+ 0.65	+ 0.65	0	0
9.0	0	100.00	0	0	0	0
9.1	+ 10	99.35	− 0.65	− 0.65	0	0
10.0	+100	93.77	− 6.23	− 6.51	+ 0.28	0.28
11.0	+200	88.05	−11.95	−13.02	+ 1.07	0.54
12.0	+300	82.80	−17.20	−19.53	+ 2.33	0.78
13.0	+400	77.96	−22.04	−26.04	+ 4.00	1.00
14.0	+500	73.51	−26.49	−32.55	+ 6.06	1.21
15.0	+600	69.42	−30.58	−39.06	+ 8.48	1.41
16.0	+700	65.64	−34.36	−45.57	+11.21	1.60
17.0	+800	62.15	−37.85	−52.08	+14.23	1.78
18.0	+900	58.92	−41.08	−58.59	+17.51	1.95

Convexity factors are not uniform; they vary depending on the size and direction of the change in yield. Exhibit 10–2 calculates the convexity factors for the 30-year U.S. Treasury bond presented in Chapter 9.

Each convexity factor scales the actual convexity by presenting the convexity effect in a "per 100BP yield change" form, which allows for comparability between the convexity factors. For example, a 300BP yield decline creates a 3.45 convexity factor for the 30-year U.S. Treasury bond (Exhibit 10–2). A 500BP yield decline generates a 6.92 convexity factor for the same bond. The larger yield change doubles the convexity effect (6.92 factor versus 3.45 factor). Since the actual yield decline is 500BP (not 300BP), the percentage effect is more than twice as great (34.60% versus 10.36%). See Exhibit 10–2.

Exhibit 10-2. The convexity of the U.S. Treasury 9⅛% due 5/15/18 for a variety of yield changes. The bond is priced at par on May 15, 1988 and has a modified duration of 10.20 years.

YTM (%)	Yield Change (in BP)	Bond Price	Percentage Change in Bond Price		Convexity (in %)	Convexity Factor
			Actual	Predicted		
0.125	−900	364.92	+264.92	+91.80	+173.12	19.24
1.125	−800	303.22	+203.22	+81.60	+121.62	15.20
2.125	−700	254.69	+154.69	+71.40	+ 83.29	11.90
3.125	−600	216.26	+116.26	+61.20	+ 55.06	9.18
4.125	−500	185.60	+ 85.60	+51.00	+ 34.60	6.92
5.125	−400	160.95	+ 60.95	+40.80	+ 20.15	5.04
6.125	−300	140.96	+ 40.96	+30.60	+ 10.36	3.45
7.125	−200	124.63	+ 24.63	+20.40	+ 4.23	2.12
8.125	−100	111.18	+ 11.18	+10.20	+ 0.98	0.98
9.025	− 10	101.03	+ 1.03	+ 1.02	+ 0.01	0.10
9.125	0	100.00	0	0	0	0
9.225	+ 10	98.99	− 1.01	− 1.02	+ 0.01	0.10
10.125	+100	90.63	− 9.37	−10.20	+ 0.83	0.83
11.125	+200	82.72	− 17.28	−20.40	+ 3.12	1.56
12.125	+300	75.98	− 24.02	−30.60	+ 6.58	2.19
13.125	+400	70.20	− 29.80	−40.80	+ 11.00	2.75
14.125	+500	65.19	− 34.81	−51.00	+ 16.19	3.24
15.125	+600	60.83	− 39.17	−61.20	+ 22.03	3.67
16.125	+700	57.00	− 43.00	−71.40	+ 28.40	4.06
17.125	+800	53.62	− 46.38	−81.60	+ 35.22	4.40
18.125	+900	50.62	− 49.38	−91.80	+ 42.42	4.71

There are three methods for arriving at a representative convexity factor for a given bond:

1. Use the convexity factor for a specific yield change (e.g., −100BP).

2. Calculate an average convexity factor for an absolute yield change (e.g., ±300BP).

3. Derive a weighted average convexity factor for a series of yield changes based on an assessment of the likelihood of various yield shifts. A brief discussion of each of these methods follows.

Choosing a single convexity factor

If a 200BP rise in interest rates is expected, the 30-year U.S. Treasury bond deserves a convexity of 1.56 (Exhibit 10-2). The identical 200BP rise in yields renders a 0.54 convexity to the 10-year U.S. Treasury bond (Exhibit 10-1). For consistent comparisons, the forecasted change in interest rates must be the same across all securities.[2] If the interest rate forecast proves incorrect, then the convexity impacts will not be as anticipated.[3]

> Using an average convexity factor
> for a given magnitude
> of change in interest rate

If interest rates are expected to fluctuate in a ±300BP range, the convexity of the 30-year U.S. Treasury bond is assessed at 2.82 (Exhibit 10-2):

$$\text{convexity} = \frac{\begin{array}{c}\text{convexity factor} \\ \text{(yields fall 300BP)}\end{array} + \begin{array}{c}\text{convexity factor} \\ \text{(yields rise 300BP)}\end{array}}{2}$$

$$= \frac{(3.45 + 2.19)}{2}$$

$$= \frac{5.64}{2}$$

$$= 2.82$$

Thus, convexity is a function of the magnitude of the yield change. The direction of the yield change is not predicted; therefore, a simple average of the up and down scenarios serves as the convexity representation.

The convexity effects in up and down markets are not identical. A decline in yields creates stronger convexity impacts

---

[2] Nonparallel yield shifts (i.e., changes in yield spread) can be incorporated into the convexity factor derivations if a nonuniform yield change is anticipated rather than a parallel yield shift.

[3] In addition, the duration effects will not be as expected.

than does an equivalent rise in yields. Exhibit 10–3 illustrates this phenomenon graphically for the 10-year U.S. Treasury bond. Exhibit 10–4 reveals that convexity effects are not only greater for long maturity bonds but are even more nonsymmetric.

Exhibit 10-3. The convexity of a 10-year U.S. Treasury bond over a variety of yield changes (data from Exhibit 10-1).

(a) On a Percentage Basis

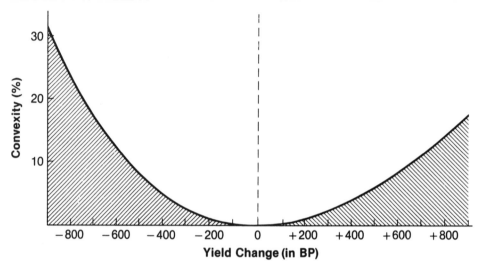

(b) Using Convexity Factors

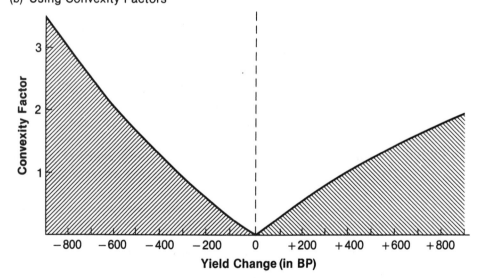

This graph plots the convexity data for the 30-year U.S. Treasury bond of previous illustrations.

Exhibit 10-4. The convexity of a 30-year U.S. Treasury bond over a variety of yield changes (data from Exhibit 10-2).

(a) On a Percentage Basis

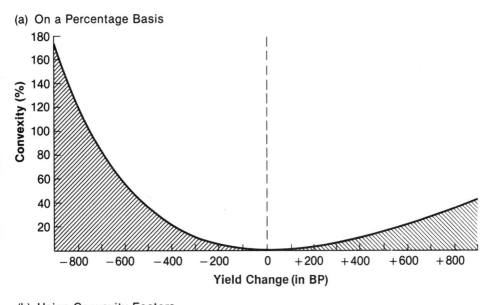

(b) Using Convexity Factors

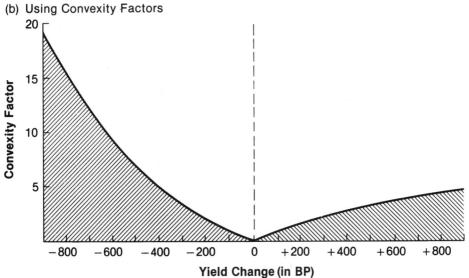

Consequently, an averaging of two convexity factors (one for an up market and one for a down market) introduces some degree of inaccuracy because the eventual outcome can be either higher or lower interest rates but not both. This error becomes greater the larger the yield change and the longer the duration of the bond under examination.

Using a probability-weighted average convexity factor

With this approach, probabilities are assigned to a series of potential interest rate changes. The probabilities, as expressed in decimal form, must add up to 1.00. A weighted average convexity figure is derived by using these subjective probabilities. For example, if U.S. Treasury bond yields currently average approximately 9%, a bullish investor might assess the future interest rate environment as follows:

Yield Level (in %)	BP Change from Current Level	Subjective Probability
5	-400	0.10
6	-300	0.20
7	-200	0.25
8	-100	0.20
9	0	0.20
10	+100	0.10
11	+200	0.05
		1.00

The 10-year U.S. Treasury bond of previous illustrations has a weighted average convexity of 0.58 (data from Exhibit 10–1):

(1) BP Yield Change from Current Level	(2) Convexity Factor	(3) Subjective Probability	(4) = (2) × 3) Weights
-400	1.29	0.10	0.129
-300	0.93	0.20	0.186
-200	0.60	0.25	0.150
-100	0.29	0.20	0.058
0	0.00	0.20	0.000
+100	0.28	0.10	0.028
+200	0.54	0.05	0.027
		Weighted average convexity =	0.580

The formula for calculating a weighted average convexity factor can be generalized as follows:

$$\begin{array}{c} \text{weighted average} \\ \text{convexity} \end{array} = \sum_{i=1}^{N} \left(\begin{array}{c} \text{convexity} \\ \text{factor}_i \end{array} \times P_i \right)$$

where

convexity factor $_i$ = the convexity factor corresponding to the ith interest rate scenario

P_i = the subjective probability assigned to the ith interest rate scenario (expressed in decimal form)

N = the number of interest rate scenarios under consideration

Forthcoming illustrations use the second approach (an average convexity factor for $\pm x$BP). The first approach is too dependent on market direction, and the third approach is too subjective.

The convexity of U.S. Treasury Bonds

Generic issues

Exhibits 10–5 through 10–8 derive the convexity factors for a series of U.S. Treasury bonds priced in a 7% yield environment: a 3-year U.S. Treasury bond (Exhibit 10–5), a 10-year U.S. Treasury bond (Exhibit 10–6), a 30-year U.S. Treasury bond (Exhibit 10–7), and a 30-year STRIPS (Exhibit 10–8). Under a ±100BP yield volatility assumption, the convexities of the bonds are as follows:

Issue	Convexity [a]
3-year bond	0.05
10-year bond	0.32
30-year bond	1.27
30-year STRIPS	4.34

[a]An average of the convexity factor for "+100BP yield change" and the convexity factor for "−100BP yield change."

Long duration bonds offer more convexity than short duration issues.

Exhibit 10-5. The convexity of the 3-year, 7% coupon U.S. Treasury bond priced at par in a 7% yield environment. The bond has a modified duration of 2.66 years.

YTM (%)	Yield Change (in BP)	Bond Price	Percentage Change in Bond Price		Convexity (in %)	Convexity Factor
			Actual	Predicted		
3	−400	111.39	+11.39	+10.64	+0.75	0.19
4	−300	108.40	+ 8.40	+ 7.98	+0.42	0.14
5	−200	105.51	+ 5.51	+ 5.32	+0.19	0.10
6	−100	102.71	+ 2.71	+ 2.66	+0.05	0.05
7	0	100.00	0	0	0	0
8	+100	97.38	− 2.62	− 2.66	+0.04	0.04
9	+200	94.84	− 5.16	− 5.32	+0.16	0.08
10	+300	92.39	− 7.61	− 7.98	+0.37	0.12
11	+400	90.01	− 9.99	−10.64	+0.65	0.16

Exhibit 10-6. The convexity of the 10-year, 7% coupon U.S. Treasury bond priced at par in a 7% yield environment. The bond has a modified duration of 7.11 years.

YTM (%)	Yield Change (in BP)	Bond Price	Percentage Change in Bond Price		Convexity (in %)	Convexity Factor
			Actual	Predicted		
3	−400	134.34	+34.34	+28.44	+5.90	1.48
4	−300	124.53	+24.53	+21.33	+3.20	1.07
5	−200	115.59	+15.59	+14.22	+1.37	0.69
6	−100	107.44	+ 7.44	+ 7.11	+0.33	0.33
7	0	100.00	0	0	0	0
8	+100	93.20	− 6.80	− 7.11	+0.31	0.31
9	+200	86.99	−13.01	−14.22	+1.21	0.61
10	+300	81.31	−18.69	−21.33	+2.64	0.88
11	+400	76.10	−23.90	−28.44	+4.54	1.14

Exhibit 10-7. The convexity of a 30-year, 7% coupon U.S. Treasury bond priced at par in a 7% yield environment. The bond has a modified duration of 12.47 years.

YTM (%)	Yield Change (in BP)	Bond Price	Percentage Change in Bond Price		Convexity (in %)	Convexity Factor
			Actual	Predicted		
3	−400	178.76	+78.76	+49.88	+28.88	7.22
4	−300	152.14	+52.14	+37.41	+14.73	4.91
5	−200	130.91	+30.91	+24.94	+ 5.97	2.99
6	−100	113.84	+13.84	+12.47	+ 1.37	1.37
7	0	100.00	0	0	0	0
8	+100	88.69	−11.31	−12.47	+ 1.16	1.16
9	+200	79.36	−20.64	−24.94	+ 4.30	2.15
10	+300	71.61	−28.39	−37.41	+ 9.02	3.01
11	+400	65.10	−34.90	−49.88	+14.98	3.75

Under a ±300BP yield volatility assumption, the convexities of the bonds increase as follows:

Issue	Convexity [a]
3-year U.S. Treasury	0.13
10-year U.S. Treasury	0.98
30-year U.S. Treasury	3.96
30-year STRIPS	13.73

[a]An average of the convexity factor for "+300BP yield change" and the convexity factor for "−300BP yield change."

Exhibit 10-8. The convexity of a 30-year STRIPS priced to yield 7% to maturity. The bond has a modified duration of 28.99 years.

YTM (%)	Yield Change (in BP)	Bond Price	Percentage Change in Bond Price		Convexity (in %)	Convexity Factor
			Actual	Predicted		
3	−400	40.93	+222.54	+115.96	+106.58	26.65
4	−300	30.48	+140.19	+ 86.97	+ 53.22	17.74
5	−200	22.73	+ 79.12	+ 57.98	+ 21.14	10.57
6	−100	16.97	+ 33.73	+ 28.99	+ 4.74	4.74
7	0	12.69	0	0	0	0
8	+100	9.51	− 25.06	− 28.99	+ 3.93	3.93
9	+200	7.13	− 43.81	− 57.98	+ 14.17	7.09
10	+300	5.35	− 57.84	− 86.97	+ 29.13	9.71
11	+400	4.03	− 68.24	−115.96	+ 47.72	11.93

The positive relationship between duration and convexity strengthens as yield volatility increases. For example, when compared to the convexities generated with a 100BP yield shift, the convexities for a 300BP yield shift are 160% greater for the 3-year bond (0.13 versus 0.05) and 212% larger for the 30-year bond (3.96 versus 1.27). (Chapter 11 elaborates on this duration: convexity relationship.)

Actual issues

Exhibit 10–9 presents the convexities of a series of U.S. Treasury bonds priced as of May 15, 1988 (assuming a 300BP yield shift). The longer the duration, the higher the convexity. The 1-year bond has virtually no convexity (0.02). The 7-year issue offers a 0.48 convexity and the 15-year bond earns a 1.36 convexity, which is almost triple that of the 7-year bond. The 30-year bonds generate convexities in the 2.38 to 2.85 range, and the long-term (20-year) zero coupon bond has a 5.78 convexity.

Exhibit 10–9. Convexities of a series of U.S. Treasury bonds as of May 15, 1988. A 300BP change in yield is assumed in the calculation of the convexity figures.

Issue Description	*Maturity Sector*	*Modified Duration*	*Convexity Factor*
U.S. Treasury 6⅞% due 5/15/89	1 year	0.94	0.02
U.S. Treasury 8 ⅛% due 5/15/91	3 years	2.61	0.13
U.S. Treasury 11¼% due 5/15/95	7 years	4.93	0.48
U.S. Treasury 9% due 5/15/98	10 years	6.51	0.86
U.S. Treasury 10¾% due 5/15/03	15 years	7.78	1.36
U.S. Treasury 11¼% due 2/15/15	30 years	9.41	2.38
U.S. Treasury 7¼% due 5/15/16	30 years	10.35	2.85
U.S. Treasury 9⅛% due 5/15/18	30 years	10.20	2.82
STRIPS 0% due 5/15/93	5 years	4.79	0.38
STRIPS 0% due 5/15/98	10 years	9.55	1.45
STRIPS 0% due 5/15/08	20 years	19.09	5.78

The convexity of noncallable corporate and federal agency bonds

Generic issues

Exhibits 10–10 through 10–13 summarize the convexities of a 3-year corporate bond, a 10-year corporate bond, a 30-year corporate bond, and a 30-year federal agency zero coupon bond. In each case, the bond is noncallable for life. A 7% U.S. Treasury yield environment is assumed to allow comparisons to the generic U.S. Treasury bonds shown earlier in Exhibits 10–5 through 10–8. The corporate bonds bear 8% coupons and are priced at par to yield 8% to maturity, a 100BP yield spread over comparable U.S. Treasury bonds. The 30-year federal agency STRIP is priced to yield 7.50%, a 50BP yield spread over a 30-year U.S. Treasury STRIPS.

Exhibit 10-10. The convexity of a 3-year, 8% coupon, noncallable corporate bond priced at par in a 7% U.S. Treasury yield environment (+100BP yield spread). The bond has a modified duration of 2.63 years. The 100BP yield spread is held constant as market yields shift.

Market Yield Change (in BP)	Bond Price	Percentage Change in Bond Price		Convexity (in %)	Convexity Factor
		Actual	*Predicted*		
−400	111.20	+11.20	+10.52	+0.68	0.17
−300	108.26	+ 8.26	+ 7.89	+0.37	0.12
−200	105.42	+ 5.42	+ 5.26	+0.16	0.08
−100	102.66	+ 2.66	+ 2.63	+0.03	0.03
0	100.00	0	0	0	0
+100	97.42	− 2.58	− 2.63	+0.05	0.05
+200	94.92	− 5.08	− 5.26	+0.18	0.09
+300	92.51	− 7.49	− 7.89	+0.40	0.13
+400	90.17	− 9.83	−10.52	+0.69	0.17

Using a 300BP yield volatility assumption, the convexities of the bonds are as follows:

Issue	Convexity [a]
3-year corporate	0.13
10-year corporate	0.91
30-year corporate	3.37
30-year federal agency strip	13.65

[a]An average of the convexity factor for "+300BP yield change" and the convexity factor for "−300BP yield change"

Once again, the long duration bonds have larger convexities than the short duration bonds. For a given U.S. Treasury yield environment (in this case, 7%), non-U.S. Treasury securities (such as federal agency bonds and corporate bonds) have lower durations than do their U.S. Treasury counterparts.

Maturity Sector	Modified Duration of:	
	U.S. Treasury	Corporate
3 years	2.66	2.63
10 years	7.11	6.80
30 years	12.47	11.31

As a result, the convexities of non-U.S. Treasury securities are generally lower than their U.S. Treasury counterparts:

Maturity Sector	Convexity of: [a]	
	U.S. Treasury	Corporate
3 years	0.13	0.13
10 years	0.98	0.91
30 years	3.96	3.37

[a] An average of the convexity factor for "+300BP yield change" and the convexity factor for "−300BP yield change."

This is an important consideration when comparing U.S. Treasuries to alternative investments. Convexity differences become even more critical when comparing noncallable U.S. Treasury bonds to callable corporate bonds and prepayable mortgage-backed securities, a subject that is addressed in Chapter 12.[4]

Exhibit 10–11. The convexity of a 10-year, 8% coupon, noncallable corporate bond priced at par in a 7% U.S. Treasury yield environment (+100BP yield spread). The bond has a modified duration of 6.80 years. The +100BP yield spread is held constant as market yields shift.

Market Yield Change (in BP)	Bond Price	Percentage Change in Bond Price		Convexity (in %)	Convexity Factor
		Actual	*Predicted*		
–400	132.70	+32.70	+27.20	+ 5.50	1.38
–300	123.38	+23.38	+20.40	+ 2.98	0.99
–200	114.88	+14.88	+13.60	+ 1.28	0.64
–100	107.11	+ 7.11	+ 6.80	+ 0.31	0.31
0	100.00	0	0	0	0
+100	93.50	– 6.50	– 6.80	+ 0.30	0.30
+200	87.54	–12.46	–13.60	+ 1.14	0.57
+300	82.07	–17.93	–20.40	+ 2.47	0.82
+400	77.06	–22.94	–27.20	+ 4.26	1.07

Exhibit 10–12. The convexity of a 30-year, 8% coupon noncallable corporate bond priced at par in a 7% U.S. Treasury yield environment (+100BP yield spread). The bond has a modified duration of 11.31 years. The +100BP yield spread is held constant as market yields shift.

Market Yield Change (in BP)	Bond Price	Percentage Change in Bond Price		Convexity (in %)	Convexity Factor
		Actual	*Predicted*		
–400	169.52	+69.52	+45.24	+24.28	6.07
–300	146.36	+46.36	+33.93	+12.43	4.14
–200	127.68	+27.68	+22.62	+ 5.06	2.53
–100	112.47	+12.47	+11.31	+ 1.16	1.16
0	100.00	0	0	0	0

[4]The differences may imply a consistent superiority of U.S. Treasury bonds vis-à-vis non-Treasury investment alternatives. This implication is not intended. In the comparison of investments, convexity features are only one consideration. Yield differences, anticipated changes in yield spread, and convexity behaviors in an up market versus a down market are important factors to assess in evaluating alternative investments. This book focuses on the duration and convexity characteristics of fixed-income securities. You are encouraged to consult Chapter 8 ("Total Return and Realized Compound Yield") and Chapter 14 ("Bond Swaps") of *Yield Curve Analysis: The Fundamentals of Risk and Return (New York: New York Institute of Finance, 1988)* for additional insights on the evaluation of potential investments.

Exhibit 10–12. (cont.)

Market Yield Change (in BP)	Bond Price	Percentage Change in Bond Price		Convexity (in %)	Convexity Factor
		Actual	*Predicted*		
0	100.00	0	0	0	0
+100	89.68	−10.32	−11.31	+ 0.99	0.99
+200	81.07	−18.93	−22.62	+ 3.69	1.85
+300	73.83	−26.17	−33.93	+ 7.76	2.59
+400	67.68	−32.32	−45.24	+12.92	3.23

Exhibit 10–13. The convexity of a 30-year federal agency zero-coupon bond priced to yield 7.50% to maturity in an environment of 7% STRIPS yields (+50BP yield spread). The bond has a modified duration of 28.92 years. The +50BP yield spread is held constant as market yields shift.

Market Yield Change (in BP)	Bond Price	Percentage Change in Bond Price		Convexity (in %)	Convexity Factor
		Actual	*Predicted*		
−400	35.31	+221.58	+115.68	+105.90	26.48
−300	26.31	+139.62	+ 86.76	+ 52.86	17.62
−200	19.64	+ 78.87	+ 57.84	+ 21.03	10.52
−100	14.68	+ 33.65	+ 28.92	+ 4.73	4.73
0	10.98	0	0	0	0
+100	8.23	− 25.05	− 28.92	+ 3.87	3.87
+200	6.18	− 43.72	− 57.84	+ 14.12	7.06
+300	4.64	− 57.74	− 86.76	+ 29.02	9.67
+400	3.49	− 68.21	−115.68	+ 47.47	11.87

Actual issues

Exhibit 10–14 presents the convexities of a series of noncallable federal agency bonds and noncallable corporate bonds priced as of May 15, 1988. Comparisons can be made to the U.S. Treasury bonds of Exhibit 10–9. The positive correlation between duration and convexity is again evident. The World Bank 9⅞% due 10/1/97 offers a 0.74 convexity. The Atlantic Richfield Company, 10⅞% due 7/15/05 provides almost twice the convexity (1.46 factor). The long maturity Canadian yankee bond (Province of Quebec 8⅝% due 12/1/26) has a sizable 2.79 convexity when compared to the short maturity issues.

Exhibit 10-14. Convexities of a sample of noncallable federal agency bonds and noncallable corporate bonds as of May 15, 1988. A 300BP change in yield (with a constant yield spread to U.S. Treasuries) is assumed in the convexity calculations.

Issue Description	Price	YTM (%)	Yield Spread[a]	Modified Duration	Convexity Factor
World Bank 9⅞% due 10/1/97	102.25	9.50	+ 50BP	6.00	0.74
Atlantic Richfield Company 10⅞% due 7/15/05	107.50	9.95	+ 75BP	7.76	1.46
Atlantic Richfield Company 9⅞% due 3/1/16	99.25	9.95	+ 75BP	9.20	2.33
Financing Corporation 9.40% due 2/8/18	92-17	10.20	+100BP	9.14	2.38
Fed. Nat. Mortgage Assoc. 8.95% due 2/12/18	90-29	9.90	+ 70BP	9.42	2.51
Province of Quebec 8⅝% due 12/1/26	87.00	9.95	+ 75BP	9.49	2.79

[a]The yield spreads are based on the U.S. Treasury 9% due 5/15/98 (9% YTM) and the U.S. Treasury 8⅞% due 8/15/17 (9.20% YTM). The World Bank issue is spread off the former, and the remaining issues are spread off the latter. Spreads reflect bid-side price quotes as of May 15, 1988.

The advantages and limitations of convexity factors

A convexity factor is useful in several respects. It provides a consistent, standardized way of assessing a bond's convexity features. This in turn allows for comparability between various issues. It can also be viewed as an accompaniment to the duration effect. A combination of the bond's modified duration and its convexity factor provides a better predictor of the bond's price:yield behavior than duration alone.[5] In addition, a weighted average of a bond's potential convexity factors can be tailored to an

---

[5] In graphic terms, this combination plots a straight line that cuts through the price:yield curve. As a result, the prediction errors are less than those from the use of a modified duration tangent line. This is true only if the yield volatility assumption is reasonably accurate.

investor's expectations regarding future interest rate direction and volatility.

Convexity factors also have limitations. First, a bond's convexity is influenced by the magnitude and direction of yield change. Any misjudgments on these variables introduces error into the convexity factor. Second, an averaging of convexity factors introduces a degree of error because the nonsymmetric nature of convexity plays a role. Despite these limitations, however, a consistent application of convexity factors does highlight the underlying return biases of a bond. These biases are not captured by modified duration.

The concept of a price volatility multiplier

Modified duration is typically used as a proxy for a bond's price sensitivity to changes in interest rates. Recall the duration:price connection:

$$\text{percentage change in bond price} = -\left(\text{modified duration}\right) \times \left(\frac{\text{BP change in yield}}{100}\right)$$

For example, a bond with a modified duration of 7.00 is expected to fluctuate by 7% in value for every 100BP shift in interest rates. In actuality, however, the price:yield connection is nonlinear, and therefore there is some degree of error in relying on the bond's modified duration as the sole influence on the bond's price behavior. Incorporating the bond's convexity into the equation allows for a better estimate of the actual price behavior:

$$\text{percentage change in bond price} = \left[-\left(\text{modified duration}\right) \times \left(\frac{\text{BP change in yield}}{100}\right)\right] +$$

duration
multiplier

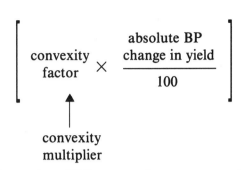

$$\left[\text{convexity factor} \times \frac{\text{absolute BP change in yield}}{100} \right]$$

↑

convexity
multiplier

A bond's price is, in essence, influenced by two multipliers: duration and convexity. The convexity influence is positive, regardless of the direction of the yield change. A bond with a modified duration of 7.00 and a convexity of 2.00 is expected to experience a 9% increase in price for every 100BP fall in yield and a 5% decrease in price for every 100BP rise in yield.

The duration and convexity effects can be combined to form a price volatility multiplier (PVM). Price volatility multipliers are derived as follows:

Falling yield environment:

$$\text{PVM} = \frac{\text{modified}}{\text{duration}} + \frac{\text{convexity}}{\text{factor}}$$

Rising yield environment:

$$\text{PVM} = \frac{\text{modified}}{\text{duration}} - \frac{\text{convexity}}{\text{factor}}$$

Convexity enhances a bond's price behavior in both bull and bear markets. In a bull market, the price volatility is increased by the convexity factor, which allows for greater-than-expected price gains. In a bear market, the price volatility is reduced by the convexity influence thereby resulting in less-than-expected price losses.[6] The effects of duration and convexity are typically

---

[6] The terms *price sensitivity* and *price volatility* are used interchangeably.

expressed as distinct quantities. A PVM is useful in that it condenses the inherent volatility of a bond investment into a single figure.

Summary

Convexity is the difference between a bond's price change and its duration-predicted price change. A convexity factor adjusts this absolute convexity for the magnitude of the market yield shift. By expressing duration in a "per 100BP yield change" form, a convexity factor is stated in the same units as modified duration. A price volatility multiplier combines a bond's duration and convexity statistics to form a better proxy for the bond's price sensitivity.

A bond has a series of convexity factors, one for each BP change in market yield. The bond's representative convexity factor can be a single convexity factor, an average convexity factor for a specific amount of yield change, or a probability-weighted average convexity factor.

The chapter illustrations support several conclusions regarding convexity. First, bonds of long duration offer more convexity than those of short duration. Second, a larger change in market yield elicits additional convexity. Third, convexity effects are not symmetric: A decline in yield creates a larger convexity than an identical rise in yield. Finally, noncallable federal agency and corporate bonds have less convexity than noncallable U.S. Treasury bonds of similar maturity. The chapter Appendix presents the mathematics of convexity and the price:yield function. Chapter 11 analyzes the factors that influence convexity.

Convexity and the Price:Yield Function

The mathematics of the price:yield function

The price:yield relationship is nonlinear by nature. Graphically, the price:yield function plots a smooth curve rather than a straight line. This function can be analyzed as a Taylor series of derivatives:

$$\Delta P = \left[\frac{dP}{dY}(\Delta Y) \right] + \left[\frac{1}{2!} \cdot \frac{d^2P}{dY^2}(\Delta Y)^2 \right] +$$

$$\left[\frac{1}{3!} \cdot \frac{d^3P}{dY^3}(\Delta Y)^3 \right] + \cdots + \left[\frac{1}{n!} \cdot \frac{d^nP}{dY^n}(\Delta Y)^n \right] (1)$$

Modified duration and convexity are defined as follows:

$$\text{modified duration} = \frac{dP/dY}{P} \tag{2}$$

$$\text{convexity} = \frac{d^2P/dY^2}{P} \tag{3}$$

Dividing each of the terms in Equation (1) by the bond price (P) renders:

$$\frac{\Delta P}{P} = \left[\frac{dP}{dY} \cdot \frac{1}{P}(\Delta Y) \right] + \left[\frac{1}{2} \cdot \frac{d^2P}{dY^2} \cdot \frac{1}{P}(\Delta Y)^2 \right] +$$

$$\left[\frac{1}{6} \cdot \frac{d^3P}{dY^3} \cdot \frac{1}{P}(\Delta Y)^3 \right] + \cdots + \left[\frac{1}{n!} \cdot \frac{d^nP}{dY^n} \cdot \frac{1}{P}(\Delta Y)^n \right] \tag{4}$$

In general:

$$\frac{\Delta P}{P} = -C_1(\Delta Y) + \frac{1}{2}C_2(DY)^2 - \frac{1}{6}C_3(DY)^3 +$$

$$\cdots + \frac{1}{n!}C_n(\Delta Y)^n \tag{5}$$

where C_1, C_2, ... C_n are the coefficients to the terms of the equation.

Using the definitions of modified duration and convexity from Equations (2) and (3):

$$\frac{\Delta P}{P} = - \left(\begin{array}{c} \text{modified} \\ \text{duration} \end{array} \right)(\Delta Y) + \frac{1}{2} \cdot \text{convexity}\,(\Delta Y)^2 + \text{residual effect} \tag{6}$$

where the third-, fourth-, and higher-order derivatives are lumped into the residual effect. Generally speaking, the residual effect is not significant.

More simply, modified duration is the first derivative of price with respect to yield, divided by the price. Convexity is the second derivative divided by the price. As the second derivative, convexity measures the rate of change in the first derivative (modified duration). Insofar as modified duration is expressed in number of years, convexity is expressed in squared years.

Estimating the price:yield relationship

The impact of yield change is often roughly estimated by using the modified duration variable:

$$\frac{\text{price change}}{\text{(in \%)}} = - \left(\begin{array}{c} \text{modified} \\ \text{duration} \end{array} \right) (\Delta Y) \qquad (7)$$

A more advanced version incorporates the convexity effect:

$$\frac{\text{price change}}{\text{(in \%)}} = - \left(\begin{array}{c} \text{modified} \\ \text{duration} \end{array} \right) (\Delta Y) + \frac{1}{2} \cdot \text{convexity} \ (\Delta Y)^2 \quad (8)$$

The residual effects are typically ignored.

Convexity is defined as the bond price action that is not attributable to the bond's modified duration. As such, the convexity figure is comparable to a modified duration and is expressed in number of years. Modified duration and convexity combine to form a price volatility multiplier, an attempt to better linearize the price:yield function.

CHAPTER 11

The Factors That Influence Convexity

Introduction

This chapter identifies the primary factors that influence a bond's convexity: duration, cash flow distribution, market yield volatility, and the direction of yield change. Generic examples highlight the importance of each specific factor. The chapter focuses on the convexity of noncallable bonds and compares the convexities of noncallable U.S. Treasury bonds and noncallable corporate bonds. The chapter Appendix analyzes the convexity of zero coupon bonds.

Duration

Convexity is positively related to the duration of the underlying bond. Long duration bonds carry higher convexities than do issues of short duration. Exhibit 11-1 plots the price:yield curves for 7% coupon U.S. Treasury bonds of 3-year, 10-year, and 30-year maturities. Graphically, the price:yield function is more cup-shaped

Exhibit 11-1. Price:yield curves for 3-, 10-, and 30-year U.S. Treasury bonds carrying 7% coupons and priced at par to yield 7% to maturity.

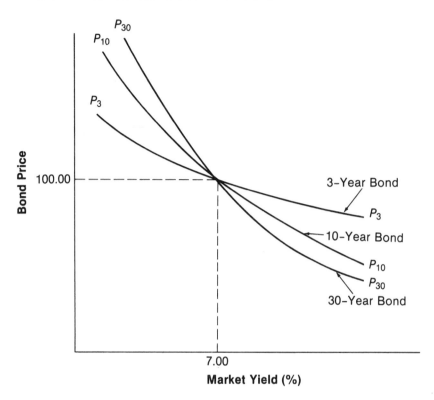

for high duration issues. The 30-year bond has superior convexity over the shorter duration 3-year and 10-year issues.

Exhibits 11–2, 11–3, and 11–4 calculate the convexities of the 3-year bond, the 10-year bond, and the 30-year bond, respectively, for yield shifts of up to 400 basis points. For a given change in yield, a higher duration bond offers more convexity than a lower duration issue. A 200BP yield decline creates a convexity return of 0.17% for the 3-year bond (modified duration = 2.67), a convexity return of 1.37% for the 10-year bond (modified duration = 7.11), and a convexity return of 5.97% for the 30-year bond (modified duration = 12.47). Exhibit 11–5 highlights the incremental convexity offered by long duration bonds by plotting

Exhibit 11-2. Price behavior of a 7% coupon, 3-year U.S. Treasury bond as attributable to duration and convexity. The bond is initially priced at par to yield 7% and has a modified duration of 2.67 years.

Yield Change (in BP)	Actual % Price Change	Modified Duration	Convexity	Convexity Factor
−400	+11.39	+10.68	+0.71	0.18
−300	+ 8.40	+ 8.01	+0.39	0.13
−200	+ 5.51	+ 5.34	+0.17	0.09
−100	+ 2.71	+ 2.67	+0.04	0.04
0	0	0	0	0
+100	− 2.62	− 2.67	+0.05	0.05
+200	− 5.16	− 5.34	+0.18	0.09
+300	− 7.61	− 8.01	+0.40	0.13
+400	− 9.99	−10.68	+0.69	0.17

the percentage convexity returns calculated in Exhibits 11–2 through 11–4.

An alternative way of deciphering the convexity:duration linkage is by using convexity factors. The convexity factors for the three bonds used in earlier illustrations are as follows (data from Exhibits 11–2, 11–3, and 11–4):

Issue	Modified Duration	Convexity Factor [a]
3-year bond	2.67	0.13
10-year bond	7.11	0.98
30-year bond	12.47	3.96

[a] Assumes a 300BP change in yield

Once again, the positive relationship between duration and convexity is exposed.

The convexity:duration relationship is perhaps best exemplified through the analysis of zero coupon bonds. Long-term STRIPS have high durations (up to 30 years) and offer sizable convexities. Exhibit 11–6 calculates the convexity of a 30-year STRIPS (modified duration = 28.99). This bond's convexity dwarfs

Exhibit 11-3. Price behavior of a 7% coupon, 10-year U.S. Treasury bond as attributable to duration and convexity. The bond is initially priced at par to yield 7% and has a modified duration of 7.11 years.

Yield Change (in BP)	Actual % Price Change	Modified Duration	Convexity	Convexity Factor
−400	+34.34	+28.44	+5.90	1.48
−300	+24.53	+21.33	+3.20	1.07
−200	+15.59	+14.22	+1.37	0.69
−100	+ 7.44	+ 7.11	+0.33	0.33
0	0	0	0	0
+100	− 6.80	− 7.11	+0.31	0.31
+200	−13.01	−14.22	+1.21	0.61
+300	−18.69	−21.33	+2.64	0.88
+400	−23.90	−28.44	+4.54	1.14

the convexity of the 3-year, 10-year, and 30-year coupon-bearing bonds of earlier illustrations. A 300BP rise in yield creates a 9.72 convexity factor for the 30-year STRIPS (Exhibit 11–6). The corresponding convexity factors for the 3-year, 10-year, and 30-year bonds are only 0.13, 0.88, and 3.01, respectively (per Exhibits 11–2, 11–3, and 11–4).

Exhibit 11-4. Price behavior of a 7% coupon, 30-year U.S. Treasury bond as attributable to duration and convexity. The bond is initially priced at par to yield 7% and has a modified duration of 12.47 years.

Yield Change (in BP)	Actual % Price Change	Modified Duration	Convexity	Convexity Factor
−400	+78.76	+49.88	+28.88	7.22
−300	+52.14	+37.41	+14.73	4.91
−200	+30.91	+24.94	+ 5.97	2.99
−100	+13.84	+12.47	+ 1.37	1.37
0	0	0	0	0
+100	−11.31	−12.47	+ 1.16	1.16
+200	−20.64	−24.94	+ 4.30	2.15
+300	−28.39	−37.41	+ 9.02	3.01
+400	−34.90	−49.88	+14.98	3.75

Exhibit 11-5. Positive convexity of 3-, 10-, and 30-year 7% coupon U.S. Treasury bonds priced at par (data from Exhibits 6-31, 6-32 and 6-33).

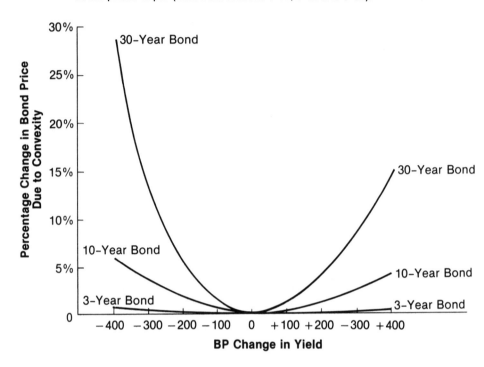

Exhibit 11-6. Price behavior of a 30-year STRIPS as attributable to duration and convexity. The bond is initially priced to yield 7% and has a modified duration of 28.99 years.

Yield Change (in BP)	Actual % Price Change	Modified Duration	Convexity	Convexity Factor
–400	+222.45	+115.96	+106.49	26.62
–300	+140.11	+ 86.97	+ 53.14	17.71
–200	+ 79.06	+ 57.98	+ 21.08	10.54
–100	+ 33.72	+ 28.99	+ 4.73	4.73
0	0	0	0	0
+100	– 25.11	– 28.99	+ 3.88	3.88
+200	– 43.84	– 57.98	+ 14.14	7.07
+300	– 57.82	– 86.97	+ 29.15	9.72
+400	– 68.28	–115.96	+ 47.68	11.92

Convexity is not only positively related to duration; it is an increasing function of duration. The convexity:duration relationship is nonlinear in nature. A bond with twice as much duration has more than double the convexity. Exhibit 11–7 presents this fact graphically, using data from prior illustrations. Exhibit 11–8 confirms this phenomenon by calculating the *convexity per year of duration* for the 3-year, 10-year and 30-year U.S. Treasury bonds used in earlier examples and for a 30-year STRIPS. Longer duration bonds have larger convexities per year of duration than do shorter duration issues.

Exhibit 11–7. The relationship between duration and convexity (data from Exhibits 11–2, 11–3, 11–4, and 11–6). The convexities assume a 400BP decline in market yield.

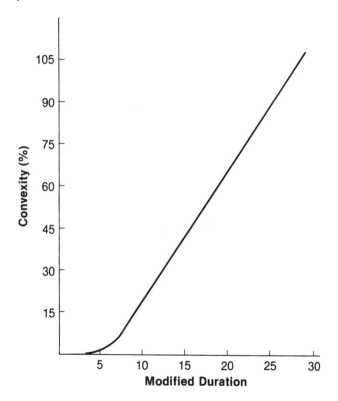

Exhibit 11-8. Calculations of the "convexity per year of duration" for 3-, 10-, and 30-year U.S. Treasury bonds and a 30-year STRIPS. An initial yield of 7% and a 300BP yield shift underlies the duration and convexity figures (data from Exhibits 11–2, 11–3, 11–4, and 11–6).

(1)	*(2)*	*(3)*	*(4) = (3)/(2)*
			Convexity per
	Modified	*Convexity*	*Year of Modified*
Issue	*Duration*	*Factor*	*Duration*
3-year U.S. Treasury bond	2.67	0.13	0.05
10-year U.S. Treasury bond	7.11	0.98	0.14
30-year U.S. Treasury bond	12.47	3.96	0.32
30-year STRIPS	28.99	13.72	0.47

As discussed in Chapter 3, duration is positively related to a bond's term to maturity. Duration is inversely related to a bond's coupon rate of interest, accrued interest, and the market yield level. A bond's convexity bears similar relationships to these underlying factors.

Cash flow distribution

Convexity is positively related to the degree of dispersion in a bond's cash flows. Given two bonds of identical duration, the bond with the wider distribution of underlying cash flows carries a higher convexity. A 30-year, 7% coupon U.S. Treasury bond priced at par has a 12.91 duration (12.47 modified duration). A zero coupon bond priced to yield 7% and maturing in exactly 12.91 years bears a 12.91 duration (12.47 modified duration). Despite their identical durations, the bonds' convexities differ because of their unique cash flows. Exhibit 11–9 illustrates the contrasting cash flow patterns in a timeline format. Exhibit 11–10 calculates the convexity of the 12.91-year zero for a variety of yield changes; the convexity of the 30-year U.S. Treasury bond was presented previously in Exhibit 11–4.

The convexity differences are significant. A 100BP yield decline creates a 52BP return advantage for the 30-year bond vis-à-vis the similar duration zero coupon bond (1.37% convexity return versus 0.85% convexity return). A 400BP yield decline generates a sizable 13.26% incremental return to the 30-year bond (28.88% convexity return versus 15.62% convexity return). Using convexity factors, the superiority of the 30-year bond again emerges:

Issue	Modified Duration	Convexity Factor[a]
30-year U.S. Treasury bond	12.47	3.96
12.91-year STRIPS	12.47	2.46

[a]Assumes a 300BP change in yield.

Exhibit 11-9. The cash flow patterns of a 30-year, 7% coupon U.S. Treasury bond priced at par to yield 7% and a 12.91-year zero coupon bond priced to yield 7%. Each bond has a 12.47 modified duration.

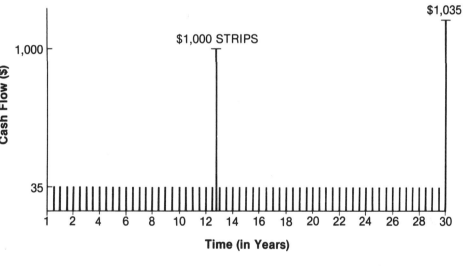

Assuming a yield swing of 300BP, the 30-year bond has 61% more convexity than its zero coupon counterpart (3.96/2.46 = 1.61).[1] Exhibit 11-11 plots the convexity advantage of the 30-year U.S. Treasury bond versus the 12.91-year STRIPS.

---

[1]This finding does not conflict with the earlier discovery that long-term STRIPS have large convexities. It merely illustrates that, for a given duration, a zero-coupon bond offers less convexity than a coupon-bearing issue. If one could create a long-term U.S. Treasury bond with a duration of 30.00 years, the bond would offer far more convexity than a 30-year STRIPS. Unfortunately, long-term U.S. Treasuries typically have durations of only 9.00 to 12.00 years.

Exhibit 11-10. Price behavior of a 12.91-year STRIPS as attributable to duration and convexity. The bond is initially priced to yield 7% and has a modified duration of 12.47 years.

Yield Change (in BP)	Actual % Price Change	Price Change (%) Due to:		Convexity Factor
		Modified Duration	Convexity	
−400	+65.50	+49.88	+15.62	3.91
−300	+45.78	+37.41	+ 8.37	2.79
−200	+28.49	+24.94	+ 3.55	1.78
−100	+13.32	+12.47	+ 0.85	0.85
0	0	0	0	0
+100	−11.70	−12.47	+ 0.77	0.77
+200	−21.98	−24.94	+ 2.96	1.48
+300	−31.03	−37.41	+ 6.38	2.13
+400	−38.99	−49.88	+10.89	2.72

Exhibit 11-11. Positive convexity of a 30-year, 7% coupon U.S. Treasury bond and a 12.91-year STRIPS. Each bond is initially priced to yield 7% to maturity and has a modified duration of 12.47 years (data from Exhibits 11-4 and 11-10). The convexity factors reflect an average of the convexity factors for up and down markets.

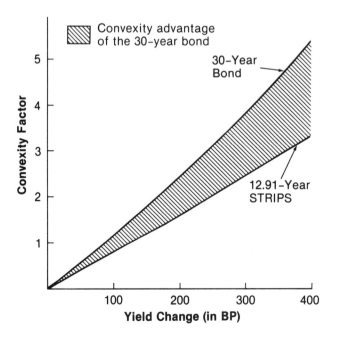

Exhibit 11-12. The convexities of cash flows of various maturities (a 7% discount rate is assumed).

(1) Cash Flow Maturity (in Years)	(2) Modified Duration	(3) Convexity Factor [a]	(4) = (3)/(2) Convexity per Year of Modified Duration
0	0.00	0.00	0.00
5	4.83	0.39	0.08
10	9.66	1.48	0.15
15	14.49	3.32	0.23
20	19.32	5.93	0.31
25	24.15	9.37	0.39
30	28.99	13.72	0.47

[a]Based on a 300BP change in the discount rate.

The rationale behind the convexity:cash flow distribution relationship lies in the fact that long-term cash flows carry progressively larger amounts of convexity. Exhibit 11-12 illustrates this phenomenon by calculating the convexities of a variety of future cash flows. The final column of this exhibit shows that long-term cash flows provide increasingly higher convexities per year of modified duration. If the convexity per year of modified duration was constant, rather than increasing, there would be no impact on a bond's convexity from the bond's distribution of cash flow.

Exhibit 11-13 shows that, for sequential 5-year extensions, a cash flow's convexity factor rises at an increasing rate. Whereas the extension from a 5-year cash flow to a 10-year cash flow is responsible for a 1.09 increase in the convexity factor, a move from a 25-year cash flow to a 30-year cash flow causes a 4.35 surge in the convexity factor.

Because a bond's convexity simply reflects the convexities of the bond's component cash flows, the wider the dispersion of cash flows the greater the convexity effects. Long-term cash flows are responsible for the incremental convexity. Using the data from Exhibit 11-12, Exhibit 11-14 plots the convexity factors for the series of cash flows analyzed. The dashed line in this exhibit represents a variety of combinations of cash assets (0.00 duration) and 30-year cash flows (30.00 duration). The weighted average combination of short-term cash flows and long-term cash flows provides a superior amount of convexity versus a single cash flow of intermediate-term maturity.

Exhibit 11-13. The incremental convexity of extending the maturity of a cash flow (data from Exhibit 11-12).

Extension (in Years)	Change in Convexity Factor
0 to 5	+0.39
5 to 10	+1.09
10 to 15	+1.84
15 to 20	+2.61
20 to 25	+3.44
25 to 30	+4.35

Exhibit 11-14. The convexity factors for a variety of individual cash flows (data from Exhibit 11-12).

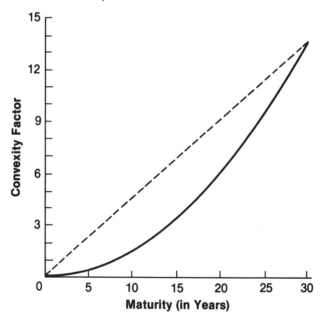

For example, a bond with a single cash flow due in 15 years carries a 3.32 convexity (see Exhibit 11-12). A similar bond with 50% of its cash flow due immediately and the remaining 50%

due in 30 years offers a similar duration (i.e., 15.00 years) but approximately twice as much convexity:

$$0.50(0.00) + 0.50(13.72) = 6.86 \text{ convexity}$$

For analogous reasons, the 30-year U.S. Treasury bond of earlier illustrations offers superior convexity to a STRIPS of similar duration.

Market yield volatility

Convexity is positively related to market yield volatility. High volatility in interest rates creates large convexity effects. Graphically, the curvature of the price:yield curve becomes more severe as the market yield shifts further away from current levels (Exhibit 11–15). Greater market volatility increases the probability of a major change in market yields.

Exhibit 11–15. Convexity is enhanced by larger shifts in yield.

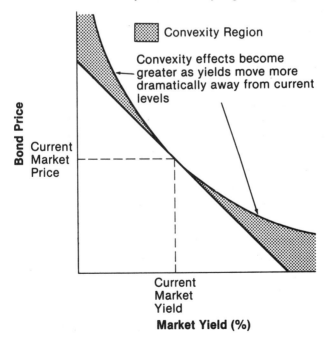

This effect is supported by the data in Exhibits 11–2, 11–3, and 11–4. For example, the 3-year U.S. Treasury bond has a convexity factor of 0.18 for a 400BP change in yield. The same bond offers only a 0.05 convexity factor for a 100BP yield shift. *The convexity:market yield volatility effect is magnified in bonds of long duration.* The 30-year U.S. Treasury bond provides a 1.27 convexity factor assuming a 100BP yield shift and a 5.49 convexity factor for a 400BP yield shift. A 30-year STRIPS experiences a 4.31 convexity factor for a 100BP yield shift and a 19.27 convexity factor under an assumption of a 400BP yield volatility.

Direction of yield change

Convexity is more positively influenced by a downward movement in yields than by an upward surge in yields. The 3-year, 10-year, and 30-year bonds of earlier illustrations help to reveal this effect (see Exhibits 11–2, 11–3, and 11–4). A 10-year U.S. Treasury bond has a 1.48 convexity factor at a 400BP decline in yield; the corresponding factor for a 400BP rise in yield is only 1.14 (see Exhibit 11–3). Graphically, convexity has nonsymmetric tendencies, with convexity effects exaggerated in declining yield environments, as can be seen in Exhibit 11–16.

Another way of observing the nonsymmetry of convexity is by analyzing the change in a bond's modified duration as interest rates rise and fall. Exhibit 11–17 calculates the modified durations of a 7% coupon, 30-year U.S. Treasury bond at a variety of yield levels. Positive convexity is reflected in the fact that the bond's modified duration lengthens as yields fall, and it shortens as yields rise. The nonsymmetry of convexity is exposed in the "change in modified duration" column of this table. A decline in yields fosters a larger expansion in modified duration than an identical rise in yields creates through a contraction. For example, a 400BP drop in yields generates a 4.21-year surge in modified duration; a corresponding 400BP increase in yields forces only a 3.30-year decline in modified duration.

The convexity:direction-of-yield change effect is magnified in bonds of long duration. Assuming a 400BP yield change, a 30-year U.S. Treasury bond has a 7.22 convexity factor in a falling

Exhibit 11-16. The nonsymmetric nature of convexity, as illustrated by a 30-year U.S. Treasury bond. Convexity effects are greater in declining yield environments than in rising yield environments (data from Exhibit 11-4).

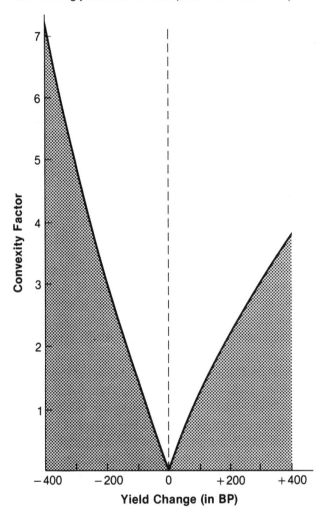

yield environment versus only a 3.75 convexity factor in a rising yield environment (see Exhibit 11–4). Assuming a 400BP yield change, a 30-year STRIPS registers a 26.62 convexity factor with declining yields in contrast to an 11.92 convexity factor with rising yields (see Exhibit 11–7).

Exhibit 11-17. The nonsymmetric behavior of the change in duration for a 7% coupon, 30-year U.S. Treasury bond priced at par (issue data from Exhibit 11-4).

Yield Change (in BP)	Modified Duration	Change in Modified Duration
−400	16.68	+4.21
−300	15.57	+3.10
−200	14.49	+2.02
−100	13.46	+0.99
− 0	12.47	0
+100	11.55	-0.92
+200	10.69	-1.78
+300	9.89	-2.58
+400	9.17	-3.30

The four primary factors that influence convexity (duration, cash flow distribution, market yield volatility, and direction of yield change) are considered in the context of a single bond (e.g., a 10-year U.S. Treasury bond). There is a variety of potential fixed-income investments available in the marketplace at a given point in time. Although the "market" yield level is represented by U.S. Treasury bonds, non-Treasury investments, such as federal agency bonds and corporate bonds, trade at higher yields than do comparable U.S. Treasuries and, therefore, have convexity features that differ from U.S. Treasuries. In the following section, the convexity implications of investing in non-Treasury securities are assessed through the analysis of a noncallable corporate bond. The convexity attributes of callable securities are discussed in Chapter 12.

The convexity of noncallable corporate bonds versus noncallable U.S. Treasury bonds

Because of underlying credit risk, a noncallable corporate bond trades at a higher yield than does a U.S. Treasury bond of similar maturity. In comparing the convexities of a noncallable corporate bond and a noncallable U.S. Treasury bond, several realities must be considered. For a corporate bond and a U.S. Treasury bond trading at identical prices, the corporate bond:

1. Carries a higher coupon rate.
2. Offers a higher yield to maturity.
3. Exposes the buyer to "spread risk" (i.e., the bond's yield spread vis-à-vis a similar U.S. Treasury bond can change).[2]

The first two factors lower the duration and convexity of the corporate bond vis-à-vis its U.S. Treasury bond counterpart. The third factor (spread risk) can have either a beneficial convexity effect (through a spread narrowing) or a detrimental convexity effect (through a spread widening). The overall impact of these factors generally shows that a noncallable corporate bond has a lower convexity than a comparable noncallable U.S. Treasury bond.

Exhibit 11–18 assesses the convexity characteristics of an 8% coupon, 30-year noncallable corporate bond. The bond is initially priced at par to yield 8%, exactly 100BP more than a comparable U.S. Treasury bond maturing in 30 years (recall Exhibit 11–4). Exhibit 11–19 plots the price:yield curves for the 30-year corporate bond and for its 30-year U.S. Treasury bond counterpart. As compared to the U.S. Treasury bond, the 30-year corporate bond has an identical price (100), a higher coupon (8% versus 7%), a higher yield (8% versus 7%), a lower modified duration (11.31 versus 12.47), and less convexity. For example, a 300BP yield decline gives the Treasury bond a 14.73% convexity effect. The identical decline in market yield generates only a 12.43% convexity effect for the corporate bond. Exhibit 11–20 summarizes the convexity impacts for both bonds under a variety of shifts in market yield. In each case, the U.S. Treasury bond offers incremental convexity over its corporate bond counterpart.

If the yield spread between the 30-year corporate bond and the 30-year U.S. Treasury bond is allowed to change from its

[2] The spread risk results from changes in credit quality (or the perception of the company's future credit trend), supply/demand imbalances in the marketplace, the yields available on alternative non-Treasury investments (e.g., mortgage passthroughs, asset-backed securities, and federal agency bonds), and the like. In addition, a callable corporate bond introduces spread risk as a result of the changing value of the underlying call option(s) that the issuer holds. Chapter 12 discusses the convexity of callable corporate bonds.

Exhibit 11-18. The price behavior of an 8% coupon, 30-year noncallable corporate bond as attributable to duration and convexity. The bond is initially priced at par to yield 8% to maturity and has a modified (and effective) duration of 11.31 years. With 30-year U.S. Treasury bonds yielding 7%, the 30-year corporate bond trades at a +100BP yield spread to comparable U.S. Treasuries. The calculations assume a constant yield spread in all interest rate scenarios.

U.S. Treasury Yield Change (in BP)	Actual % Price Change	Price Change (%) Due to:		Convexity Factor
		Effective Duration	*Convexity*	
−400	+69.52	+45.24	+24.28	6.07
−300	+46.36	+33.93	+12.43	4.14
−200	+27.68	+22.62	+ 5.06	2.53
−100	+12.47	+11.31	+ 1.16	1.16
0	0	+ 0	+ 0	0
+100	−10.32	−11.31	+ 0.99	0.99
+200	−18.93	−22.62	+ 3.69	1.85
+300	−26.18	−33.93	+ 7.75	2.58
+400	−32.32	−45.24	+12.92	3.23

Exhibit 11-19. A comparison of the price:yield curves of a 30-year noncallable corporate bond and a 30-year noncallable U.S. Treasury bond (data from Exhibits 11-4 and 11-18). The corporate bond is priced at a +100BP yield spread to the U.S. Treasury bond in all interest rate scenarios.

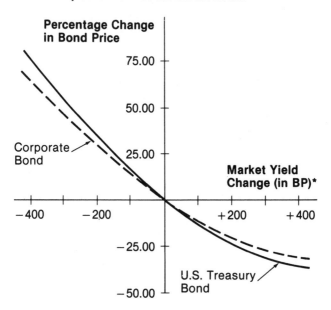

Exhibit 11-20. The convexities of a current coupon, noncallable 30-year U.S. Treasury bond and a current coupon, noncallable 30-year corporate bond for a variety of market yield shifts. The corporate bond is assumed to maintain a constant 100BP yield spread over the U.S. Treasury bond as the market yield changes (data from Exhibits 11-4 and 11-18).

Market Yield Change (in BP)[a]	Convexity Effect (in %)	
	30-Year U.S. Treasury	30-Year Corporate
−400	+28.88	+24.28
−300	+14.73	+12.43
−200	+ 5.97	+ 5.06
−100	+ 1.37	+ 1.16
0	0	0
+100	+ 1.16	+ 0.99
+200	+ 4.30	+ 3.69
+300	+ 9.02	+ 7.75
+400	+14.98	+12.92

[a]Market yield is the YTM of a comparable noncallable U.S. Treasury bond.

current level of 100BP, convexity is affected. Exhibit 11–21 calculates the percentage changes in price (and the related convexity

Exhibit 11-21. The price behavior and convexity effects of an 8% coupon, 30-year noncallable corporate bond as U.S. Treasury yields change from the current 7% level. The corporate bond's yield spread (a) narrows 20BP to +80BP, (b) remains stable at +100BP, or (c) widens 20BP to +120BP.

U.S. Treasury Yield Change (in BP)	Actual % Price Change if the Yield Spread:			Convexity Effect (in %) if the Yield Spread:		
	Narrows 20BP	Is Unchanged	Widens 20BP	Narrows 20BP	Is Unchanged	Widens 20BP
−400	+74.80	+69.52	+64.48	+29.56	+24.28	+19.24
−300	+50.60	+46.36	+42.30	+16.67	+12.43	+ 8.37
−200	+31.11	+27.68	+24.38	+ 8.49	+ 5.06	+ 1.76
−100	+15.27	+12.47	+ 9.78	+ 3.96	+ 1.16	− 1.53
0	+ 2.31	0	− 2.22	+ 2.31	0	− 2.22
+100	− 8.41	−10.32	−12.17	+ 2.90	+ 0.99	− 0.86
+200	−17.33	−18.93	−20.48	+ 5.29	+ 3.69	+ 2.14
+300	−24.82	−26.18	−27.49	+ 9.11	+ 7.75	+ 6.44
+400	−31.17	−32.32	−33.44	+14.07	+12.92	+11.80

components) for an 8% coupon, 30-year corporate bond if the bond's yield spread vis-à-vis U.S. Treasuries (1) narrows 20BP, (2) remains constant at 100BP, or (3) widens 20BP. A variety of general market yield shifts is considered (−400BP to +400BP). The corporate bond's convexity is enhanced by a narrowing in the yield spread. If the yield spread remains the same or widens, the corporate bond offers less convexity than its U.S. Treasury bond counterpart. If the yield spread narrows to 80BP, the convexity of the corporate bond exceeds that of a comparable U.S. Treasury bond in eight of the nine interest rate scenarios considered.

Summary

There are four major influences on a bond's convexity: duration, cash flow distribution, market yield volatility, and the direction of yield change. Convexity is positively related to the duration of the underlying security. Convexity is an increasing function of duration, as reflected in the higher "convexity per year of duration" statistics of long duration investments. Convexity is enhanced by a wider dispersion in a bond's cash flows because long-term cash flows have disproportionately large amounts of convexity.

Convexity is positively related to market yield volatility. Greater volatility creates more convexity. This effect is magnified in long duration bonds. Convexity is stronger in a bull market than in a bear market. A decline in yields elicits a more substantial convexity effect than a yield increase of similar magnitude. This effect is especially pronounced in long duration bonds. A noncallable corporate bond has less convexity than a noncallable U.S. Treasury bond of similar maturity because the former carries a lower duration (because of its higher coupon rate and higher market yield).

The chapter Appendix explains convexity for zero coupon bonds. Chapter 12 analyzes the convexity of callable corporate bonds and mortgage-backed securities. It introduces the concept of negative convexity and identifies the factors that influence negative convexity.

The Convexity of Zero Coupon Bonds

The convexity of zero coupon bonds is particularly interesting. The single cash flow nature of zeroes and the wide range of potential durations available with them make the analysis understandable and illustrate the power of convexity. The positive relationship between duration and convexity becomes quite clear.

Exhibit 11–22 calculates the convexities of a series of STRIPS. A long maturity STRIPS offers substantial convexity advantages over a short maturity STRIPS. For example, a 5-year STRIPS has more than five times as much convexity as a 2-year STRIPS (0.39 versus 0.07); a 10-year STRIPS offers much more convexity than a 5-year STRIPS (1.48 versus 0.39); a 20-year STRIPS provides four times the convexity of a 10-year STRIPS (5.93 versus 1.48); a 30-year STRIPS contains over twice the convexity of a 20-year STRIPS (13.72 versus 5.93). Exhibit 11–23 plots the findings of Exhibit 11–22.

When compared to a similar maturity U.S. Treasury bond, a STRIPS has superior convexity. Exhibit 11–24 shows this comparison for a range of possible maturities. The higher duration of the STRIPS (versus its similar maturity U.S. Treasury bond) explains the STRIPS' convexity advantage.

Exhibit 11-22. The convexity of STRIPS of a variety of maturities. A 300BP yield change is assumed with an initial yield of 7%.

Issue	Modified Duration	Convexity Factor
1-year STRIPS	0.97	0.02
2-year STRIPS	1.93	0.07
3-year STRIPS	2.90	0.15
5-year STRIPS	4.83	0.39
10-year STRIPS	9.66	1.48
20-year STRIPS	19.32	5.93
30-year STRIPS	28.99	13.72

Exhibits 11-25 and 11-26 further illustrate the positive relationship between duration and convexity. Exhibit 11-25 derives the convexities of a series of STRIPS as expressed on a "per year of duration" basis. Convexity is an increasing, not

Exhibit 11-23. The relationship between duration and convexity for a variety of STRIPS (data from Exhibit 11-22).

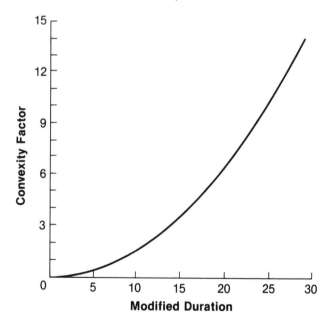

Exhibit 11-24. A comparison of the convexity of STRIPS versus coupon-bearing U.S. Treasuries of similar maturity. Each bond initially yields 7% and the U.S. Treasuries are priced at par. The convexity factors assume a 300BP shift in yield.

Maturity Sector (in Years)	Convexity Factor for a:	
	STRIPS	U.S. Treasury Bond
1 year	0.02	0.02
2 year	0.07	0.07
3 year	0.15	0.13
5 year	0.39	0.32
10 year	1.48	0.98
20 year	5.93	2.55
30 year	13.72	3.96

a constant, function of duration. A long STRIPS produces more convexity per year of duration than a short-maturity STRIPS. Exhibit 11-26 tabulates the return attributions for a series of STRIPS (a 300BP yield decline is assumed). Convexity accounts

Exhibit 11-25. The convexity of a variety of STRIPS, as expressed on a "per year of duration" basis (data from Exhibit 11-22).

Issue	Convexity per Year of Duration
1-year STRIPS	0.02
2-year STRIPS	0.04
3-year STRIPS	0.05
5-year STRIPS	0.08
10-year STRIPS	0.15
20-year STRIPS	0.31
30-year STRIPS	0.47

Exhibit 11-26. The total return attributions for a series of STRIPS. An instantaneous 300BP yield decline is assumed. The initial yield level is 7%.

Issue	Return % Due to	
	Duration	Convexity
1-year STRIPS	98	2
3-year STRIPS	95	5
10-year STRIPS	85	15
30-year STRIPS	62	38

for an increasing proportion of return for longer duration securities. For example, convexity explains only 2% of the return on a 1-year STRIPS. Convexity describes 15% of the return on a 10-year STRIPS and accounts for 38% of the return on a 30-year STRIPS. Exhibit 11–27 plots the findings of Exhibit 11–26 in a bar chart form.

Exhibit 11-27. The total return attributions for a variety of STRIPS (data from Exhibit 11–26).

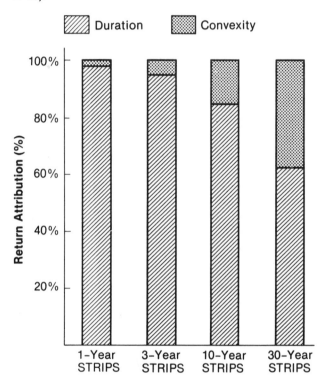

CHAPTER 12

Negative Convexity

Introduction

Chapters 9 through 11 introduced the concept of convexity and analyzed the convexity of noncallable bonds. This chapter assesses the convexity of callable bonds; these have elements of both positive convexity and negative convexity. This chapter also defines negative convexity, illustrates the negative convexity of corporate bonds and mortgage-backed securities, and discusses the factors that affect negative convexity.

Defining negative convexity

Convexity is defined as the difference between a bond's actual price (or actual price change) and the bond's duration-predicted price (or price change):

$$\begin{matrix} \text{convexity} \\ \text{(in \$)} \end{matrix} = \begin{matrix} \text{actual bond} \\ \text{price} \end{matrix} - \begin{matrix} \text{duration-predicted} \\ \text{bond price} \end{matrix}$$

$$\begin{matrix} \text{convexity} \\ \text{(in \%)} \end{matrix} = \begin{matrix} \text{actual price} \\ \text{change (in \%)} \end{matrix} - \begin{matrix} \text{duration-predicted} \\ \text{price change (in \%)} \end{matrix}$$

The duration of choice may be modified duration or, preferably, effective duration. A positive difference is termed positive convexity; a negative difference is called *negative convexity.*

A numeric illustration of negative convexity

Exhibit 12–1 calculates the convexities of the noncallable 30-year U.S. Treasury bond (9% due 11/15/18).[1] Noncallable bonds have positive convexity characteristics. The 30-year U.S. Treasury bond, for example, offers a 10.38% convexity if yields decline by 300BP:

$$\begin{array}{ccc} \text{convexity} & \text{actual price} & \text{duration-predicted} \\ \text{(in \%)} = \text{change (in \%)} - \text{price change (in \%)} \end{array}$$

$$= 40.98\% - 30.60\%$$

$$= 10.38\%$$

Exhibit 12–1. The convexity of the U.S. Treasury 9% due 11/15/18. The bond is priced at par on December 30, 1988, and has a modified (and effective) duration of 10.20 years.

Market Yield Change (in BP)	Bond Price	Percentage Change in Bond Price		Convexity (in (%)	Convexity Factor
		Actual[a]	Predicted[b]		
–300	141.44	+40.98%	+30.60%	+10.38	3.46
–200	124.90	+24.62	+20.40	+ 4.22	2.11
–100	111.28	+11.16	+10.20	+ 0.96	0.96
0	100.00	0	0	0	0
+100	90.52	– 9.38	–10.20	+ 0.82	0.82
+200	82.54	–17.27	–20.40	+ 3.13	1.57
+300	75.74	–23.99	–30.60	+ 6.61	2.20

[a]Reflects the percentage change in the bond's full price (including accrued interest).
[b]Based on a modified (and effective) duration of 10.20 years.

[1]The convexities in this book were derived by the author. The effective durations and projected price behaviors of callable securites were provided by Capital Management Sciences unless otherwise indicated. The CMS data serve as the basis for the author's calculations of the convexity factors for callable bonds.

Exhibit 12-2. The convexity of the Anheuser-Busch 10% due 7/1/18. The bond is priced at 99.50 on December 30, 1988 and carries an 8.97 modified duration and a 6.83 effective duration. The bond has a 110 current cash call and a 105 refunding call (on 7/1/98).[a]

Market Yield Change (in BP)	Bond Price	Percentage Change in Bond Price		Convexity (in %)	Convexity Factor
		Actual[b]	Predicted[c]		
−300	110.96	+10.97%	+20.49%	− 9.52	−3.17
−200	110.54	+10.57	+13.66	− 3.09	−1.55
−100	106.36	+ 6.56	+ 6.83	− 0.27	−0.27
0	99.50	0	0	0	0
+100	92.06	− 7.13	− 6.83	− 0.30	−0.30
+200	84.89	−13.99	−13.66	− 0.33	−0.17
+300	78.33	−20.27	−20.49	+ 0.22	+0.07

[a]Price data courtesy of Capital Management Sciences.

[b]Reflects the percentage change in the bond's full price (including accrued interest).

[c]Based on a modified (and effective) duration of 6.83 years.

A 300BP rise in yields elicits a 6.61% convexity from the bond:

$$\frac{\text{convexity}}{\text{(in \%)}} = -23.99\% - (-30.60\%)$$
$$= 6.61\%$$

A callable bond has both positive and negative convexity features. Exhibit 12-2 projects the price behavior of the Anheuser-Busch 10% due 7/1/18. The bond's effective duration is 6.83 years. In a bull market, the bond suffers from negative convexity. A 300BP decline in market yield creates a −9.52% convexity effect:

$$\frac{\text{convexity}}{\text{(in \%)}} = \frac{\text{actual price}}{\text{change (in \%)}} - \frac{\text{duration-predicted}}{\text{price change (in \%)}}$$
$$= 10.97\% - 20.49\%$$
$$= -9.52\%$$

A market collapse, on the other hand, gives the bond a small positive convexity. A 300BP rise in interest rates generates a 0.22% convexity:

$$\frac{\text{convexity}}{\text{(in \%)}} = -20.27\% - (-20.49\%)$$

$$= 0.22\%$$

The convexity characteristics of a callable bond are exaggerated when modified duration, rather than effective duration, is used to derive the convexity effects. Using the same Anheuser-Busch 10% bond as an illustration, Exhibit 12–3 calculates the divergent convexities of a callable bond in a bull market versus a bear market by using modified duration as the bond's price predictor. A 300BP market rally is responsible for a –15.94% convexity effect:

$$\frac{\text{convexity}}{\text{(in \%)}} = 10.97\% - 26.91\%$$

$$= -15.94\%$$

A 300BP surge in market yield creates a distinctly positive convexity of 6.64%:

$$\frac{\text{convexity}}{\text{(in \%)}} = -20.27\% - (-26.91\%)$$

$$= 6.64\%$$

Exhibit 12–3. The convexity of the Anheuser-Busch 10% due 7/1/18, based on its 8.97 modified duration (data from Exhibit 12–2).

Market Yield Change (in BP)	Bond Price	Percentage Change in Bond Price		Convexity (in %)	Convexity Factor
		Actual[a]	Predicted[b]		
−300	110.96	+10.97%	+26.91%	−15.94	−5.31
−200	110.54	+10.57	+17.94	− 7.37	−3.69
−100	106.36	+ 6.56	+ 8.97	− 2.41	−2.41
0	99.50	0	0	0	0
+100	92.06	− 7.13	− 8.97	+ 1.84	+1.84
+200	84.89	−13.99	−17.94	+ 3.95	+1.98
+300	78.33	−20.27	−26.91	+ 6.64	+2.21

[a]Reflects the percentage change in the bond's full price (including accrued interest).
[b]Based on a modified (and effective) duration of 8.97 years.

Convexity effects are more dramatic and more divergent when modified duration, rather than effective duration, serves as the measure of bond risk. By acting as a superior proxy for a callable bond's price sensitivity, effective duration reduces the unexpected price changes (i.e., convexity). Consequently, the illustrations in this book use effective duration to derive convexity effects and convexity factors.[2]

The average convexity factor for a callable bond

The nonsymmetric nature of convexity warrants caution when interpreting an average convexity factor. For a noncallable bond, the average factor understates the bond's convexity in a bull market and overstates the bond's convexity in a bear market. The 30-year U.S. Treasury bond of Exhibit 12–1 has a 2.83 average convexity factor (for a 300BP change in market yield):

$$\text{average convexity factor} = \frac{\text{convexity factor}_{(-300BP)} + \text{convexity factor}_{(+300BP)}}{2}$$

$$= \frac{3.46 + 2.20}{2}$$

$$= 2.83$$

This factor underestimates the bond's convexity in a falling yield environment (3.46) and overestimates the bond's convexity in a rising yield environment (2.20).

For a callable bond, the nonsymmetry of convexity can be severe. The average convexity factor for the Anheuser Busch bond used in Exhibit 12–2 is –1.55 for a 300BP change in market yield:

---

[2] For a noncallable bond, of course, effective duration and modified duration are synonymous. Therefore, the illustrations in Chapters 9 through 11 are consistent with this methodology.

$$\begin{array}{c} \text{average} \\ \text{convexity} \\ \text{factor} \end{array} = \frac{-3.17 \; + \; 0.07}{2}$$

$$= -1.55$$

This average factor understates the bond's negative convexity in a bull market (–3.17) and misrepresents the bond's positive convexity in a bear market (0.07).

Using modified duration as the proxy for a callable bond's price sensitivity (the traditional approach) makes the average convexity factor difficult to interpret. The Anheuser-Busch 10% due 7/1/18 has a –1.55 average convexity factor for a 300BP shift in market yield (refer back to Exhibit 12–3):

$$\begin{array}{c} \text{average} \\ \text{convexity} \\ \text{factor} \end{array} = \frac{-5.31 \; + \; 2.21}{2}$$

$$= -1.55$$

This average statistic, however, blunts the bond's sizable negative convexity in a rallying market (–5.31) and hides the bond's positive convexity in a declining market (2.21). Chapter 10 highlighted the dangers of convexity factors. These dangers are magnified in the convexity factors of callable bonds.

A graphical presentation of negative convexity

Negative convexity is an unexpected price effect that creates a lower bond price than suggested by the bond's duration (modified or effective). On a graph convexity is the area between a bond's price:yield curve and the bond's modified (or effective) duration line. For a noncallable bond, convexity effects are always positive and the price:yield curve lies above the modified (and effective) duration tangent line (see Exhibit 12–4).[3] Negative convexity exists

---

[3] It is also true that putable bonds offer only positive convexity.

Exhibit 12-4. Positive convexity.

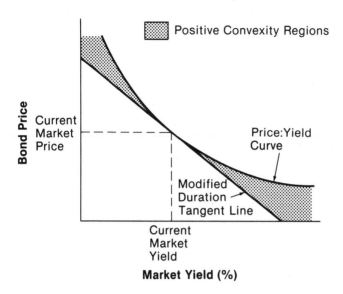

when the modified duration tangent line lies above the price:yield curve (see Exhibit 12–5).

A callable bond has convexity effects that are positive in some areas and negative in other areas. Exhibits 12–6 and 12–7 illustrate the positive and negative convexity regions for a new-issue, long maturity callable bond using modified duration and effective duration, respectively, as the estimators of the bond's price sensitivity to yield change. Exhibits 12–8 and 12–9 provide similar graphics for a long maturity callable bond that has 5 years of call protection remaining.

Negative convexity and callable corporate bonds

Factors that influence the negative
convexity of callable bonds

There are five primary factors that affect a callable bond's negative convexity: (1) call features; (2) the divergence between

Exhibit 12–5. Negative convexity.

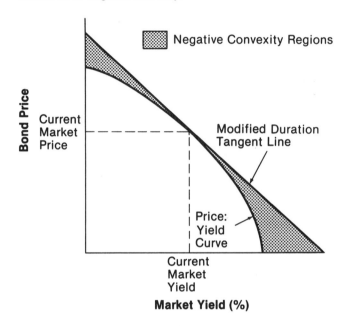

the bond's modified duration to call (DTC) and the bond's modified duration to maturity (DTM); (3) the bond's market price relative to its call price; (4) the expected trend in interest rates; and (5) market yield volatility. Each of these factors is discussed in turn.

Call features. Restrictive call provisions enhance the effects of negative convexity. Immediate cash calls, short periods of refunding call protection, sinking funds (and options to increase the sinking fund payment), and low call prices contribute to a callable bond's negative convexity. Less restrictive call provisions mitigate some of the negative convexity effects.

The divergence between modified duration to call (DTC) and modified duration to maturity (DTM). A wider divergence magnifies the impact of negative convexity. This influence is related to the first factor (i.e., call features). A bond's effective duration has more potential to change considerably if the DTC to DTM difference is large. A bond's modified DTM grossly overstates

Exhibit 12-6. The price:yield curve and convexity regions for a new-issue, 30-year callable bond priced at par. The bond has a current cash call at a premium. The convexity regions are determined by the bond's modified duration. For a callable bond, the modified duration line is *not* tangent to the price:yield curve as it is for a noncallable bond.

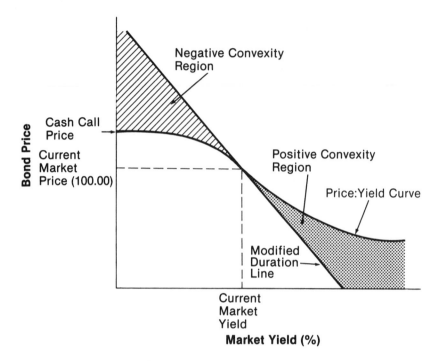

the bond's upside price potential if market yields decline measurably.

The market price of the bond relative to its call price. The closer the market price and the call price, the greater the influence of negative convexity. When a bond trades at its call price, the call option is "at-the-money." The bond's effective duration can shift considerably as the option moves "out-of-the-money" or "in-the-money." When a bond trades well above its call price, the call option is significantly in-the-money, and the bond's effective duration stabilizes near the bond's modified duration to call. When a bond trades well below its call price, the call option is significantly

Exhibit 12-7. The price:yield curve and convexity regions for a new-issue, 30-year callable bond priced at par. The bond has a current cash call at a premium. The convexity regions are determined by the bond's effective duration. The effective duration line is flatter than the modified duration line; as a result, convexity regions are smaller (compare to Exhibit 12-6).

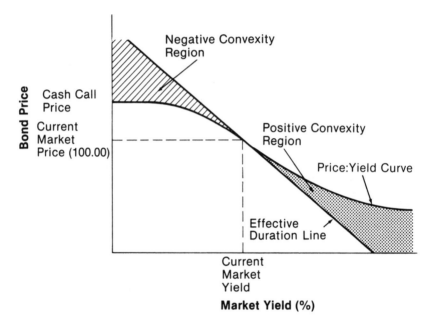

out-of-the-money, and the bond's effective duration hovers near the bond's modified duration to maturity. Negative convexity is positively related to the sensitivity of a bond's effective duration to changes in interest rates. This potential variability is maximized when the call option is at-the-money.

The expected trend in interest rates. Negative convexity is enhanced by a trend to lower interest rates. Conversely, a trend to higher interest rates reduces or eliminates the negative convexity effect.

Market yield volatility. Greater volatility magnifies the effect of negative convexity. The potential for early redemption is increased by a high degree of market yield volatility.

Exhibit 12-8. The price:yield curve and convexity regions for a new-issue, 30-year callable bond priced at par. The bond is noncallable for 5 years. The convexity regions are determined by the bond's modified duration. A bond with a period of call protection (in this case, 5 years) has less negative convexity than a currently callable bond (compare to Exhibit 12-6).

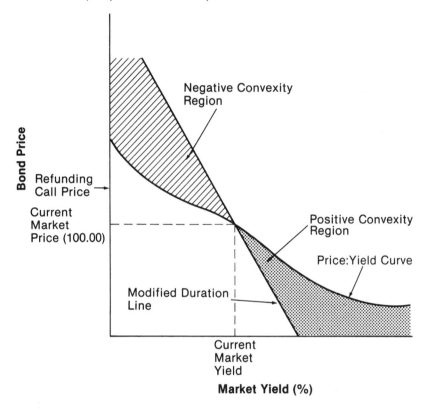

Illustrations of corporate bonds

Exhibit 12–10 summarizes the convexity factors for a variety of callable bonds, including corporates, municipals, and callable U.S. Treasuries (this table contains the same issues as does Exhibit 6–11, see page 90). For comparative purposes, Exhibit 12–11 provides the convexity factors for a series of noncallable U.S. Treasury bonds and STRIPS of various maturities. Exhibit 12–11 shows that noncallable bonds always have positive convexities,

Exhibit 12-9. The price:yield curve and convexity regions for a new-issue, 30-year callable bond priced at par. The bond is noncallable for 5 years. The convexity regions are determined by the bond's effective duration. The effective duration line is flatter than the modified duration line; as a result, convexity regions are smaller (compare to Exhibit 12-8).

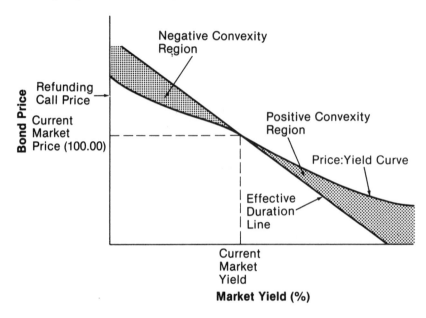

with long duration issues offering larger amounts of convexity than short duration issues.[4] Callable bonds, on the other hand, usually carry negative convexities.

Bonds trading at modest premiums to par and having current cash calls (or current refunding calls) suffer from sizable negative convexities. For example, the Capital Cities Broadcasting 11⅝% due 8/15/15 has a –2.38 convexity, and the Texas Utilities Electric 12% due 9/1/15 bears a –2.23 convexity. Premium coupon bonds that have a period of call protection remaining offer negative convexities as well. For example, the Southern Bell Telephone 10¾% due 12/18/25 (callable on 12/18/90) carries a –1.73 convexity, and the Citicorp 10⅞% due 6/15/10 (callable on 6/15/90) has a –1.84 convexity.

---

[4] It is also true that putable bonds offer only positive convexity.

Exhibit 12-10. Effective durations and convexities of a series of callable bonds. Data as of December 30, 1988, and from Exhibit 6-11. Convexities assume a 300BP shift in market yield.

Intermediate Maturity Issues

Ratings	Issue Description	Price	YTM (%)	Effective Duration	Convexity Factor
AAA/AAA	International Business Machines 9% due 5/1/98	98.00	9.32	5.56	0.36
AAA/AA+	African Development Bank 10% due 11/1/97	101.85	9.68	5.72	0.67
Baa1/BBB+	Commonwealth Edison 10⅛% due 5/1/98	99.75	10.16	5.47	−0.95

Long-Maturity Issues

Ratings	Issue Description	Price	YTM (%)	Effective Duration	Convexity Factor
Callable U.S. Treasuries:					
AAA/AAA	U.S. Treasury 14% due 11/15/11	141–20	9.21[a]	8.00	1.52
AAA/AAA	U.S. Treasury 10⅜% due 11/15/12	101–12	9.20[a]	8.62	1.66
AAA/AAA	U.S. Treasury 11¾% due 11/15/14	124–04	9.14[a]	8.80	1.88
Industrials:					
AA3/AA−	Anheuser-Busch 10% due 7/1/18	99.50	10.05	6.83	−1.55
A1/A+	Capital Cities Broadcasting 11⅝% due 8/15/15	108.75	10.63	2.55	−2.38
A1/A+	Atlantic Richfield Company 10⅞% due 7/15/05	108.75	9.80	7.61	1.40
A1/A+	Atlantic Richfield Company 9⅞% due 3/1/16	100.75	9.79	9.15	2.31
A3/BBB+	Georgia-Pacific 9½% due 2/15/18	90.50	10.55	7.67	−0.26
Telephone utilities:					
AAA/AAA	Southern Bell Telephone 8⅝% due 9/1/26	88.75	9.75	8.15	0.27
AAA/AAA	Southern Bell Telephone 10¾% due 12/18/25	105.63	10.16	4.82	−1.73
AA3/AA−	Southwestern Bell Telephone 11⅞% due 10/18/21	110.75	10.68	4.30	−1.29
AA3/A+	Pacific Telephone and Telegraph 9⅝% due 7/15/18	95.50	10.10	7.07	−1.28

Exhibit 12-10. (cont.)

Ratings	Issue Description	Price	YTM (%)	Effective Duration	Convexity Factor
Electric utilities:					
Baa1/BBB+	Commonwealth Edison				
	11⅛% due 5/1/18	102.75	10.81	5.93	–1.86
Baa1/BBB	Texas Utilities Electric				
	12% due 9/1/15	106.25	11.25	4.30	–2.23
Yankees:					
AA2/AA–	British Columbia Hydro				
	15½% due 11/15/11	134.25	9.74[a]	5.39	0.53
AA3/AA–	Province of Quebec				
	8⅝% due 12/1/26	91.00	9.51	10.21	3.09
Bank and finance:					
A1/AA–	Citicorp 10⅞% due 6/15/10	103.00	10.52	4.35	–1.84
Original issue discounts (OIDs):					
AA2/AA	Dupont 6% due 12/1/01	72.75	9.75	7.68	0.73
AA3/AA–	General Motors Acceptance				
	Corporation				
	6% due 4/1/11	65.50	9.85	9.26	1.46
High yield corporates:					
BA3/B+	Gulf States Utilities				
	12⅜% due 9/1/15	101.25	12.21	5.66	–1.28
B3/CCC+	Federated Department Stores				
	16% due 11/1/00	90.25	18.00	4.80	0.57
Municipals:					
A1/A	New Jersey Turnpike				
	7.20% due 1/1/18	95.63	7.58	7.94	–0.20

[a] The issue is trading on a YTC basis; therefore, the YTC is shown rather than the YTM.

Discount coupon bonds, with deep out-of-the money call options, offer positive convexities. For example, the Southern Bell Telephone 8⅝% due 9/1/26 has a 0.27 convexity, and the GMAC 6% due 4/1/11 carries a 1.46 convexity. Super-premium coupon bonds, with deep in-the-money call options, typically have positive convexities. For example, the U.S. Treasury 14% due 11/15/11 (callable at 100 on 11/15/06) has a 1.52 convexity, and the British Columbia Hydro 15½% due 11/15/11 (callable at 106.64 on 11/15/96) offers a 0.53 convexity. Noncallable corporate bonds

Exhibit 12-11. The convexity factors for a variety of noncallable U.S. Treasury bonds and STRIPS (data as of December 30, 1988). The convexity factors assume a 300BP change in market yield.

Issue Description	Price	YTM (%)	Effective Duration	Convexity Factor
U.S. Treasury 6⅞% due 12/31/90	95–16	9.13	1.76	0.06
U.S. Treasury 9% due 11/15/93	99–16	9.11	3.77	0.27
U.S. Treasury 11½% due 11/15/95	111–16	9.20	4.77	0.45
U.S. Treasury 8⅞% due 11/15/98	98–08	9.15	6.38	0.83
U.S. Treasury 9⅜% due 2/15/06	102–20	9.07	8.28	1.62
U.S. Treasury 11¼% due 2/15/15	121–28	9.05	9.34	2.34
U.S. Treasury 9% due 11/15/18	100–00	9.00	10.20	2.83
STRIPS 0% due 11/15/08	17.382	9.00	19.02	5.74
STRIPS 0% due 11/15/18	7.853	8.70	28.63	13.36

have positive convexities. For example, the Atlantic Richfield Company 10⅞% due 7/15/05 carries a 1.40 convexity and the Province of Quebec 8⅝% due 12/1/26 has a 3.09 convexity.

Another approach
to discovering negative convexity

In Chapter 10, the positive convexity of a noncallable bond was illustrated as the natural (and beneficial) change in the bond's duration as yields shift: A decline in yields increases the bond's duration; a rise in yields decreases the bond's duration. The negative convexity of a callable bond can be observed in a similar analysis. A callable bond's effective duration changes as interest rates shift. However, the effects are the opposite of those experienced by a noncallable bond. The effective duration of a callable bond falls as yields decline (and early redemption becomes more probable) and increases as yields rise (and early redemption becomes less probable).

For example, the Citicorp 10⅞% due 6/25/10 (callable on 6/15/90 at 106.53) was priced at 103 on December 30, 1988. The bond's effective duration is 4.35 years (see Exhibit 12–10). As market yields change, the bond's effective duration varies as follows:

Market Yield Change (in BP)	Effective Duration of Citicorp 10⅞% Bond
−300	0.57
−200	1.01
−100	2.43
− 50	3.40
0	4.35
+ 50	5.16
+100	5.77
+200	6.47
+300	6.72

The callable bond's effective duration shortens in a market rally and lengthens in a market decline. Each of these behaviors works to the detriment of the bondholder. The more severe the duration change, the more negative the convexity characteristics of the bond.

A price volatility multiplier
for corporate bonds

A price volatility multiplier (PVM) combines a bond's duration and convexity statistics into a single figure. For a callable bond:

$$PVM = \frac{effective}{duration} + \frac{convexity}{factor}$$

The PVM is a better proxy for a bond's price sensitivity than the bond's effective duration because it considers the bond's inherent convexity attributes.

Using data from Exhibit 12-10, the Pacific Telephone and Telegraph 9⅝% due 7/15/18 has a 5.79 PVM:

$$PVM = 7.07 + (-1.28)$$

$$= 5.79$$

The Capital Cities Broadcasting 11⅜% due 8/15/15 has a 0.17 PVM:

$$PVM = 2.55 + (-2.38)$$
$$= 0.17$$

The noncallable Province of Quebec 8⅝% due 12/1/26 offers a sizable 13.30 PVM:

$$PVM = 10.21 + 3.09$$
$$= 13.30$$

Negative convexity and mortgage-backed securities

Factors influencing
the negative convexity
of mortgage-backed securities

Five primary factors affect an MBS negative convexity: the type of MBS, the market price of the MBS, the prepayment rate assumption, the expected trend in interest rates, and market yield volatility. Each of these factors is discussed in turn with the focus on mortgage passthroughs, which make up the largest component of the mortgage marketplace.

1. *The type of MBS.* Examples are mortgage passthrough (GNMA versus FNMA, 15-year collateral versus 30-year collateral), traditional CMO, PAC CMO, TAC CMO, IO strip, PO strip, CARS, and CARDS. Specific types of MBS have specific cash flow characteristics and specific sensitivities to changes in interest rates.

2. *The market price of the MBS.* Mortgages are prepayable at par value. The negative convexity of a mortgage passthrough is greatest for current coupon issues (i.e., passthroughs trading close to par). The implicit call option on these issues is at-the-money when the security's market value is 100-00. Negative convexity dissipates as a passthrough's price falls to a sizable discount to par (and the call option is deeply out-of-the-money). Negative convexity also evaporates as a passthrough's price surges to a significant premium to par (and the call option is deeply in-the-money).

3. *The prepayment rate assumption.* For discount coupon MBS, a lower prepayment rate reduces the security's actual return, mitigating some or all of the discount's positive convexity. For current coupon MBS and premium coupon MBS, a higher prepayment rate increases negative convexity. The prepayment rate assumption is affected by factors including seasonality, general economic activity, housing activity (e.g., housing starts and sales of existing homes), inflation, real interest rates, the geographic distribution of the underlying mortgages, and prepayment burnout.

4. *The expected trend in interest rates.* Negative convexity is enhanced by a trend to low interest rates. Conversely, a trend to high interest rates reduces or eliminates the negative convexity effect.

5. *Market yield volatility.* The greater the volatility the more magnified is the effect of negative convexity. The potential for early redemption (through prepayments) is increased by a greater degree of market yield volatility.

Illustrations of mortgage-backed securities

Mortgage passthroughs. Exhibit 12–12 presents the convexity factors for a series of 30-year mortgage passthroughs. Current coupon issues suffer the greatest degree of negative convexity. The FHLMC 11s (trading at 99.040) carry a –1.42 convexity, and the FHLMC 11½s (trading at 100.853) offer a –1.48 convexity. Deep discount issues and super-premium issues have more positive convexity than current coupon issues. The discount coupon FHLMC 8s (trading at 87.025) have a 0.68 positive convexity. The super-premium coupon FHLMC 13s (trading at 104.872) have a –0.52 convexity. The convexity patterns of 15-year mortgage passthroughs are similar to those of 30-year passthroughs, although the sizes of the effects are less dramatic.

Derivative mortgage products. In general, the greater the potential variation in a callable security's effective duration, the larger the underlying negative convexity of the instrument. A traditional CMO has minimal convexity in its short maturity tranches but has negative convexity hidden in its long maturity

Exhibit 12-12. The price, yield, effective duration, and convexity statistics for a series of 30-year mortgage passthroughs.[a]

Issue Description	Price	Cash Flow Yield (%)	Effective Duration	Convexity Factor
FHLMC 8s	87.025	10.32	5.47	0.68
FHLMC 9s	91.840	10.44	5.51	-0.16
FHLMC 10s	95.756	10.78	5.23	-0.92
FHLMC 11s	99.040	11.16	3.87	-1.42
FHLMC 11½s	100.853	11.15	2.86	-1.48
FHLMC 12s	102.699	10.88	1.83	-1.31
FHLMC 13s	104.872	10.46	1.11	-0.52

[a]Data as of March 31, 1989 and courtesy of Capital Management Sciences.

tranche(s). A PAC CMO is virtually devoid of negative convexity. A TAC CMO has a modest amount of negative convexity because its effective duration extends in a bear market and, after a period of prepayment protection, contracts in a bull market. Both CARS and CARDS are immune to convexity effects (positive or negative) because of their short effective durations and high degree of predictability of their cash flows.

A PO strip has a large effective duration. The convexity attributes of a PO strip are influenced by the type of underlying collateral (e.g., regular passthrough collateral versus synthetic passthrough collateral) and the coupon rate attached to the underlying collateral. Exhibit 12-13 calculates the convexities of three PO strips that are backed by 30-year FNMA single-family mortgage passthroughs of various coupons (8%, 9%, and 10%). Each strip has a minor degree of negative convexity in a bull market and a modest amount of positive convexity in a bear market. The price of a PO strip is highly sensitive to changes in interest rates.

An IO strip carries a negative effective duration. As with a PO strip, the type of mortgage collateral and the coupon rate of the underlying mortgage passthroughs affect the IO strip's convexity features. Exhibit 12-14 derives the convexities of a series of IO strips backed by 30-year FNMA single-family mortgage passthroughs. Three classes of coupon collateral are illustrated (8%, 9%, and 10%). Each IO strip has a large amount of negative convexity in both bull and bear markets. The price of an IO strip is highly sensitive to changes in interest rates and its price moves in the same direction as interest rates.

Exhibit 12-13. The convexities of a series of PO strips for a variety of yield shifts. The underlying collateral is FNMA 30-year, single-family mortgages. The convexities are based on the difference between the projected 1-year total returns and the effective duration-predicted total returns.[a]

(a) FNMA Trust #54 PO

Price:	48–31
Collateral:	FNMA 8s
WAC:	8.88%
Effective duration:	14.50

Market Yield Change (in BP)	1-Year Return (%)	Incremental Return (%)	Duration-Predicted Return (%)	Convexity (in %)
–200	36.23	27.69	29.00	–1.31
–100	22.21	13.67	14.50	–0.83
0	8.54	0	0	0
+100	– 4.73	–13.67	–14.50	1.23
+200	–17.42	–25.96	–29.00	3.04

(b) FNMA Trust #1 PO

Price:	50–16
Collateral:	FNMA 9s
WAC:	9.69%
Effective duration:	13.87

Market Yield Change (in BP)	1-Year Return (%)	Incremental Return (%)	Duration-Predicted Return (%)	Convexity (in %)
–200	36.10	25.99	27.74	–1.75
–100	22.84	12.73	13.87	–1.14
0	10.11	0	0	0
+100	– 2.04	–12.15	–13.87	1.72
+200	–13.71	–23.82	–27.74	3.92

(c) FNMA Trust #29 PO

Price:	53–16
Collateral:	FNMA 10s
WAC:	10.75%
Effective duration:	14.56

Market Yield Change (in BP)	1-Year Return (%)	Incremental Return (%)	Duration-Predicted Return (%)	Convexity (in %)
–200	37.92	27.51	29.12	–1.61
–100	23.55	13.14	14.56	–1.42
0	10.41	0	0	0
+100	– 2.18	–12.59	–14.56	1.97
+200	–14.01	–24.42	–29.12	4.70

[a]Data as of March 22, 1989, and courtesy of Goldman, Sachs & Co.

Exhibit 12-14. The convexities of a series of IO strips for a variety of yield shifts. The underlying collateral is FNMA 30-year single-family mortgages. The convexities are based on the difference between the projected 1-year total returns and the effective duration-predicted total returns.[a]

(a) FNMA Trust #54 IO

Price:	39–24
Collateral:	FNMA 8s
WAC:	8.88%
Effective duration:	–4.68

Market Yield Change (in BP)	1-Year Return (%)	Incremental Return (%)	Duration-Predicted Return (%)	Convexity (in %)
–200	– 2.57	–14.85	–9.36	–5.49
–100	6.39	– 5.89	–4.68	–1.21
0	12.28	0	0	0
+100	16.08	3.80	4.68	–0.88
+200	18.23	5.95	9.36	–3.41

(b) FNMA Trust #1 IO

Price:	40–31
Collateral:	FNMA 9s
WAC:	9.69%
Effective duration:	–6.77

Market Yield Change (in BP)	1-Year Return (%)	Incremental Return (%)	Duration-Predicted Return (%)	Convexity (in %)
–200	– 7.45	–19.17	–13.54	–5.63
–100	3.92	– 7.80	– 6.77	–1.03
0	11.72	0	0	0
+100	16.94	5.22	6.77	–1.55
+200	20.46	8.74	13.54	–4.80

(c) FNMA Trust #29 IO

Price:	42–17
Collateral:	FNMA 10s
WAC:	10.75%
Effective duration:	–10.49

Market Yield Change (in BP)	1-Year Return (%)	Incremental Return (%)	Duration-Predicted Return (%)	Convexity (in %)
–200	–17.05	–28.50	–20.98	–7.52
–100	0.03	–11.42	–10.49	–0.93
0	11.45	0	0	0
+100	19.49	8.04	10.49	–2.45
+200	24.96	13.51	20.98	–7.47

[a]Data as of March 22, 1989, and courtesy of Goldman, Sachs & Co.

Summary

Negative convexity is a negative difference between the actual price behavior of a callable bond and its duration-predicted price behavior. Negative convexity stems from the call features implicitly attached to a callable bond or a (prepayable) mortgage-backed security. Negative convexity reveals itself when a callable bond's effective duration falls when interest rates decline (for a noncallable bond, effective duration lengthens when interest rates decline). A call provision restricts a callable bond's price advance in a bull market. Its effect diminishes in a bear market, allowing a callable bond to exhibit positive convexity over certain ranges of interest rates. The nonsymmetric nature of a callable bond's convexity can be severe. As a result, interpreting the average convexity factor for a callable bond is difficult. A callable bond's price volatiliy multiplier, which combines the bond's duration and convexity statistics, is equally misleading.

Several factors affect the negative convexity of a callable corporate bond: call features; the divergence between the bond's modified DTC and the bond's modified DTM; the bond's market price relative to its call price; the expected trend in interest rates; and market yield volatility. For a mortgage-backed security, the influential factors are the type of MBS, the market price of the MBS, the prepayment rate assumption, the expected trend in interest rates, and market yield volatility. For a derivative mortgage product, the type of product (e.g., IO strip versus CARS) is the most critical variable. Chapter 13 applies the convexity discoveries of Chapters 9 through 12 to bond portfolios.

CHAPTER 13

Portfolio Convexity

Introduction

This chapter explores the convexity of a bond portfolio. A portfolio's convexity reflects the convexities of the portfolio members and quantifies the price return effects that are not captured by the portfolio's duration. The chapter illustrates the calculation of portfolio convexity and discusses the limitations of portfolio convexity.

Portfolio convexity: The concept

Convexity is defined as the price return that is not explained by modified (or effective) duration. For a portfolio of securities, convexity is calculated as follows:

$$\begin{array}{ccccc} \text{portfolio} & & \text{actual price} & & \text{duration-predicted} \\ \text{convexity} & = & \text{return} & - & \text{price return} \\ \text{(in \%)} & & \text{(in \%)} & & \text{(in \%)} \end{array}$$

$$\begin{array}{c} \text{portfolio} \\ \text{convexity} \\ \text{factor} \end{array} = \dfrac{\dfrac{\text{portfolio convexity (in \%)}}{\text{absolute BP change in yield}}}{100}$$

Portfolio convexity is affected by the nature of the underlying securities (e.g., noncallable, callable corporate, or mortgage-backed), the durations of the portfolio components, the cash flow distributions of the individual bonds (e.g., coupon rates, sinking funds, or final maturities), the current level of interest rates, the volatility of interest rates, and the direction in which interest rates change. Exhibit 13–1 illustrates portfolio convexity graphically by plotting the price:yield pairings for a sample portfolio in a wide variety of interest rate environments.

Portfolio convexity: Calculations

Exhibit 13–2 presents a $100 million portfolio consisting solely of noncallable U.S. Treasury bonds. The portfolio's internal rate of return (IRR) is 8.97%, and its modified (and effective) duration is 4.50 years.[1] Based on this information, Exhibit 13–3 tabulates the portfolio's convexity for a variety of yield shifts. For a 300BP yield decline, the portfolio's convexity is calculated as 2.22%:

$$\begin{array}{ccc} \text{portfolio} & \text{actual price} & \text{duration-predicted} \\ \text{convexity} = & \text{return} & - & \text{price return} \\ \text{(in \%)} & \text{(in \%)} & \text{(in \%)} \end{array}$$

$$= 15.72\% - 13.50\%$$

$$= 2.22\%$$

The portfolio's average convexity factor for a 300BP yield shift is 0.66.

---

[1] Modified duration (to maturity) and effective duration are identical for a noncallable security or for a portfolio of noncallable securities.

Exhibit 13-1. Portfolio convexity in a graphical context.

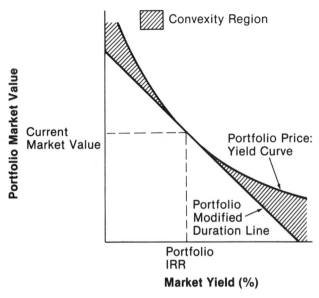

Exhibit 13–4 displays the portfolio's cash flow distribution and derives the portfolio's Macaulay's duration (4.70) and modified duration (4.50). The *discounted cash flow (DCF) yield* (in this case, 8.97%) is the single discount rate that, when applied to all of the portfolio's future cash flows, equates the present value of the cash

Exhibit 13-2. A portfolio of noncallable U.S. Treasury bonds (data as of May 15, 1988).

Par Amount ($000)	Issue	Price	YTM (%)	Effective Duration	Market Value ($000)	% of Portfolio
24,000	U.S. Treasury 11¾% due 5/15/89	104–00	7.52	0.93	24,960	0.2496
26,630	U.S. Treasury 8% due 11/15/90	100–00	8.00	2.23	26,630	0.2663
12,000	U.S. Treasury 9% due 5/15/98	100–00	9.00	6.51	12,000	0.1200
4,000	U.S. Treasury 11¼% due 5/15/95	112–12	8.84	4.93	4,495	0.0450
26,000	U.S. Treasury 12% due 5/15/05	122–24	9.31	8.06	31,915 100,000	0.3192

Exhibit 13-3. Market value changes for a five-bond portfolio as attributable to duration and convexity. The portfolio is initially priced at an 8.97% DCF yield and has a modified (and effective) duration of 4.50 years (data from Exhibit 13-2).[a]

Market Yield Change (in BP)	Actual % Change in Market Value	Market Value Change (%) Due to:		Convexity Factor
		Effective Duration	*Convexity*	
−400	+22.16	+18.00	+4.16	1.04
−300	+15.72	+13.50	+2.22	0.74
−200	+ 9.94	+ 9.00	+0.94	0.47
−100	+ 4.72	+ 4.50	+0.22	0.22
0	0	0	0	0
+100	− 4.29	− 4.50	+0.21	0.21
+200	− 8.19	− 9.00	+0.81	0.41
+300	−11.76	−13.50	+1.74	0.58
+400	−15.03	−18.00	+2.97	0.74

[a]The DCF yield is exactly 8.966%, which rounds to 8.97%.

flows to the portfolio's current market value ($100 million). The DCF yield is the portfolio's internal rate of return. Exhibit 13–5 analyzes a bond portfolio that includes callable corporate bonds and mortgage-backed securities. The portfolio has a –0.15 convexity.

Exhibit 13–6 assesses the portfolio's total return behavior in a variety of interest rate scenarios. The return simulation reveals the unique convexity attributes of the portfolio. The "income effect" column calculates the coupon (and reinvestment) return over the 1-year holding period. The income effect is enhanced in high yield environments when the reinvestment rate increases. The "parallel effect" column shows the portfolio's return caused by a parallel shift in the U.S. Treasury yield curve (for as large as a 400BP shift); the effects of call provisions are incorporated into the results. Over a 1-year horizon, there is a 90% chance that U.S. Treasury yields will end the year within 200BP of the beginning-of-year level ("10% to 90% confidence interval").

The "nonparallel effect" column summarizes the portfolio's return that is attributable to nonparallel shifts in the U.S. Treasury yield curve. These yield curve twists (between long-term bond yields

Exhibit 13-4. Calculation of the duration of the portfolio of Exhibit 13-2. The present value factors are based on a 8.966% DCF yield.

(1) t (Yrs)	(2) Cash Flow CF_t ($000)	(3) Present Value Factor	(4) = (2) × (3) $PV(CF_t)$ ($000)	(5) = (4) / PMV^a Present Value Weight	(6) = (1) × (5) Present Value Weighted t
0.5	4,800	0.9571	4,594	0.0459	0.0230
1.0	28,800	0.9160	26,381	0.2638	0.2638
1.5	3,390	0.8767	2,972	0.0297	0.0446
2.0	3,390	0.8391	2,845	0.0285	0.0570
2.5	30,020	0.8031	24,109	0.2411	0.6028
3.0	2,325	0.7686	1,787	0.0178	0.0534
3.5	2,325	0.7357	1,711	0.0171	0.0599
4.0	2,325	0.7041	1,637	0.0164	0.0656
4.5	2,325	0.6739	1,567	0.0157	0.0707
5.0	2,325	0.6450	1,500	0.0150	0.0750
5.5	2,325	0.6173	1,435	0.0144	0.0792
6.0	2,325	0.5908	1,374	0.0137	0.0822
6.5	2,325	0.5655	1,315	0.0132	0.0858
7.0	6,325	0.5412	3,423	0.0342	0.2394
7.5	2,100	0.5180	1,088	0.0109	0.0818
8.0	2,100	0.4958	1,041	0.0104	0.0832
8.5	2,100	0.4745	996	0.0100	0.0850
9.0	2,100	0.4541	954	0.0095	0.0855
9.5	2,100	0.4346	913	0.0091	0.0865
10.0	14,100	0.4160	5,866	0.0587	0.5870
10.5	1,560	0.3981	621	0.0062	0.0651
11.0	1,560	0.3811	595	0.0060	0.0660
11.5	1,560	0.3647	569	0.0057	0.0656
12.0	1,560	0.3491	545	0.0055	0.0660
12.5	1,560	0.3341	521	0.0052	0.0650
13.0	1,560	0.3198	499	0.0050	0.0650
13.5	1,560	0.3060	477	0.0048	0.0648
14.0	1,560	0.2929	457	0.0046	0.0644
14.5	1,560	0.2803	437	0.0044	0.0638
15.0	1,560	0.2683	419	0.0042	0.0630
15.5	1,560	0.2568	401	0.0040	0.0620
16.0	1,560	0.2458	383	0.0038	0.0608
16.5	1,560	0.2352	367	0.0037	0.0611
17.0	27,560	0.2251	6,204	0.0620	1.0540
			100,000	1.0000	4.6980
			Portfolio Market Value (in $000)		Portfolio Duration (Macaulay's)

^{a}Portfolio market value.

Exhibit 13-5. A sample portfolio and its duration and convexity characteristics as of December 30, 1988. Convexity calculations reflect a 300BP volatility assumption.[a]

Par Amount ($000)	Issue	Price	Effective Duration	Convexity Factor	Market Value ($000)	% of Portfolio
10,000	U.S. Treasury 8⅝% due 8/31/90	99–04	1.48	0.05	10,200	0.1409
20,000	Texas Utilities Electric 12% due 9/1/15	106.25	4.30	−2.23	22,050	0.3047
10,000	GNMA 10% due 6/15/16	98–04	4.55	−0.88	9,850	0.1361
20,000	U.S. Treasury 9⅛% due 5/15/18	101–00	10.13	2.78	20,425	0.2822
10,000	Pacific Telephone and Telegraph 9⅝% due 7/15/18	94.10	7.21	−1.01	9,850	0.1361
	Portfolio averages ⟶		5.98	−0.15	72,375	

[a]Data courtesy of Capital Management Sciences.

and short-term bond yields) are typically less than 150BP over a 1-year holding period ("10% to 90% confidence interval"). The "quality spread effect" column ascertains the impact of a general change in quality spreads. Over a 1-year horizon, quality spreads are expected to remain within 100BP of the beginning-of-year levels ("10% to 90% confidence interval").

The "passthrough spread effect" is the incremental portfolio return due to shifts in mortgage passthrough spreads. Passthrough spreads are likely to remain within 100BP of the beginning-of-year levels ("10% to 90% confidence interval"). The simulated return for the portfolio is a combination of the income effect, the parallel effect, the nonparallel effect, the quality spread effect, and the passthrough spread effect.

A portfolio convexity based on a total return simulation is superior to a DCF yield-based convexity because the former recognizes that not all cash flows behave similarly. Nonparallel

Exhibit 13-6. A component-by-component total return simulation for the bond portfolio of Exhibit 13-5. A 1-year horizon is assumed.[a]

Interest Rate Change (in BP)	Income Effect(%)	Parallel Effect (%)	Nonparallel Effect (%)	Quality Spread Effect (%)	Pass-through Spread Effect (%)
-400	10.164	20.938	0.854	2.110	1.491
-350	10.190	18.292	0.775	2.086	1.367
300	10.215	15.798	0.698	2.063	1.265
-250	10.240	13.429	0.622	2.028	1.184
-200	10.265	11.034[b]	0.544	1.924	1.091
-150	10.291	8.530	0.458[b]	1.728	0.930
-100	10.316	5.898	0.353	1.407[b]	0.685[b]
- 50	10.341	3.034	0.200	0.832	0.358
0	10.367	0.000[c]	0.000[c]	0.000[c]	0.000[c]
50	10.392	- 3.077	-0.230	-0.995	-0.365
100	10.417	- 6.079	-0.475	-2.073[b]	-0.705
150	10.443	- 8.985	-0.726[b]	-3.183	-1.051
200	10.468	-11.757[b]	-0.980	-4.306	-1.389
250	10.493	-14.335	-1.231	-5.410	-1.692
300	10.518	-16.716	-1.474	-6.471	-1.981
350	10.544	-18.910	-1.711	-7.498	-2.257
400	10.569	-20.902	-1.939	-8.474	-2.521

[a]Calculations courtesy of Capital Management Sciences.

[b]10% to 90% confidence interval.

[c]Mean interest rate change.

yield shifts occur between sectors of the market (e.g., callable bonds versus noncallable bonds, high quality bonds versus low quality bonds, or short-term bonds versus long-term bonds). The total return simulation is designed to capture all the real-world effects of a general shift in interest rates. Convexity behaviors in bull markets can differ sizably from convexity behaviors in bear markets. A total return simulation brings these divergent results to light, whereas an average portfolio convexity statistic melds the two types of results into a single, sometimes meaningless, figure.

Estimating portfolio convexity

Portfolio convexity can be estimated by the weighted average convexity of the portfolio members:

$$\text{portfolio convexity} = \sum_{i=1}^{N} (C_i \times w_i)$$

where

C_i = the convexity of the ith security

w_i = the market value weight of the ith security (expressed in decimal form)

N = the number of securities in the portfolio

Exhibit 13–7 lists the holdings of a seven-bond portfolio of U.S. Treasury bonds and corporate bonds. The portfolio has a 7.93 modified duration, a 5.33 effective duration, and a –0.60 convexity:

portfolio duration = 3.77(.0458) + 6.38(.0994) + 7.61(.1706) +
(modifed)   7.78(.1362) + 8.39(.2262) + 8.97(.2088) +
                       8.80(.1131)

= 7.93

portfolio duration = 3.77(.0458) + 6.38(.0994) + 7.61(.1706) +
(effective)   5.39(.1362) + 2.55(.2262) + 6.83(.2088) +
                       4.30(.1131)

= 5.33

portfolio convexity = 0.27(.0458) + 0.83(.0994) + 1.40(.1706) +
(based on effective   0.53(.1362) + (–2.38) (.2262) +
duration)   (–1.55) (.2088) + (–1.29) (.1131)

= –0.60

A portfolio of bonds can have a zero convexity or a negative convexity if a large proportion of the portfolio holdings are concentrated in callable corporate bonds and/or high coupon mortgage-backed securities.

Exhibit 13-7. The duration and convexity characteristics of a seven-bond, $100 million portfolio of U.S. Treasuries and corporates as of December 30, 1988. Convexity calculations reflect a 300BP volatility assumption.[a]

Par Amount ($000)	Issue	Price	Modified Duration	Effective Duration	Convexity Factor	Market Value ($000)	% of Portfolio
4,470	U.S. Treasury 9% due 11/15/93	99–16	3.77	3.77	0.27	4,580	0.0458
10,000	U.S. Treasury 8⅞% due 11/15/98	98–08	6.38	6.38	0.83	9.935	0.0994
15,000	Atlantic Richfield Co. 10⅞%, due 7/15/05	108.75	7.61	7.61	1.40	17,060	0.1706
10,000	British Columbia Hydro 15½% due 11/15/11	134.25	7.78	5.39	0.53	13,620	0.1362
20,000	Capital Cities Broadcasting 11⅜% due 8/15/15	108.75	8.39	2.55	−2.38	22,620	0.2262
20,000	Anheuser-Busch 10% due 7/1/18	99.50	8.97	6.83	−1.55	20,875	0.2088
10,000	Southwestern Bell Tel. 11⅞% due 10/18/21	110.75	8.80	4.30	−1.29	11,310	0.1131
	Portfolio averages ⎯⎯⎯⎯⎯>		7.93	5.33	−0.60	100,000	

[a]Data courtesy of Capital Management Sciences.

Summary

Portfolio convexity is simply the difference between a bond portfolio's actual price behavior and its duration-predicted price behavior. The duration-predicted behavior is based on either modified duration or, preferably, effective duration. Portfolio convexity is estimated by a weighted average of the convexities of the portfolio members. Portfolio convexity can be positive, negative, or zero. A portfolio's convexity is often represented by an average of the convexity factors for a rise and fall in interest rates of equal magnitude (e.g., ±300BP).

A total return simulation is a useful supplement to a portfolio convexity statistic because the portfolio's convexity behaviors can vary dramatically in different interest rate environments. Such a simulation can isolate the portfolio's sensitivity to other real-world influences such as nonparallel shifts in yield curves and changes in sector spreads. Chapter 14 concludes the convexity section of the book with applications of convexity to bond portfolio management.

Convexity and Bond Portfolio Management Strategy

Introduction

This chapter applies convexity to bond portfolio management by discussing and illustrating both passive and active bond portfolio strategies. Passive bond portfolio management approaches include cash flow matching, bond immunization, and bond indexation. Active bond portfolio management strategies come in two primary types: risk-controlled styles and risk-altering styles. The structure of the chapter parallels that of Chapter 8, which analyzed the duration of bond portfolios.

Passive management strategies

Passive strategies for bond management typically include a target or a benchmark portfolio such as a liability stream or a bond index. The passive manager attempts to satisfy the investment objectives of the portfolio while minimizing portfolio turnover and transaction costs. Three passive management approaches are prevalent: cash flow matching, bond immunization, and bond indexation.

Cash flow matching

Cash flow matching, or dedication, is a passive management technique in which a bond portfolio is structured to match the cash flows of a future set of obligations. Cash flow matching is generally achieved with U.S. Treasury bonds and STRIPS. These issues are attractive because of their noncallability, lack of credit risk, and widespread availability in the marketplace. Because the maturities of the portfolio cash flows are matched to the maturities of the liability cash flows, the duration and convexity of the bond portfolio are identical to those of the liability stream. *A cash flow match assures a convexity match as well as a duration match.*[1]

Bond immunization

Bond immunization is a revised version of cash flow matching in which the average duration of the bond portfolio is matched to the average duration of a stream of future liabilities. Periodic rebalancing maintains the duration match until the liabilities are fully paid. Convexity differences can arise, however, because of the nonlinearity of convexity. Convexity is positively related to cash flow dispersion and duration. Dumbbell bond portfolios offer greater convexity than intermediate maturity bond portfolios of similar average duration (to be discussed later in this chapter). *Consequently, convexity differences can exist in immunized bond portfolios.*

Exhibit 14–1 calculates the convexities of STRIPS that mature in 10, 20, and 30 years. A bond portfolio with an average duration of 20.00 years immunizes a liability that is due in 20.00 years. Exhibit 14–2 illustrates two portfolios that can immunize a 20-year liability: a portfolio of 20-year STRIPS and a portfolio equally invested in 10-year STRIPS and 30-year STRIPS. Although the

---

[1] If a perfect cash flow match cannot be achieved, therre will be mismatches of duration and convexity as well. Serious problems can arise if the cash flows of either the assets (i.e., the bond portfolio) or the liabilities change. Credit risk or call risk can influence the former; changes in actuarial assumptions or plan benefits can affect the latter. The cash flow variability of the asset stream is eliminated by using noncallable U.S. Treasury bonds and STRIPS. Variability in liability cash flows is minimized by dedicating (i.e., cash flow matching) only the known retired lives liabilities of a defined benefit plan.

Exhibit 14-1. Price, yield, duration, and convexity statistics for a 10-year STRIPS, a 20-year STRIPS, and a 30-year STRIPS (data as of November 15, 1988). The convexity factors assume a 300BP yield shift.

Issue	*Price*	*YTM (%)*	*Macaulay's Duration*	*Convexity Factor*
STRIPS 0% due 11/15/98	41.069	9.10	10.00	1.45
STRIPS 0% due 11/15/08	16.867	9.10	20.00	5.80
STRIPS 0% due 11/15/18	7.550[a]	8.80	30.00	12.46

[a]Although not actively traded until December 1988, this price reflects an estimate of where the bond would have traded on 11/15/88 (at a 20BP lower yield than the current coupon 30-year U.S. Treasury bond).

portfolio durations are identical (20.00), their convexities differ (5.78 and 6.98 respectively). A 10-year STRIPS/30-year STRIPS combination has superior convexity versus a 20-year liability cash flow. Convexity differences are magnified if callable bonds are used in the immunization process.

The primary objective of an immunization strategy is protection from the adverse effects of general shifts in interest rates. Call risk and credit risk should be minimized in order to eliminate unexpected interruptions in cash flow. Carefully selected discount coupon corporate bonds or mortgage-backed securities can be used in modest quantities to reduce the cost of the immunization and to add incremental yield.

Bond indexation

Bond indexation is a passive management technique in which a portfolio is structured and maintained with the risk and return characteristics of a particular bond index. The index may be a

Exhibit 14-2. The convexities of two immunized bond portfolios. Each portfolio has a Macaulay's duration of 20.00 years. (Convexity data from Exhibit 14-1.)

Portfolio	*Portfolio Convexity*
20-year STRIPS	5.80
10-year STRIPS/30-year STRIPS combination	6.96

broad-based bond market index such as the Shearson Lehman Hutton Aggregate Bond Index, or it may be a customized index tailored to specific risk and return parameters. In either case, the average duration of the bond portfolio is targeted to that of the underlying benchmark. In addition, the characteristics of the bond index are matched on a weighted market value basis: issuer sector distribution, quality distribution, coupon distribution, maturity distribution, and duration distribution.

The bond index may be impossible to match perfectly because of the unavailability of issues or the prohibitive cost of implementing an exact duplicate. Sampling techniques are used to best mimic the risk and return behaviors of the benchmark. *While the duration match is maintained, convexity differences can arise as a result of differing degrees of call risk (e.g., a mismatch in coupon distribution) and cash flow distribution (e.g., a mismatch in maturity distribution or duration distribution).* Credit risk differences can emerge through a mismatch in the quality distribution or through an inability to replicate the weightings of individual issuers.

Exhibit 14–3 presents descriptive information on the Shearson Lehman Hutton Government Corporate (SLHGC) bond index as of June 30, 1989. This table shows the wide variety of characteristics that must be matched to eliminate duration and convexity discrepancies between an indexed portfolio and the underlying bond index. In other cases (e.g., an all-Treasury bond index), a perfect or near-perfect match can be achieved with an indexed portfolio. Exhibit 14–4 describes the Shearson-Lehman Hutton Long-Term U.S. Treasury bond index as of June 30, 1989. The availability of the underlying issues and the lack of credit risk make this index easy to mimic with a sample portfolio. Duration and convexity differences between the indexed portfolio and the actual index can be minimized.

Active management strategies

Actively managed bond portfolios require daily attention. The turnover rate of an active bond portfolio exceeds that of a passively managed portfolio because the active manager constantly pursues market opportunities. To take advantage of changing market

Exhibit 14-3. Descriptive data on the Shearson Lehman Hutton Government/ Corporate Bond Index as of June 30, 1989.[a]

Number of issues	4,977	Average YTM (%)	8.54
Average duration (Macaulay's)	5.30	Average maturity (years)	9.79
Average duration (effective)	4.78	Market value (millions)	$1,894

Description:

1. All public obligations of the U.S. Treasury except for flower bonds and foreign-targeted issues.
2. All publicly issued debt of agencies of the U.S. government, quasi-federal corporations, and corporate debt guaranteed by the U.S. government (excluding mortgage-backed securities).
3. All public, fixed rate, nonconvertible investment grade domestic corporate debt.
4. All U.S. dollar denominated, SEC registered, public, nonconvertible debt issued or guaranteed by foreign sovereign governments, foreign municipalities, foreign governmental agencies, or international agencies.

Only notes and bonds with a minimum outstanding principal of $25 million and a minimum remaining term to maturity of one year are included in the index.

Issuer Sector Distribution	Index Weighting (in %)	Maturity Distribution (in Years)	Index Weighting (in %)
U.S. Treasury	62.84	0– 1	0.00
Federal agency	10.68	1– 2	17.68
Industrial	7.30	2– 3	11.03
Bank and finance	7.68	3– 4	8.95
Utility	8.17	4– 5	7.72
Yankee	3.33	5– 6	5.82
		6– 7	6.09
		7– 8	3.86
Quality Distribution		8– 9	3.56
U.S. Treasury	62.84	9–10	4.05
Federal agency	10.68	10–15	6.13
AAA	3.65	15–20	5.98
AA	7.55	20–25	4.91
A	9.42	25–30	13.30
BBB	5.87	30+	0.92
Below BBB	0.00		

Coupon Rate Distribution		Effective Duration Distribution (in Years)	
0– 6	1.26	0– 1	1.56
6– 7	3.28	1– 2	20.01
7– 8	13.64	2– 3	14.15
8– 9	30.35	3– 4	13.61
9–10	24.01	4– 5	11.10
10–11	9.13	5– 6	9.85
11–12	8.46	6– 7	8.43
12–13	4.53	7– 8	4.39
13+	5.33	8– 9	4.18
		9–10	3.80
		10–11	3.56
		11–12	5.11
		12+	0.26

[a]Data courtesy of Shearson Lehman Hutton Inc.

Exhibit 14-4. Descriptive data on the Shearson Lehman Hutton Long-Term U.S. Treasury Bond Index as of June 30, 1989.

Number of issues	47
Average duration (Macaulay's)	9.88
Average duration (effective)	9.66
Average YTM (%)	8.23
Average maturity (years)	22.81
Market value (millions)	$327

Description: All U.S. Treasury bonds with maturities of ten years or greater; $25 million minimum principal outstanding; excludes flower bonds and foreign-targeted issues.

Maturity Distribution (in Years)	Index Weighting (in %)
10–15	14.09
15–20	16.68
20–25	18.99
25–30	50.24

Coupon Rate Distribution (in %)	Index Weighting (in %)
0– 7	0.00
7– 8	12.17
8– 9	20.49
9–10	13.88
10–11	13.89
11–12	16.78
12–13	12.23
13+	10.56

[a]Data courtesy of Shearson Lehman Hutton Inc.

conditions and shifting relative values, an active manager needs the flexibility to move in and out of various market sectors and individual issues. Up-to-date and thorough analyses of the fundamentals of various issuer credits is important.

Active management techniques can be classified into two basic types. Risk-controlled techniques attempt to monitor closely the overall interest rate risk of the bond portfolio while adding value through sector rotation and security selection. Risk-altering techniques pursue an investment objective (such as maximizing convexity) while allowing the interest rate risk of the portfolio to change in the process. The following two sections discuss several active strategies, and the concluding section gives some additional factors to consider when actively managing a bond portfolio.

Risk-controlled bond management techniques

Risk-controlled techniques handle portfolio risk by maintaining a portfolio duration equal to that of a benchmark (e.g., a bond index, a customized index, or a fixed number). Adept sector rotation and security selection garner incremental total returns. The illustrations that follow assume convexity maximization as the investment objective.[2]

Exhibit 14–5 lists some of the potential bond market sectors from which an active manager can select: U.S. Treasury bonds, federal agency bonds, corporate bonds of various quality, foreign currency bonds, futures, options, preferred stock, and so on. Exhibit 14-6 reveals the size of several of the bond market sectors.

Exhibit 14-5. A sampling of bond market sectors.

U.S. Treasury bills	Floating rate notes
U.S. Treasury notes and bonds	Foreign currency bonds
STRIPS	High-yield (below investment
Federal agency notes and bonds	grade) bonds
Mortgage-backed securities	Money-market investments
Industrial bonds	Preferred stock
Utility bonds	Futures
Bank/Finance bonds	Options
Yankee bonds	Municipal bonds
Eurodollar bonds	Asset-backed securities

[2] A convexity maximization objective is a form of total return maximization. The purpose here is to focus on enhancing convexity, the concept of interest in this section of the book. As will be noted later in the chapter, incremental convexity is not always a desirable trait. The price of convexity is sometimes too dear, and less convex instruments are more attractive. Nonparallel yield shifts and yield spread changes can also eliminate the desire for incremental convexity. You are cautioned to consider convexity in light of the investment objective(s) of the portfolio and in light of current market conditions.

Exhibit 14-6. The size of a selection of bond market sectors (as of December 31, 1988).

Bond Market Sector	Approximate Market Value ($ Billion)
U.S. Treasury bills	425
U.S. Treasury notes/bonds	1,250
Investment grade corporates	420
High-yield corporates	190
Municipals	760
Mortgage passthroughs	610
Foreign currency bonds	5,500
Federal agency bonds	310
Yankee bonds	60
Eurodollar bonds	415
Money-market investments [a]	950

[a]Includes CP, BAs, and CDs (domestic and Euro).

The sheer size of these sectors implies that there is a large potential pool of individual issues from which to choose. The selection is vast. For example, there are approximately 30 U.S. Treasury bills, 200 U.S. Treasury notes and bonds, 60 STRIPS, 600 federal agency notes and bonds, 400 yankee bonds, 4,500 investment-grade domestic corporate bonds, and 2 million municipals. Issue selection, therefore, provides opportunities for total return enhancement, yield enhancement, convexity enhancement, and other types of enhancement.

Adding convexity vis-à-vis a benchmark. Firms such as Capital Management Sciences offer analytical software packages that assist in constructing a bond portfolio that matches the average duration of a bond market index (or a customized bond index) while providing convexity enhancements. Exhibit 14–7 lists the holdings of a sample portfolio that offers more convexity than the Salomon Brothers Broad Investment Grade (BIG) bond index (data as of December 30, 1988). The portfolio of 19 bonds includes noncallable U.S. Treasuries, discount coupon mortgage passthroughs, and discount coupon corporates. The portfolio's average effective duration is virtually identical to the effective duration of the Salomon Brothers' index (4.69 versus 4.67), and the portfolio's average convexity is almost three times as great as the average convexity of the Salomon Brothers' index (0.27 versus 0.10).

The total return simulations of Exhibit 14–7 confirm the superior convexity of the active bond portfolio as the U.S. Treasury yields shift in a parallel fashion over a 1-year investment horizon. Larger yield changes amplify the convexity of the portfolio vis-à-vis the index. A 100BP decline in interest rates renders an 18BP total return advantage to the portfolio as a result of its convexity features. A 300BP drop in yields rewards the portfolio with 139BP in added return vis-à-vis its index counterpart.

Dumbbell portfolios versus bullet portfolios. A *dumbbell portfolio* is a combination of bonds of short and long maturities. A *bullet portfolio*, on the other hand, is a collection of bonds of intermediate maturities. A dumbbell portfolio offers more convexity than a bullet portfolio of the same average duration because of the convexity characteristics of the former portfolio's underlying cash flows.

Convexity is an increasing function of duration. Long-term cash flows have disproportionately large amounts of convexity. A portfolio that is concentrated in long-term cash flows offers superior convexity. A portfolio consisting solely of long-term bonds carries a high duration and considerable convexity. A dumbbell portfolio that has a partial exposure to long-term bonds offers convexity that is superior to a portfolio of bonds of intermediate-term maturities.

Exhibit 14–8 calculates the convexities of two U.S. Treasury bond portfolios. The dumbbell portfolio consists of a combination of 2-year bonds and 30-year bonds; the bullet portfolio holds only 7-year bonds. The 2-year bond/30-year bond portfolio provides more than twice as much convexity as the 7-year bond portfolio (1.09 versus 0.48). Positive convexity is particularly enhanced by dumbbell combinations of short-term STRIPS and long-term STRIPS.

In a portfolio of noncallable securities, cash flow dispersion enhances convexity. When callable bonds are introduced into a portfolio, the dumbbell:bullet generalizations stated earlier no longer apply. Long-term callable bonds often have severely negative convexities, rather than strongly positive convexities, particularly in a bull market.

Exhibit 14-7. Analysis of a bond portfolio designed to match the risk characteristics of the Salomon Brothers' Broad Investment Grade (BIG) bond index while enhancing convexity.

COMPARE System, Portfolio Appraisal Report

Par Amount ($000)	CUSIP	Issuer	Quality	Coupon (%)	Maturity	12/30/88 Price	Market Value ($000)	Percentage of Portfolio	Yield to Maturity[b] (%)	Duration (years)			Pass-through Spread	Convexity
										Parallel	Non-Parallel	Quality Spread		
3500	912827TL	U.S. Treasury	GOV	7.250	3/31/90	97.674	3482	3.6	9.245	1.20	0.84	0.00	0.00	0.01
1000	912827VZ	U.S. Treasury	GOV	7.375	3/31/90	97.763	9961	10.2	9.294	1.20	0.84	0.00	0.00	0.01
5000	202795CZ	Commonwealth Edison	BBB	8.125	4/15/90	97.456	4957	5.1	10.257	1.23	0.85	1.23	0.00	0.01
3000	173034DM	Citicorp	A	8.375	5/1/90	98.386	2993	3.1	9.674	1.28	0.87	0.96	0.00	0.01
9500	912827RY	U.S. Treasury	GOV	11.375	5/15/90	102.641	9886	10.1	9.266	1.30	0.88	0.00	0.00	0.01
9500	912827QA	U.S. Treasury	GOV	11.500	10/15/90	103.512	10061	10.3	9.307	1.64	0.98	0.00	0.00	0.01
5000	171205BZ	Chrysler Financial	BBB	7.875	11/1/91	94.996	4814	4.9	9.934	2.56	1.14	2.56	0.00	0.03
2000	171205CC	Chrysler Financial	BBB	7.625	3/10/92	93.800	1923	2.0	9.929	2.82	1.13	2.82	0.00	0.04
5000	44065AT	Hospital Corp.	BBB	7.875	8/15/93	90.582	4677	4.8	10.492	3.80	1.01	3.80	0.00	0.08
5000	744567CD	Public Service Electric & Gas	A	7.500	4/1/96	87.992	4492	4.6	9.852	5.49	0.57	4.12	0.00	0.14
5000	293561AA	Enron Corp.	BBB	7.000	2/15/99	78.523	4057	4.2	10.488	6.79	0.23	6.79	0.00	0.28
1190	FH080007	FHLMC	AGY	8.000	6/15/07	90.289	1078	1.1	10.302	4.88	0.72	0.00	4.88	0.34
4794	FH075007	FHLMC	AGY	7.500	6/15/07	88.109	4239	4.3	10.288	4.90	0.71	0.00	4.90	0.37
5104	FN075012	FNMA	AGY	7.500	6/15/12	87.344	4474	4.6	10.230	5.40	0.59	0.00	5.40	0.47
7500	912810DW	U.S. Treasury	GOV	7.250	5/15/16	82.021	6220	6.4	9.031	10.78	0.00	0.00	0.00	0.96
5000	624284AU	Mountain States Telephone & Telegraph	AA	8.000	9/15/17	80.320	4133	4.2	10.109	9.08	0.01	4.54	0.00	0.42
10000	912810EA	U.S. Treasury	GOV	9.125	5/15/18	100.893	10203	10.4	9.036	10.57	0.00	0.00	0.00	0.94
2000	845335BH	Southwestern Bell Telephone	AA	8.750	11/1/24	85.664	1742	1.8	10.257	8.43	0.03	4.21	0.00	0.26
5000	451794AQ	Illinois Bell Telephone	AA	8.500	4/22/26	83.883	4274	4.4	10.177	8.85	0.01	4.42	0.00	0.38

[a]Data and analysis courtesy of Capital Management Sciences.

[b]Cash flow yield for mortgage passthroughs.

309

Exhibit 14-7. (cont.)

COMPARE System
Sensitivity Analysis
1.00 Year Horizon
Portfolio vs. Salomon BIG Index
Total Return Differences

Interest Rate Change (in BP)	Income Effect (%)	Parallel Effect (%)	Non-Parallel Effect (%)	Quality Spread Effect (%)	Pass-through Spread Effect (%)
−400	−0.000	2.658	0.058	2.782	−1.826
−350	−0.002	2.044	0.009	2.388	−1.667
−300	−0.003	1.510	−0.028	2.007	−1.489
−250	−0.004	1.057	−0.053	1.639	−1.291
−200	−0.005	0.685[c]	−0.066	1.285	−1.073
−150	−0.006	0.393	−0.068[c]	0.944	−0.835
−100	−0.007	0.181	−0.057	0.616[c]	−0.576[c]
− 50	−0.008	0.050	−0.034	0.301	−0.298
0	−0.009	0.000[d]	0.000[d]	0.000[d]	0.000[d]
50	−0.010	0.030	0.046	−0.288	0.318
100	−0.011	0.140	0.105	−0.563[c]	0.656[c]
150	−0.012	0.331	0.175[c]	−0.824	1.015
200	−0.013	0.603[c]	0.257	−1.073	1.393
250	−0.014	0.955	0.351	−1.307	1.791
300	−0.015	1.387	0.456	−1.529	2.209
350	−0.016	1.900	0.574	−1.738	2.647
400	−0.017	2.494	0.704	−1.933	3.105

[c]10% to 90% confidence interval

[d]Mean interest rate change.

Exhibit 14-7. (cont.)

COMPARE System
Portfolio Summary Report
Four Factor Duration
Portfolio vs. Salomon BIG Index

	Yield to Maturity (%)	Duration in Years				
		Parallel	Non-Parallel	Quality Spread	Pass-through Spread	Convexity
Portfolio	9.672	4.69	0.61	1.39	0.51	0.27
Salomon BIG Index	9.680	4.67	0.69	0.77	1.16	0.10
Difference	−0.008	0.02	−0.08	0.62	−0.65	0.17

Exhibit 14-8. The price, yield, duration, and convexity statistics for two U.S. Treasury bond portfolios (data as of December 30, 1988). The convexity factors assume a 300BP shift in yield.

Dumbbell portfolio

Portfolio Weighting (in %)	Issue	Price	YTM (%)	Effective Duration	Convexity Factor
0.643	U.S. Treasury 6⅝% due 12/31/90	95–16	9.13	1.76	0.06
0.357	U.S. Treasury 9% due 11/15/18	100–00	9.00	10.20	2.83
	Portfolio averages ⟶			4.77	1.05

Bullet portfolio

Issue	Price	YTM (%)	Effective Duration	Convexity Factor
U.S. Treasury 11½% due 11/15/95	111–16	9.20	4.77	0.45

*Duration-weighted swaps that add incremental convex-
ity.* Active swapping of bonds can increase the convexity of a
bond portfolio. In a risk-controlled management style, bond swaps
are duration-weighted in order to stabilize the market risk of the
bond portfolio. Three types of duration-weighted swaps are
common: a bullet-to-dumbbell swap (noncallable bonds), a down-
in-coupon swap (callable bonds), and a callable bond-to-
noncallable bond swap.

BULLET-TO-DUMBBELL SWAP (NONCALLABLE BONDS). A duration-
weighted bullet-to-dumbbell swap from an intermediate maturity
bond into a short maturity bond/long maturity bond combination
adds convexity (as previously illustrated). A swap from a STRIPS
into a coupon-bearing U.S. Treasury bond of similar duration
adds convexity (recall the illustration in Chapter 11, see page 253).

DOWN-IN-COUPON SWAP (CALLABLE BONDS). A move into a lower
coupon (i.e., a better call-protected) bond adds convexity to a
bond portfolio.[3] The rationale for such a strategic move includes
expectations of the following:

1. *A widening in coupon spreads.* If the yield spreads between
    low coupon callable bonds and high coupon callable bonds
    are narrow on a historical basis, the incentive to hold high-
    coupon issues no longer exists. In all likelihood, coupon spreads
    will widen in the future.

2. *An increase in interest rate volatility.* Greater volatility in
    interest rates leads to a cheapening of high coupon bonds vis-
    à-vis low coupon issues. The value of embedded call options
    causes this change in relative prices.

3. *An impending decline in interest rates.* The negative convexity
    associated with high coupon bonds is inflamed during periods
    of falling yields. Under such conditions, high coupon bonds
    are likely to underperform their low coupon counterparts.

The Southern Bell Telephone (SBT) 10¾% bond due 12/18/25

---

[3] For noncallable bonds, a duration-weighted down-in-coupon swap reduces
convexity.

(refundable at 108.40 on 12/18/90) was recently quoted at a 105.63 price to yield 10.16% to maturity. At the same time, the SBT 8⅝% bond due 9/1/26 (refundable at 104.69 on 9/1/91) was trading at an 88.75 price to yield 9.75% to maturity. A swap down in coupon from the 10¾% issue to the 8⅝% issue requires a 41BP giveup in yield.

Exhibit 14–9 calculates the convexities of the two SBT issues. The low coupon issue offers substantially more convexity than the high coupon bond (0.27 versus –1.73). A duration-weighted swap out of the SBT 10¾% bond into the SBT 8⅝% bond adds 1.99 units of convexity on the dollars involved in the trade.[4] Exhibit 14–10 shows that the low coupon bond (8⅝%) outperforms the high coupon bond (10¾%) if the yield spread widens for any of the aforementioned reasons. If the spread expands to 51BP, for example, the 8⅝% bond provides approximately 95BP in incremental return versus the 10¾% issue. A more dramatic widening in the coupon spread rewards the 8⅝% issue with additional return.

CALLABLE-BOND-TO-NONCALLABLE BOND SWAP. A duration-weighted swap from a callable bond into a noncallable bond of similar maturity enhances the convexity of a bond portfolio. Exhibit 14–11 presents the convexities of the callable SBT 10¾% bond and the noncallable 30-year U.S. Treasury bond (9% due 11/15/18). The noncallable bond offers superior convexity when compared to the callable issue (2.83 versus –1.73). A duration-weighted trade out of the SBTs into the U.S. Treasuries renders a 4.37 pickup in convexity.[5]

Exhibit 14-9. The convexities of the Southern Bell Telephone 8⅝% due 9/1/26 and the Southern Bell Telephone 10¾% due 12/18/25 (data as of December 30, 1988). Convexity calculations assume a 300BP shift in yield.

Issue	Price	YTM (%)	Modified Duration	Convexity Factor
Southern Bell Tel. 8⅝% due 9/1/26	88.75	9.75	9.75	0.27
Southern Bell Tel. 10¾% due 12/18/25	105.63	10.16	9.51	–1.73

[4] A small cash position with a zero convexity is incorporated into the results. Bond convexities are given in Exhibit 14-9.

[5] A small cash position with a zero convexity is incorporated into the results. Bond convexities are given in Exhibit 14-11.

Exhibit 14-10. The total return advantages of the Southern Bell Telephone 8⅝%
due 9/1/26 vis-a-vis the Southern Bell Telephone 10¾% due 12/18/25 (issue data
from Exhibit 14-9). Total returns assume a modified duration-weighted trade and
an instantaneous change in yield spread.

Yield Spread (in BP)	Yield Spread Change (in BP)	Incremental Return of the 8⅝% Issue (in %)
71	+30	2.85
61	+20	1.90
51	+10	0.95
41	0	0.00

Swapping from a callable corporate bond into a noncallable
corporate bond of similar maturity generates similar results. The
rationale for a callable bond-to-noncallable bond swap is the
expectation of a widening in yield spreads between callable bonds
and noncallable bonds. This expectation is based on a bias toward
lower interest rates, greater degrees of market yield volatility,
or wider yield spreads between callable bonds and noncallable
bonds.

Risk-altering management techniques

Risk-altering strategies allow the market risk of a bond
portfolio to be shifted while in the pursuit of additional convexity.
The two typical methods of adding convexity are: extending the
average maturity (and average duration) of the portfolio and
lowering the average coupon rate of the portfolio.

*Adding convexity by extending maturity (noncallable
bonds).* Duration is positively related to a bond's remaining term

Exhibit 14-11. The convexities of the U.S. Treasury 9% due 11/15/18 and the
Southern Bell Telephone 10¾% bond due 12/18/25 (data as of December 30, 1988).
Convexity calculations assume a 300BP shift in yield and are based on effective
durations.

Issue	Price	YTM (%)	Effective Duration	Convexity Factor
U.S. Treasury 9% due 11/15/18	100–00	9.00	10.20	2.83
Southern Bell Tel. 10¾% due 12/18/25	105.63	10.16	4.82	−1.73

to maturity; convexity is, in turn, positively related to a bond's duration.[6] By extending a portfolio's duration, one enhances the portfolio's convexity. Exhibit 14-12 shows that a swap from a 2-year U.S. Treasury bond into a 30-year U.S. Treasury bond adds 2.77 units of convexity to the proceeds involved. At the same time, however, additional market risk is undertaken because the modified (and effective) duration of the 30-year bond is almost six times that of the 2-year bond. A small rise in interest rates quickly offsets any positive convexity effects garnered in the maturity extension. A swap into a long maturity STRIPS offers the largest convexity enhancement but poses the greatest danger in the event of an increase in interest rates.

Exhibit 14-12. The convexities of a 2-year U.S. Treasury bond (6⅝% due 12/31/90) and a 30-year U.S. Treasury bond (9% due 11/15/18). Data as of December 30, 1988. Convexity calculations assume a 300BP shift in yield.

Issue	*Price*	*YTM (%)*	*Effective Duration*	*Convexity Factor*
U.S. Treasury 6⅝% due 12/31/90	95–16	9.13	1.76	0.06
U.S. Treasury 9% due 11/15/18	100–00	9.00	10.20	2.83

Exhibit 14-13 summarizes two portfolios: portfolio "short" is heavily invested in short-term securities; portfolio "long" is concentrated in long-term issues. The long maturity portfolio has a higher degree of market risk than its short maturity counterpart (13.79 effective duration versus 2.87 effective duration, respectively). In addition, portfolio "long" offers more convexity (3.94) than portfolio "short" (0.21).

Adding convexity by trading down in coupon. Discount coupon callable bonds have convexity advantages over their premium coupon counterparts. Low coupon issues also carry long durations; therefore, a down-in-coupon swap not only enhances convexity but adds market risk to a bond portfolio. For example, a proceeds trade from SBT 10¾% due 12/18/25 into SBT 8⅝%

---

[6] These notions apply to noncallable bonds. Long maturity callable bonds typically have negative convexity.

Exhibit 14–13. The duration and convexity statistics for a short maturity (and low duration) portfolio and a long maturity (and high duration) portfolio (data as of December 30, 1988). Convexity calculations assume a 300BP yield.

Portfolio "Short"

Par Amount ($000)	Issue Description	Price	Effective Duration	Convexity Factor	Market Value ($000)	Percentage of Portfolio
30,000	U.S. Treasury 12¾% due 11/15/89	103–00	0.81	0.02	31,375	0.3138
10,000	U.S. Treasury 6⅝% due 12/31/90	95–16	1.76	0.06	9,880	0.0988
35,300	U.S. Treasury 9% due 11/15/93	99–16	3.77	0.27	36,160	0.3616
20,000	U.S. Treasury 11½% due 11/15/95	111–16	4.77	0.45	22,585	0.2259
					$100,000	
	Portfolio averages ——————>		2.87	0.21		

Portfolio "Long"

Par Amount ($000)	Issue Description	Price	Effective Duration	Convexity Factor	Market Value ($000)	Percentage of Portfolio
250,000	STRIPS 0% due 11/15/08	17.382	19.02	5.74	43,455	0.4346
20,000	U.S. Treasury 11¼% due 2/15/15	121–28	9.34	2.34	25,215	0.2522
10,000	U.S. Treasury 9¼% due 2/15/16	102–04	9.70	2.55	10,555	0.1056
25,025	U.S. Treasury 7¼% due 5/15/16	82–04	10.33	2.83	20,775	0.2078
					$100,000	
	Portfolio averages ——————>		13.79	3.94		

due 9/1/26 adds 2.00 units of convexity (recall Exhibit 14–9). The 8⅝% issue has a 9.75 modified duration, a modest difference from the 9.51 modified duration of the 10¾% issue. Exhibit 14–14 shows that a proceeds swap from the U.S. Treasury 11¼% due 2/15/15 into the U.S. Treasury 7¼% due 5/15/16 enhances convexity by 0.49 units.[7] At the same time, effective duration increases by 0.99 year (10.33 versus 9.34).

---

[7] This convexity enhancement arises from the longer duration of the 7¼% bond. Recall that with noncallable bonds, low coupon issues have *less* convexity than high coupon bonds of similar duration. For a further discussion of bond swaps (e.g., proceeds swaps and duration-weighted swaps), consult Chapter 14 ("Bond Swaps") of *Yield Curve Analysis: The Fundamentals of Risk and Return* (New York: New York Institute of Finance, 1988).

Exhibit 14-14. The convexities of the U.S. Treasury 11¼% due 2/15/15 and the U.S. Treasury 7¼% due 5/15/16 (data as of December 30, 1988). Convexity calculations assume a 300BP shift in yield.

Issue	Price	YTM (%)	Effective Duration	Convexity Factor
U.S. Treasury 11¼% due 2/15/15	121–28	9.05	9.34	2.34
U.S. Treasury 7¼% due 5/15/16	82–04	9.02	10.33	2.83

Exhibit 14–15 compares two bond portfolios. Portfolio "high" contains a series of high coupon bonds; portfolio "low" holds a selection of low coupon bonds. The low coupon portfolio offers superior convexity in comparison to its high coupon counterpart (3.23 versus –1.05). Portfolio "low" is concentrated in noncallable bonds and carries more market risk than portfolio "high" (12.23 effective duration versus 5.26 effective duration).

Other considerations

In implementing active management strategies designed to enhance convexity, several additional factors should be considered before executing a bond swap. These factors can mitigate some (or all) of the desired convexity effect. They are discussed in the context of the objective of total return maximization.

Exhibit 14-15. The duration and convexity statistics for a low coupon (and high duration) portfolio and a high coupon (and low duration) portfolio (data as of December 30, 1988). Convexity calculations assume a 300BP yield.

Portfolio "Low"

Par Amount ($000)	Issue Description	Price	Effective Duration	Convexity Factor	Market Value ($000)	Percentage of Portfolio
150,000	STRIPS 0% due 11/15/08	17.382	19.02	5.74	26,075	0.2608
20,000	General Motors Acceptance Corp. 6% due 4/1/11	65.50	9.26	1.46	13,400	0.1340
34,250	U.S. Treasury 7¼% due 5/15/16	82–04	10.33	2.83	28,440	0.2844
10,000	Southern Bell Tele. 8⅝% due 9/1/26	88.75	8.15	0.27	9,160	0.0916
25,000	Providence of Quebec due 12/1/26	91.00	10.21	3.09	22,925	0.2293
					$100,000	
	Portfolio averages ————>		12.23	3.23		

Exhibit 14–15. (cont.)

Portfolio "High"

Par Amount ($000)	Issue Description	Price	Effective Duration	Convexity Factor	Market Value ($000)	Percentage of Portfolio
20,130	U.S. Treasury 14% due 11/15/11	141–20	8.00	1.52	28,860	0.2886
30,000	Capital Cities Broadcasting, 11⅞% due 8/15/15	108.75	2.55	−2.38	33,930	0.3393
25,000	Commonwealth Edison, 11⅛% due 3/1/18	102.75	5.93	−1.86	26,610	0.2661
10,000	Southern Bell Telephone, 10¾% due 12/18/25	105.63	4.82	−1.73	10,600	0.1060
					$100,000	
	Portfolio averages ———>		5.26	−1.05		

Transaction costs. Transaction costs, as reflected by the bid-offer spread on a bond, detract from the incremental returns offered by the bond. The wider the bid-offer spread (e.g., 1 point versus 1/8 point) and the shorter the investment holding period (e.g., 3 months versus 3 years), the more dramatic the impact of transaction costs. Less liquid bonds, such as corporate bonds or Eurodollar bonds, require larger bid-offer spreads and attach a greater initial cost to a given swap. Bonds that become less liquid over the holding period of the investment (e.g., U.S. Treasury bonds moving from on-the-run status to off-the-run status) suffer similar penalties.

Nonparallel yield curve shifts. Convexity factors typically assume a parallel shift in the U.S. Treasury yield curve. A nonparallel shift in the curve alters the convexity effects of a dumbbell portfolio versus a bullet portfolio. A steepening yield curve reduces or eliminates the superior convexity of the dumbbell portfolio. A flattening (or inverting) yield curve enhances the superior convexity of the dumbbell portfolio.

Unexpected changes in yield spreads. If the yield spread fails to move in the anticipated direction (e.g., the yield spread narrows instead of widens), the convexity impact is adversely affected. The same effect is visible if the yield spread changes in the expected direction but fails to shift as much as desired (e.g., the yield spread widens 5BP instead of 20BP).

Importance of yield differential over time. A bond offering superior convexity typically trades at a lower yield than a similar duration bond with less convexity. The yield giveup trade into a more convex security (e.g., a down-in-coupon swap) reduces realized total return if the yield difference is not more than offset by incremental price appreciation. Thus, the element of time works against the profitability of a yield giveup swap.

The price of convexity. The cost, or price, of convexity is reflected in the yield spread between callable bonds and better call-protected (or noncallable) bonds. There are times when convexity is cheap; that is, the yield giveups to more convex issues are slim. During these periods, convexity enhancements should be undertaken. However, there are also instances in which convexity is expensive; that is, the yield giveups required to increase convexity are too great. At these times, securities offering less convexity (or offering negative convexity) should be sought.

For example, in late 1985, convexity was inexpensive. Newly issued, AAA-rated, 40-year telephone utility bonds were priced at approximately 70BP over U.S. Treasury bond yields. The 70BP incremental yield was hardly enough compensation for the 5-year call provision on the telephone bonds. Treasury bonds offered sizable convexity advantages for only a modest giveup in yield.

By April 1986, convexity had become expensive. Newly issued, AAA-rated, 40-year telephone utility bonds were priced at approximately 150BP over U.S. Treasury bond yields, a more than adequate incentive to accept the call risk (and negative convexity) associated with the telephone bonds. Convexity should not be pursued without regard for its cost.

The importance of duration effects versus convexity effects. The underlying duration difference between two bonds often has a greater influence on the relative performance of the two issues than their convexity difference does. Convexity influences typically require a large shift in yield (e.g., 100BP or more) to have a measurable impact, especially for noncallable bonds and short maturity issues. The duration-related price change from such a shift is more important. An incorrect judgment call on the direction of future interest rates outweighs the beneficial effect of convexity.

Exhibit 14–16 illustrates the duration and convexity impacts of a parallel shift in U.S. Treasury yields on a 2-year U.S. Treasury bond and a 30-year U.S. Treasury bond. Although the 30-year issue offers substantially more convexity than the 2-year issue (2.83 versus 0.06), a rising interest rate environment eliminates the return advantage of the 30-year bond. In addition, the 30-year bond's longer effective duration (10.20 versus 1.76) makes it susceptible to yield increases, despite its superior convexity.

Exhibit 14-16. The total returns attributable to duration and convexity for a 2-year U.S. Treasury bond (6⅞% due 12/31/90) and a 30-year U.S. Treasury bond (9% due 11/15/18). Data as of December 30, 1988 and from Exhibit 14-12. The total returns assume an instantaneous, parallel shift in U.S. Treasury yields.

	2-Year U.S. Treasury Bond			30-Year U.S. Treasury Bond		
		Return Attributable to:			Return Attributable to:	
Yield Change	*Total*			*Total*		
(in BP)	*Return(%)*	*Duration*	*Convexity*	*Return(%)*	*Duration*	*Convexity*
−300	+5.48	+5.28	+0.20	+40.98	+30.60	+10.38
−100	+1.78	+1.76	+0.02	+11.16	+10.20	+ 0.96
− 10	+0.18	+0.18	+0.00	+ 1.02	+ 1.02	+ 0.00
0	0	0	0	0	0	0
+ 10	−0.18	−0.18	+0.00	− 1.02	− 1.02	+ 0.00
+100	−1.74	−1.76	+0.02	− 9.37	−10.20	+ 0.83
+300	−5.10	−5.28	+0.18	−23.99	−30.60	+ 6.61

For example, a 10BP rise in yields renders a −1.02% total return to the long-term U.S. Treasury bond versus a −0.18% total return for the short-term U.S. Treasury bond. Such a small change in yield renders each bond's convexity attributes powerless. Duration accounts for the discrepancies in total return. A 100BP rise in yields creates a −9.37% total return for the 30-year bond and warrants a –1.74% total return for the 2-year bond. Although the superior convexity of the 30-year bond generates a 0.83% total return boost (versus only 0.02% for the 2-year bond), the duration of the 30-year bond forces its return down by 10.20% (versus only 1.76% for the 2-year bond). Duration risk can dramatically overwhelm convexity attributes in a rising interest rate environment.

Rebalancing away the potential convexity effects. Convexity effects are typically assessed in the context of an instantaneous change in yield. In reality, yield shifts occur over time. This time interval may put pressure on the investor to make transactions that offset some (or all) of the intended convexity effect. For example, a duration-targeted portfolio is rebalanced if its duration drifts too far from the duration of the underlying benchmark. However, a duration-weighted convexity enhancement swap may entail an increase in duration (as yields shift) in order for the convexity effect to be realized. If this duration surge occurs instantly, the convexity effect is captured and the trade is reversed. If, however, the duration shift occurs over time, offsetting duration-shortening (and convexity-reducing) moves are made in the interim period, eliminating the convexity effect.

Using effective duration to make active management decisions. Modified duration is a useful surrogate for the price sensitivity of noncallable bonds such as U.S. Treasuries and federal agencies, but it is not as suitable for callable bonds such as corporate bonds and mortgage-backed securities. By incorporating many of a callable bond's convexity behaviors into its derivation, effective duration is a better proxy for the price sensitivity of a callable bond than is modified duration. As of this writing, a standardized form of effective duration does not exist, and its implementation is not yet widespread among investors. Until the technology of effective duration derivation becomes more available and more agreed-on, individual securities (and portfolios of securities) will be analyzed using modified duration, and convexity impacts will continue to be predicated on the (less accurate) price behaviors predicted by modified duration.

Summary

Convexity is an important element in developing effective bond
portfolio strategy. Passive management strategies include cash flow
matching, bond immunization, and bond indexation. Active
management strategies include risk-controlled techniques and risk-
altering techniques.

A cash flow matching strategy guarantees a convexity match
as well as a duration match. Bond immunization assures a duration
match but not necessarily a convexity match. A portfolio of a
given duration can have a variety of convexities, depending on
how the portfolio is structured (bullet portfolio, dumbbell
portfolio, laddered portfolio). A bond indexation approach to
passive management introduces mismatches of convexity if the
underlying bond index is not duplicated with actual portfolio
holdings. Convexity differences arise because of divergences with
regard to call risk (e.g., a mismatched coupon distribution) or
cash flows (e.g., a mismatched maturity distribution or duration
distribution).

Risk-controlled active management techniques enhance a
portfolio's convexity (1) versus an established performance
benchmark, (2) through the use of a dumbbell portfolio structure,
and (3) through duration-weighted swaps. Swaps designed to add
convexity include the bullet-to-dumbbell bond swap (using
noncallable bonds), the down-in-coupon swap (using callable
bonds), and the callable bond-to-noncallable bond swap. Risk-
altering active management techniques increase a bond portfolio's
convexity through maturity extensions (using noncallable bonds)
and by trading down in coupon.

Active management strategies designed to enhance convexity
are affected by several additional factors: transaction costs,
nonparallel yield curve shifts, unexpected changes in yield spreads,
yield differentials, the price of convexity, duration effects, and
rebalancing effects. Effective duration is superior to modified
duration in executing both passive and active management
strategies. Convexity effects should be assessed in the context of
a portfolio's underlying effective duration.

Glossary

ABS: *See* asset-backed security.

AVGDUR: *See* Weighted average duration.

Accrued interest: The interest earned but not yet paid on a bond.

Active management strategies: Bond management strategies that focus on active trading to enhance a portfolio's investment objective(s). Active strategies include interest rate anticipation, sector rotation, and security selection.

Annual-pay bond: A bond that makes coupon payments on an annual basis.

Asset-backed security (ABS): A security backed by assets such as automobile loan receivables, credit card receivables, truck loan receivables, pleasure boat loan receivables, and the like.

At-the-money option: An option with an underlying security that is currently trading at the strike price.

Average convexity factor: The average of a bond's convexity factor for a specific basis point rise in yield (e.g., +300BP) and the bond's convexity factor for an identical basis point fall in yield (e.g., -300BP).

Average life: *See* Weighted average life.

Average maturity: *See* Weighted average maturity.

BP: *See* Basis point.

Bank and finance bond: A bond issued by a bank (or a bank holding company) or a finance company.

Basis point (BP): 1/100th of 1% (i.e., 0.01%).

Bond convexity: *See* Convexity.

Bond duration: *See* Duration.

Bond immunization strategy: A passive management strategy in which a bond portfolio's duration is matched to the duration of a liability stream.

Bond index portfolio: *See* Indexed bond portfolio.

Bond indexation strategy: A passive management strategy in which a bond portfolio is structured to mimic the risk and return characteristics of a specific bond index (e.g., the Shearson Lehman Hutton Government/ Corporate Bond Index).

Bond price: A bond's current market value (excluding accrued interest) expressed as a percentage of the bond's par value (e.g., a $985.00 market value deserves a 98.50 price). Fractional amounts are quoted in 32nds (U.S. Treasury bonds, federal agency bonds, and mortgage-backed securities) or 8ths (municipal bonds, corporate bonds, and Eurodollar bonds).

Bond price sensitivity: The sensitivity of a bond's price to a general shift in market yields.

Bond price volatility: *See* Bond price sensitivity.

Bond swap: A trade from one bond to another bond.

Bond yield: *See* Yield.

Bond's current market value: A bond's current value in the marketplace as expressed in dollars (e.g., $875.00, $1,015.00); this value includes any accrued interest.

Bond's full price: A bond's current market value (including accrued interest) expressed as a percentage of the bond's par value (e.g., a $1,175.00 market value deserves a 117.50 full price).

Bullet bond: *See* Option-free bond.

Bullet portfolio: A bond portfolio consisting solely of intermediate maturity bonds.

Bullet-to-dumbbell bond swap: A swap from an intermediate maturity bond into a combination of a short maturity bond and a long maturity bond; this swap adds convexity and reflects an expected flattening of the yield curve.

CARS: *See* Certificates for automobile receivables.

CARDS: *See* Certificates for amortizing revolving debts.

CMO: *See* Collateralized mortgage obligation.

Call: *See* Call option.

Call date: The prespecified future date on which the call option can be exercised.

Call date bond: A bullet bond that matures on the call date of the bond under analysis.

Call option: The right to buy a bond at a prespecified price on a prespecified future date. *See* Cash call, Refunding call, and Sinking fund.

Call option component: The component of a callable bond represented by the underlying call option(s).

Call option value: The value of a call option as determined by an option valuation model; it can be expressed in points (e.g., $3\frac{1}{2}$ points) or in dollars (e.g., $35.00).

Call price: The bond price at which a call option can be exercised.

Call protection period: The period during which a bond is protected from early redemption.

Call provision: An issuer's right to redeem a bond issue at a prespecified price on a prespecified future date. Call provisions include cash calls, refunding calls, and sinking fund calls.

Call risk: The risk that a bond will be redeemed before final maturity. *See also* Reinvestment risk.

Callable bond: A bond with one or more call options granted to the issuer of the bond.

Callable bond-to-noncallable bond swap: A swap from a callable bond into a noncallable bond of similar maturity; this swap reflects an expected widening in the yield spread between callable bonds and noncallable bonds.

Cash call: The issuer's right to redeem a bond at a prespecified price over a prespecified period. A cash call cannot be funded with lower-cost debt.

Cash flow distribution: The distribution of a bond's cash flows; also applicable to a bond portfolio.

Cash flow matching strategy: A passive management strategy in which a bond portfolio is structured to match the cash flows of a future liability (or a set of future liabilities).

Cash flow yield: *See* Discounted cash flow yield.

Certificates for amortizing revolving debts (CARDS): An asset-backed security collateralized by credit card loan receivables.

Certificates for automobile receivables (CARS): An asset-backed security collateralized by automobile loan receivables.

Collateralized mortgage obligation (CMO): A multitranche derivative mortgage product collateralized by mortgage passthroughs.

Convexity: The price return that is not explained by modified (or effective) duration; the difference between a bond's actual price and its duration-predicted price; the second derivative of the price:yield function. *See* Positive convexity and Negative convexity.

Convexity effect: *See* Convexity.

Convexity factor: A bond's convexity expressed as a percentage per 100BP change in yield.

Convexity match: An identical convexity.

Convexity maximization: An investment objective to maximize the convexity of a bond portfolio.

Corporate bond: A bond issued by a corporation in the U.S. securities market. Corporate bonds include industrial bonds, electric and gas utility bonds, telephone utility bonds, and bank and finance bonds. *See also* Yankee bond and Eurodollar bond.

Coupon-bearing bond: A bond that makes periodic coupon payments before final maturity.

Coupon distribution: A distribution of the securities comprising a bond portfolio, as sorted by coupon rate. This distribution is based on either market values or duration contributions.

Coupon rate: The stated rate of interest on a bond. For example, a 10% coupon bond pays $100.00 ($1,000.00 par × 10% = $100.00) in interest per annum.

Credit risk: The risk that the credit quality of the issuer of a bond will deteriorate. In the extreme case, the issuer fails to make interest and principal payments and defaults on the debt issue.

Crossover price: For a callable bond, the price at which the yield to call and the yield to maturity are equal. For a putable bond, the price at which the yield to put and the yield to maturity are equal.

Crossover yield: The yield corresponding to the crossover price.

Current coupon bond: *See* Par bond.

Current income: *See* Current yield.

Current income maximization: An investment objective to maximize the current yield of a bond portfolio.

Current yield: A bond's annual coupon income expressed as a percentage of the bond's market price.

Curvilinear relationship: *See* Nonlinear relationship.

DTC: *See* Duration to call.

DTM: *See* Duration to maturity.

DTP: *See* Duration to put.

Dedicated bond portfolio: A bond portfolio with cash flows that match those of a stream of future liabilities.

Dedication strategy: *See* Cash flow matching strategy.

Deferred interest bond: A CMO class that accrues income at its specified coupon rate of interest but defers any principal or interest payments until all prior classes are fully paid. During the interest deferral period, the principal amount of the deferred interest tranche increases by the amount of interest earned (but not yet paid). At the end of the interest deferral period, both principal and interest are paid as a function of scheduled and unscheduled mortgage cash flows. Also called a *Z-Bond.*

Derivative mortgage product: A mortgage-backed security created from mortgage passthroughs. Derivative mortgage products include CMOs and stripped mortgage-backed securities.

Discount: The excess of a bond's par value over the bond's price.

Discount bond: A bond with a market price below par value.

Discount factor: *See* Present value factor.

Discount rate: The interest rate used to translate, or discount, a future value into a present value. *See also* Internal rate of return.

Discounted cash flow (DCF) yield: The internal rate of return of a sinking fund bond or a mortgage-backed security.

Down-in-coupon swap: A swap to a lower coupon bond.

Dumbbell portfolio: A bond portfolio that consists of a combination of short maturity bonds and long maturity bonds.

Duration: A measure of the average life of an investment; the weighted average maturity of a bond's cash flows, where the present values of the cash flows serve as the weights; the fulcrum of the timeline of a bond's cash flows; the term to maturity of a bond's zero coupon equivalent; the future point in time at which, on average, an investor will have received half of the original investment, adjusted for the time value of money.

Duration contribution: The portion of a bond portfolio's duration that is attributable to a specific security or market sector.

Duration distribution: A distribution of the securities that comprise a bond portfolio, as sorted by duration (e.g., effective duration, modified duration, or Macaulay's duration). The distribution is based on either market values or duration contributions.

Duration dollars: The product of a bond's duration and the bond's market value (in dollars); also applicable to bond portfolios.

Duration drift: The natural tendency of a bond's duration to gradually fall as time passes and the bond's maturity nears.

Duration match: An identical duration.

Duration to call (DTC): The duration of a callable bond, assuming that the call option will be exercised.

Duration to maturity (DTM): The duration of a bond, assuming that the bond will be held to maturity.

Duration to put (DTP): The duration of a putable bond, assuming that the put option will be exercised.

Duration-predicted price: A bond price predicted by modified duration or effective duration.

Duration-weighted bond swap: A bond swap that maintains a similar degree of market risk by matching the average duration of the bond(s) sold to the average duration of the bond(s) purchased.

Duration-weighted maturity contraction: A duration-weighted swap to a shorter maturity bond(s).

Duration-weighted maturity extension: A duration-weighted swap to a longer maturity bond(s).

Early redemption provision: A provision to redeem a bond issue (or a portion of a bond issue) before its final maturity. Early redemption provisions include cash calls, refunding calls, and sinking fund calls.

Effective duration: A measure of the price sensitivity of a callable (or putable) bond; the average maturity of a callable bond's cash flows; a sophisticated version of the weighted average duration.

Electric (or gas) utility bond: A bond issued by an electric utility company or a gas utility company.

Eurobond: *See* Eurodollar bond.

Eurodollar bond: A dollar-denominated bond issued outside the U.S. securities market. The issuer may be a corporation, a sovereign entity, or a supranational organization.

Exercise price: *See* Strike price.

FHLMC: *See* FHLMC passthrough.

FHLMC gnome: A passthrough security backed by a pool of Federal Home Loan Mortgage Corporation (FHLMC) 15-year, single-family mortgages.

FHLMC passthrough: A security backed by a pool of Federal Home Loan Mortgage Corporation (FHLMC) 30-year, single-family mortgages.

FNMA: *See* FNMA passthrough.

FNMA dwarf: A passthrough security backed by a pool of Federal National Mortgage Association (FNMA) 15-year, single-family mortgages.

FNMA passthrough: A security backed by a pool of Federal National Mortgage Association (FNMA) 30-year, single-family mortgages.

Face: *See* Par value.

Face amount: *See* Par value.

Face value: *See* Par value.

Factor sensitivity: The sensitivity of duration to

a change in an underlying factor (e.g., remaining term to maturity, coupon rate, or market yield).

15-year passthrough: A mortgage passthrough backed by a pool of single-family mortgages with original terms of 15 years. A 15-year passthrough includes GNMA midgets, FHLMC gnomes, and FNMA dwarfs.

Final maturity: *See* Term to maturity.

Fixed-rate mortgage passthrough: A mortgage passthrough backed by a pool of fixed-rate mortgages.

Flat yield curve: A yield curve in which short-term bond yields, intermediate-term bond yields, and long-term bond yields are identical.

Floating-rate mortgage passthrough: A mortgage passthrough backed by a pool of adjustable-rate mortgages.

Foreign currency bond: *See* Nondollar bond.

Full price: *See* Bond's full price.

Future value (FV): The dollar value of a cash flow at a specified future point in time.

GNMA: *See* GNMA passthrough.

GNMA midget: A passthrough security backed by a pool of Government National Mortgage Association (GNMA) 15-year, single-family mortgages.

GNMA passthrough: A security backed by a pool of Government National Mortgage Association (GNMA) 30-year, single-family mortgages.

Generic issue: A bond with standard features.

High yield corporate bond: A corporate bond that is rated below investment grade; also called a junk bond.

Historical (or actual) volatility: The observed variability in bond prices or bond yields.

IO: *See* Interest-only strip.

IRR: *See* Internal rate of return.

Immunized bond portfolio: A bond portfolio with a duration that matches the duration of a stream of future liabilities.

Implied volatility: The market variability implied in the prices of fixed-income options.

In-the-money option: A call option with an underlying security that is currently trading at a market price above the call price: a put option with an underlying security that is currently trading at a market price below the put price.

Income effect: The total return (in percentage) attributable to coupon income and reinvestment (derived by Capital Management Sciences).

Indexed bond portfolio: A bond portfolio designed to replicate the risk and return characteristics of a specific bond index (e.g., the Shearson Lehman Hutton Government/ Corporate Bond Index).

Industrial bond: A bond issued by an industrial corporation.

Inflation: A general increase in the prices of goods and services.

Interest rate anticipation: An active management strategy in which a bond portfolio's duration is shifted in anticipation of a general movement in interest rates. A bullish inclination warrants a duration extension; a bearish bias justifies a duration contraction.

Interest rate risk: *See* Market risk.

Interest-only (IO) strip: A derivative mortgage product that receives the interest cash flows generated by the underlying mortgage passthrough collateral.

Internal rate of return (IRR): The discount rate that equates the present value of an investment's cash flows with the investment's current market value. *Also see* Discounted cash flow yield, Yield to average life, Yield to call, and Yield to maturity.

Inverted yield curve: A yield curve in which short-term bond yields exceed long-term bond yields.

Linear relationship: A relationship that is drawn as a straight line.

Long coupon: A coupon payment that is larger than normal because of a long period of interest accrual.

Long position: Purchasing, or going long, a security.

MBS: *See* Mortgage-backed security.

Macaulay's duration: *See* Duration.

Market price: *See* Bond price.

Market risk: The risk attributable to general movements in interest rates. *Also called* Interest rate risk.

Market sinker: A sinking fund that allows the issuer to purchase bonds in the open market in order to satisfy the sinking fund requirement.

Market value weight: The percentage of the total market value, expressed in decimal form.

Market volatility: *See* Market yield volatility.

Market yield: The general level of interest rates on risk-free securities: the yield to maturity of a comparable noncallable U.S. Treasury bond.

Market yield level: *See* Market yield.

Market yield volatility: The degree of variability in market yields.

Maturity date bond: A bullet bond that matures on the maturity date of the callable (or putable) bond under analysis.

Maturity distribution: A distribution of the securities comprising a bond portfolio, as sorted by the remaining term to maturity. The distribution is based on either market values or duration contributions.

Modified AVGDUR: For a callable bond, the weighted average duration of the bond's modified duration to call and its modified duration to maturity. For a putable bond, the weighted average duration of the bond's modified duration to put and its modified duration to maturity.

Modified DTC: *See* Modified duration to call.

Modified DTM: *See* Modified duration to maturity.

Modified DTP: *See* Modified duration to put.

Modified duration: A revised version of Macaulay's duration; a measure of bond price sensitivity. Expresses the estimated percentage change in a bond's price resulting from a 100BP change in market yield (e.g., a 5.00 modified duration suggests a 5% rise in price if yields fall 100BP and a 5% decline in price if yields rise 100BP). The slope of the line tangent to a bond's price:yield curve at the current price:yield combination.

Modified duration line: The tangent line to a bond's price:yield curve at the bond's current price:yield combination.

Modified duration to call: The modified duration of a callable bond, assuming that the call option will be exercised.

Modified duration to maturity: The modified duration of a bond, assuming that the bond will be held to maturity.

Modified duration to put: The modified duration of a putable bond, assuming that the put option will be exercised.

Mortgage-backed security (MBS): A security collateralized by mortgage passthroughs.

Mortgage passthrough: A security with cash flows derived directly from a pool of mortgages (e.g., GNMAs, FHLMCs, FNMAs).

Municipal bond: A bond issued by a municipality.

Negative convexity: The negative difference between a bond's actual price (or actual price return) and its duration-predicted price (or duration-predicted price return); common to current coupon callable corporate bonds and current coupon mortgage passthroughs.

Nominal: Stated amount.

Nominal cash flow: The stated (face) amount of cash flow that has not been adjusted for the time value of money.

Noncallable: Not redeemable under any circumstances.

Noncallable bond: A bond that cannot be redeemed before final maturity. *Also known as a* Bullet bond.

Noncallable bond component: The component of a callable bond represented by a noncallable bond that matures on the callable bond's final maturity date.

Nondollar bond: A bond denominated in a foreign currency. *Also called a* Foreign currency bond.

Nonlinear relationship: A relationship that is drawn as a curve rather than as a straight line. *Also termed a* Curvilinear relationship.

Nonparallel duration: The price sensitivity of a bond or bond portfolio to a nonparallel shift in the U.S. Treasury yield curve (derived by Capital Management Sciences).

Nonparallel effect: The total return (in percentage) attributable to a nonparallel shift in the U.S. Treasury yield curve (derived by Capital Management Sciences).

Nonrefundable: Not redeemable with new, lower-cost debt.

Nonsymmetric relationship: A relationship that has unequal effects in a rising yield environment versus a falling yield environment.

Non-PAC tranche: *See* PAC support bond.

Non-TAC tranche: *See* TAC support bond.

OID: *See* Original issue discount.

Off-the-run bond: Any bond that is not an on-the-run bond.

On-the-run bond: The most actively traded bond in a given maturity and issuer sector; typically the most recently issued security in that sector; *also called the* Benchmark issue.

Option-adjusted duration: *See* effective duration.

Option-free bond: A bond lacking any option provisions (e.g., puts or calls).

Option valuation model: A mathematical model that derives the values of options such as calls and puts.

Original issue discount (OID): A bond originally issued at a sizable discount to par value.

Out-of-the-money option: A call option with an underlying security that is currently trading at a market price below the call price; a put option with an underlying security that is currently trading at a market price above the put price.

PAC CMO: *See* Planned amortization class CMO.

PAC support bond: A CMO tranche that supports the PAC CMO tranche(s) of a specific CMO deal by incurring additional cash flow uncertainty.

PO: *See* Principal-only strip.

PV: *See* Present value.

PV factor: *See* Present value factor.

PVM: *See* Price volatility multiplier.

Par: *See* Par value.

Par bond: A bond priced at par value.

Par value: The stated principal amount of a bond, typically $1,000,00. In price terms, par value is 100% of the principal amount, or 100. *Also known as*, Par, Face, Face amount, Face value, and Principal amount.

Parallel duration: The option-adjusted duration of a bond or a bond portfolio as derived by Capital Management Sciences.

Parallel effect: The total return (in percentage) attributable to a parallel shift in the U.S. Treasury yield curve (derived by Capital Management Sciences).

Passive bond management strategies: Bond management strategies that minimize portfolio turnover. Passive strategies include cash flow matching, bond immunization, and bond indexation.

Passthrough spread duration: The price sensitivity of a bond or a bond portfolio to a change in mortgage passthrough yield spreads (derived by Capital Management Sciences).

Passthrough spread effect: The total return (in percentage) attributable to a change in mortgage passthrough yield spreads (derived by Capital Management Sciences).

Planned amortization class (PAC) CMO: A CMO tranche with cash flows that are stable in both rising and falling yield environments. This cash flow certainty is created and maintained by the use of PAC support bonds in the CMO structure.

Point: 1% of a bond's par value.

Portfolio convexity: The convexity of a bond portfolio; estimated by the weighted average convexity of the portfolio's component securities; calculated as the portfolio's actual price (or actual price return) less the portfolio's duration-predicted price (or duration-predicted price return).

Portfolio duration: The Macaulay's duration of a bond portfolio; estimated by the weighted average duration of the portfolio's component securities.

Portfolio IRR: The internal rate of return for a bond portfolio.

Portfolio modified duration: The modified duration of a bond portfolio; estimated by the weighted average modified duration of the portfolio's component securities.

Portfolio rebalancing: Adjusting a portfolio's holdings to regain a duration match, a convexity match, a bond index match, and so on.

Portfolio turnover: The annual turnover (expressed in percentage) attributable to trading activity (e.g., 50%, 100%, 300%).

Positive convexity: A positive difference between a bond's actual price (or actual price return) and its duration-predicted price (or duration-predicted price return); common to noncallable bonds, particularly long duration issues. *Also called* Convexity.

Positive yield curve: A yield curve in which long-term bond yields exceed short-term bond yields.

Prediction error: The difference between a bond's actual price (or actual price return) and its duration-predicted price (or duration-predicted price return). *See* Convexity.

Premium: The excess of a bond's price over the bond's par value.

Premium bond: A bond with a market price exceeding par value.

Prepayment burnout: The tendency of prepayments to fall short of expectations because of a prior period of refinancing activity.

Prepayment rate assumption: The assumed rate of unscheduled principal repayments (i.e., prepayments) on a mortgage passthrough.

Prepayments: The unscheduled repayments of principal on a mortgage passthrough.

Present value (PV): The value of a future cash flow as expressed in current dollars.

Present value (PV) factor: The factor that translates a future value into a present value; this factor is also called a Discount factor and is always less than 1.00.

Price volatility multiplier (PVM): A combination of a bond's duration and convexity statistics; designed to provide a more accurate measure of bond price sensitivity than duration.

Price:yield curve: The curve representing the price:yield combinations for a bond.

Price:yield relationship: The relationship between a bond's price and the market yield level. *Also see* Price:yield curve.

Pricing speed: The prepayment rate assumption used to price a CMO.

Principal amount: *See* Par value.

Principal-only (PO) strip: A derivative mortgage product that receives the principal cash flows generated by the underlying mortgage passthrough collateral.

Pro-rata sinker: A sinking fund that retires a pro-rata share of the bonds outstanding.

Probability-weighted average convexity factor: A weighted average of several convexity factors, where the weights are subjectively determined.

Protected range: The range of prepayment rates over which the average life of a planned amortization class (PAC) CMO or a targeted amortization class (TAC) CMO is unchanged.

Put: *See* Put option.

Put date: The prespecified future date on which the put option can be exercised.

Put date bond: A bullet bond that matures on the put date of the bond under analysis.

Put option: The right to sell a bond at a prespecified price on a prespecified future date.

Put option component: The component of a putable bond represented by the underlying put option(s).

Put option value: The value of a put option as determined by an option valuation model; can be expressed in points (e.g., 3½ points) or in dollars (e.g., $35.00).

Put price: The bond price at which a put option can be exercised.

Putable bond: A bond that gives the investor the right to sell, or put, the bond back to the issuer on a prespecified future date at a prespecified price (typically par value).

Quality distribution: A distribution of the securities that make up a bond portfolio that is sorted by quality rating. The distribution is based on either market values or duration contributions.

Quality spread duration: The price sensitivity of a bond or a bond portfolio to a change in quality yield spreads (derived by Capital Management Sciences).

Quality spread effect: The total return (in percentage) attributable to a change in quality yield spreads (derived by Capital Management Sciences).

Random walk (of interest rates): Interest rate movements are completely at random; there is no more likelihood of a downward move than an upward move. Predicting the future direction of interest rates is a futile exercise.

Real interest rate: The nominal interest rate less the inflation rate.

Refunding call: The issuer's right to redeem a bond at a prespecified price over a prespecified period. The refunding call can be executed with the issuance of new, lower-cost debt.

Reinvestment rate risk: *See* Reinvestment risk.

Reinvestment risk: The risk that interest rates will decline and the actual reinvestment rate will be lower than the assumed reinvestment rate.

Remaining term to maturity: The number of years remaining until the final maturity of a bond.

Risk-adjusted return: A return measure that adjusts for the degree of risk undertaken to achieve the return.

Risk-altering bond management: An active management style that allows the market risk of a bond portfolio to change while the manager is in pursuit of the investment objective. *See also* Interest rate anticipation.

Risk-altering techniques: Active management techniques that change the market risk of a portfolio in order to achieve the portfolio's investment objective(s).

Risk-controlled bond management: An active management strategy that controls the market risk of a bond portfolio while achieving the investment objective(s) through sector positioning and security selection.

Risk-controlled techniques: Investment tech-niques undertaken to implement a risk-controlled management style.

Risk-free rate of interest: The interest rate on a riskless investment such as a U.S. Treasury bill or a U.S. Treasury bond.

STRIPS: Separate Trading of Registered Interest and Principal of Securities; a zero coupon bond that is backed by the U.S. Govenment. *See also* Zero coupon bond.

Salomon Brothers' Broad Investment Grade (BIG) Bond Index: A market value-weighted index of U.S. Treasury bonds, federal agency bonds, U.S. corporate bonds, yankee bonds, and mortgage passthroughs. Each issue is a fixed-rate, dollar-denominated security with at least 1 year remaining until maturity and a minimum of $25 million par amount outstanding.

Scheduled principal payments: The mandatory principal repayments required on a mortgage passthrough.

Seasonality: The tendency for a factor (e.g., mortgage prepayments) to vary as a function of the time of the year. For example, mortgage prepayments rise in the spring and summer months as housing turnover increases; conversely, prepayments fall in the winter months as housing activity slows.

Sector rotation: An active management technique in which a portfolio's market sector exposure is shifted on the basis of relative values.

Security selection: An active management technique in which undervalued securities are purchased and overvalued securities are sold.

Semiannual-pay bond: A bond that makes coupon payments on a semiannual basis.

Shearson Lehman Hutton Aggregate (SLHAGG) Bond Index: A market value-weighted index of U.S. Treasury bonds, federal agency bonds, U.S. corporate bonds, yankee bonds, and mortgage passthroughs. Each issue is a fixed-rate, dollar-denominated security with at least 1 year remaining until maturity and a minimum of $25 million par amount outstanding.

Shearson Lehman Hutton Government/Corpo-rate (SLHGC) Bond Index: A market value-weighted index of U.S. Treasury bonds, federal agency bonds, U.S. corporate bonds, and yankee bonds. Each issue is a fixed-rate, dollar-denominated security with at least 1 year remaining until maturity and a minimum of $25 million par amount outstanding.

Shearson Lehman Hutton Long-Term U.S. Treasury (SLHLT) Bond Index: A market value-weighted index of all U.S. Treasury bonds (excluding flower bonds) with remaining terms to maturity of greater than ten years. Each issue has a minimum of $25 million par amount outstanding.

Short coupon: A coupon payment that is smaller than normal because of a short period of interest accrual.

Short position: Selling a security short.

Sinking fund: A schedule of mandatory principal repayments.

Sinking fund bond: A bond that repays principal in a series of payments rather than as a single payment at maturity.

Sinking fund call: The requirement of an issuer to retire a prespecified number of bonds according to a prespecified schedule. The sinking fund call is exercised at par value. *See also* Market sinker *and* Pro-rata sinker.

Sinking fund provision: A provision to retire a specified number of bonds over a specified time. Retirements are made at par value.

Sovereign bond: A bond issued by a foreign government or a governmental agency.

Spread risk: The risk that a yield spread will change in an unexpected manner, thereby reducing a bond portfolio's return.

Strike price: The prespecified price at which an option can be exercised. *See also* Call price *and* Put price.

Stripped MBS: A derivative mortgage product that receives either the interest payments (IO strip) or the principal payments (PO strip) from the underlying mortgage pass-through(s).

Super-premium coupon bonds: A callable bond with a market price that is significantly greater than the bond's call price.

Supranational bond: A bond issued by a supranational organization such as the World Bank, the African Development Bank, the Asian Development Bank, the Inter-American Development Bank, or the European Economic Community.

Symmetric relationship: A relationship that has equal effects in a rising yield environment and a falling yield environment.

TAC CMO: See Targeted amortization class CMO.

TAC support bond: A CMO tranche that supports the TAC CMO tranche(s) of a specific deal by incurring additional cash flow uncertainty.

Tangent line: A line that touches, but does not intersect, a curve at a specific point along that curve.

Targeted amortization class (TAC) CMO: A CMO tranche with a modest degree of call protection. A TAC CMO's cash flows are stable in a falling yield environment; however, the TAC CMO's average maturity extends in a rising yield environment as prepayments slow. A TAC CMO's call protection is created through the use of TAC support bonds in the CMO structure.

Telephone utility bond: A bond issued by a telephone utility company.

Term to maturity: The original term of a bond (e.g., 5 years, 10 years, 30 years).

30-year passthrough: A mortgage passthrough backed by a pool of single-family mortgages with original terms of 30 years. A 30-year passthrough includes GNMAs, FHLMCs, and FNMAs.

Time value of money: The principle that time has a monetary value; a dollar today has more value than a dollar received at some point in the future because today's dollar can be invested at a risk-free rate of interest over the interim.

Total return maximization: An investment objective to maximize the total return of a bond portfolio.

Total return simulation: A projection of the total return behavior of a bond (or of a bond portfolio) in a variety of interest rate environments.

Trading down in coupon: *See* Down-in-coupon swap.

Trading up in coupon: *See* Up-in-coupon swap.

Traditional CMO: A standard, multitranche CMO lacking any specialized classes such as planned amortization classes or targeted amortization classes.

Tranche: A single class of a CMO.

Transaction cost: The cost of executing a bond trade; measured by the bid-to-offer dollar spread on a specific security.

Unscheduled principal payments: *See* Prepayments.

Up-in-coupon swap: A swap into a higher coupon bond.

WACF: *See* Weighted average cash flow.

WAM: *See* Weighted average maturity.

Weighted average cash flow (WACF): The weighted maturity of a bond's cash flows, where the nominal values serve as the weights. *Also termed* Weighted average life *and* Weighted average term to maturity.

Weighted average convexity factor: *See* Probability-weighted average convexity factor.

Weighted average duration (AVGDUR): For a callable bond, the weighted average of the bond's duration to call and the bond's duration to maturity; for a putable bond, the weighted average duration of the bond's duration to put and the bond's duration to maturity.

Weighted average life: The weighted average maturity of a bond's cash flows, where the nominal values serve as the weights. *Also called* Average life, Weighted average cash flow, *and* Weighted average term to maturity.

Weighted average maturity (WAM): The weighted average maturity of a bond's principal cash flows, where the nominal values serve as the weights.

Weighted average term to maturity (WATM): *See* Weighted average cash flow.

Whole loans: A pool of mortgages packaged by a private entity rather than by a federal agency. Whole loans typically carry either a "AAA" rating or a "AA" rating.

YTAL: *See* Yield to average life.

YTC: *See* Yield to call.

YTM: *See* Yield to maturity.

Yankee bond: A bond issued in the U.S. securities market by a non-U.S. entity (e.g., a foreign corporation, a foreign government/agency, or a supranational organization).

Yield: *See* Yield to maturity.

Yield curve: A plot of the market yields of bonds that are alike in every respect except for their remaining terms to maturity.

Yield curve risk: The risk that the U.S. Treasury yield curve will shift in an adverse manner, thereby reducing a bond portfolio's return.

Yield differential: The yield difference between two bonds or between two bond portfolios.

Yield maximization: An investment objective to maximize the yield of a bond portfolio.

Yield spread: The yield difference between two individual securities or between two sectors of the bond market.

Yield to average life (YTAL): The internal rate of return of a sinking fund bond, where the entire principal repayment is assumed to occur on the average life date.

Yield to call (YTC): The internal rate of return of a callable bond, assuming that the bond is called on a prespecified call date at a prespecified call price.

Yield to maturity (YTM): The internal rate of return of a standard bond, assuming that the bond is held to maturity. *Also called* Yield.

Yield volatility: *See* Market yield volatility.

Z-Bond: *See* Deferred interest bond.

Zero coupon bond: A bond that makes no periodic coupon payments; *also known as a* Pure discount bond. *See also* STRIPS.

Index